A Shining Beacon

A Shining Beacon

Fifty Years of the
National Technical
Institute for the Deaf

RIT PRESS Rochester, NY

Edited by James K. McCarthy

A Shining Beacon: Fifty Years of the National Technical Institute for the Deaf

Published and distributed by:

RIT Press
90 Lomb Memorial Drive
Rochester, New York 14623
http://ritpress.rit.edu

Cover photograph: *LBJ at Twilight*, Scott C. Hooker. The front entrance to NTID's Lyndon Baines Johnson Hall is captured just after sunset.

Book design by Marnie Soom

Printed in the U.S.A.

ISBN 978-1-939125-49-1

Library of Congress Cataloging-in-Publication Data

Names: McCarthy, James K., 1985– editor.
Title: A shining beacon : fifty years of the National Technical Institute for
   the Deaf / edited by James K. McCarthy.
Description: Rochester, New York : RIT Press, [2018] | Includes index.
Identifiers: LCCN 2017047268 | ISBN 9781939125491 (alk. paper)
Subjects: LCSH: National Technical Institute for the Deaf. |
   Deaf–Education–United States–History.
Classification: LCC HV2561.N73 R675 2018 | DDC 371.91/2840974789–dc23
LC record available at https://lccn.loc.gov/2017047268

"NTID...shall be a lustrous beacon...of such magnitude, dignity, and décor...
that will illuminate the hearts of all who come to be served here."

Dr. S. Richard Silverman
Director, Central Institute for the Deaf
NTID Dedication Ceremony, 1974

Contents

NTID Founding Figures

Thanks to the following individuals whose generosity, service and commitment to NTID made this book possible and helped NTID become the outstanding academic institution it is today.

Gold Level:
Gary, '81, and Jeanne (Sheffer), '81, Behm
Dr. Gerard J. Buckley, '78
Dr. William E. Castle
Dr. Robert R. Davila
Dr. James J. DeCaro
Dr. D. Robert Frisina
Dr. T. Alan and Vicki T. Hurwitz, '83, '93
The family of Dr. Robert F. Panara

Silver Level:
Charmaine, '94, and Gregory Hlibok
Ms. Linda A. Iacelli
Kathryn L. Schmitz, '95, Ph.D.
Christopher, '94, and Staci, '92, Wagner

Foreword

Dr. Gerard J. Buckley

On June 8, 1965, President Lyndon B. Johnson sat at a desk in the White House Rose Garden, flanked by a crowd of onlookers that included Senator Robert F. Kennedy, to sign a bill drafted by New York Congressman Hugh L. Carey. With President Johnson's signature, that bill became Public Law 89–36, creating the National Technical Institute for the Deaf (NTID).Just three years later, NTID enrolled its first class of 70 students on the campus of Rochester Institute of Technology (RIT). NTID's first director, D. Robert Frisina, assembled in short order a faculty and staff that included Robert F. Panara, William E. Castle, and others who came to join what Dr. Frisina called The Grand Experiment.

Six years after that, I arrived on campus as a wide-eyed member of the Summer Vestibule Program of 1974 (SVP '74). I did not dream then, and I suspect that not even Dr. Frisina could have imagined, what NTID would become. When NTID opened its doors on the RIT campus, the college revolutionized education for deaf and hard-of-hearing students. Never before had there been a postsecondary institution that offered degree programs designed specifically to enable deaf and hard-of-hearing individuals to enter technical and professional fields, and to propel them to success in their careers and in life.

Much has changed since I arrived at RIT/NTID as an undergraduate student, but what has not changed is the energy, excitement, and enthusiasm of our students to learn, to grow, and to take advantage of the opportunities available to them at RIT/NTID. Many of our students travel a great distance to attend RIT/NTID and to prepare themselves for a successful future. They recognize the value of the career education and the unparalleled services and support we provide. They also understand that finding a community where they can fit in and feel comfortable is essential for an enjoyable and successful college experience.

Everything we do at RIT/NTID is centered on providing the education and experiences that students need to pursue their goals and to lead productive, rewarding lives. And our alumni are doing exactly that. They are pursuing successful careers around the country and the world in business, industry, education, government, and many other sectors. They are contributing to the economy and to the communities in which they live.

Since its establishment, NTID has graduated more than 8,000 deaf and hard-of-hearing students, and I am proud to be one of them. I am prouder still to lead the college now as we continue to help students earn degrees and hit the ground running in scientific, technical, and professional careers.

Seeing our students graduate and start their careers is a tremendous source of pride for all of us at RIT/NTID. With each individual success story, our mission is fulfilled. But our work is never done. We continue to welcome new students and to help them on their journey to successful careers and lives. It is not just what we do. It is who we are. And it all began with the signing of PL 89–36.

As we reflect on the past 50 years, we thank those—too numerous to name here—who have contributed to NTID's ongoing success. The college would not be where it is today without them. NTID is a federal program that is clearly working and benefitting deaf and hard-of-hearing citizens of our nation in a manner consistent with our mission and the reasons we were established that June day 50 years ago.

May the next 50 years be just as fruitful for NTID and those we serve.

Dr. Gerard J. Buckley, '74, '78
NTID President
RIT Vice President and Dean

Introduction
RIT/NTID Alumni Make Their Mark

Loriann Macko

As we commemorate the first 50 years of the National Technical Institute for the Deaf (NTID), there is much to celebrate and recognize regarding the changes that have taken place through the years. With RIT/NTID enrolling and graduating increasingly larger classes of students, alumni numbers have grown to approximately 9,000 spread across the United States and other countries throughout the world. It's amazing to think that the days when NTID did not yet have any alumni are still within recent memory. The first class of students enrolled in 1968. They are just now entering their 70s and enjoying active retirement, taking time to give back in volunteer roles, and helping to support younger alumni and current students.

Since alumni weave such an integral thread through NTID's history, many of the other chapters in this book will mention alumni who have played roles in the shaping of NTID. They have all done things that have changed the face of this unique institution.

Being an NTID alum means different things to different people: community, investment, involvement, and success. It also means being in the driver's seat of NTID's headlong plunge into the future and making a very real impact on that future. This chapter will uncover a few ways that NTID alumni have given back to the community that nurtured them as young adults, as well as some of the ways that NTID has taken these gifts and leveraged them in creating a ladder for each new generation of deaf and hard-of-hearing adults.

As we look back on the beginnings of NTID and the successive years in which each new generation of alumni have emerged, a metaphor that comes to mind is that of a dandelion—the cultivation, growth, and eventual spreading of the dandelion wisps—to flower new places and new fields. Alumni who attended in the earlier years will remember the large metal dandelion sculptures in the open-air LBJ courtyard, prior to the creation of the Dyer Arts Center. It seems to be an appropriate image to use in describing NTID and its alumni.

Growing Our Own Talent

These days, many of NTID's alumni have come back to work in and lead the college's various departments and programs, bringing their alumni perspective and their first-hand experiences as former students. Nearly half of NTID faculty and staff members also are alumni.

Even after 50 years, NTID is still considered a "young" institution, and the prominence of NTID alumni in institutional governance is still new. For example, the first alum to take the highest administrative office at NTID did so in 2010: Dr. Gerard Buckley. A member of SVP '74 and a 1978 graduate of RIT's Bachelor of Science degree program in Social Work, Buckley represents the classical arc that often takes alumni from "highly-engaged student" to "institutional leader." His role as a leader within the NTID community began with his tenure as president of the NTID Student Congress (NSC) and has continued to grow over more than 20

Golden Dandelions by Harry Bertoia.

group that focuses on developing classroom access technologies for deaf and hard-of-hearing students.

CAT is one of the primary sources of technological innovations relating to access technologies at NTID. The students who work there frequently win innovation and business-related competitions—at NTID, RIT, and nationally—with their cutting-edge ideas. Upon graduating, alums have gone on to work for Fortune 500 companies, move to Silicon Valley, or start their own companies. In this way, Behm, himself a product of NTID, continues to encourage and nurture future generations of successful RIT/NTID alumni. More information on this process can be found in "Big Ideas Everywhere" by W. Scot Atkins.

Christopher Knigga (SVP '89, '93) is the Director of NTID Facilities Services and Sustainability. His chief responsibilities center around integrating best practices in environmental sustainability with NTID facilities operations, maintaining and upgrading NTID facilities, and guiding all aspects of the planning process required to ensure that NTID facilities continue to be the best in their class. In this way, his hand shapes the face of NTID in a very real sense. This is reflected in the recent Panara Theatre renovations (detailed in "Finding a Home on Stage" by Bonnie Meath-Lang et al.), the recent upgrades to the Information & Computing Studies hallway, and the sustainability awards won for the construction of the Sebastian and Lenore Rosica Hall (as further detailed in "Buildings of the National Technical Institute for the Deaf" by Erwin Smith).

At the helm of NTID's Center on Employment (NCE) is John Macko (SVP '85, '91, '98). John has worked for NCE since 1993, when he began as an Employment Advisor. Working his way up the ladder over the years, he has served as director of the department since 2007. You can read more about employment efforts in "From Classrooms to the Workforce" by Mary Ellen Tait and John Macko. Says Macko of his time as a student, "RIT and NTID really shaped who I am today. Benefiting from the educational system and social opportunities was exceptional, and it means a lot to be able to work here in this capacity and help students advance toward their own paths to success."[1]

Filling a vital and creative role at NTID is a recent addition to the "alumni returning home" family, Fred

years spent working at NTID in various capacities.

Buckley's status as an NTID alum has allowed him to bring a perspective to the role of NTID president that has never been seen before at the college. Having been a student, a faculty member, and a leader of NTID's outreach efforts, he has seen life at NTID through many lenses, and he brings a uniquely personal understanding to his dealings with all campus constituencies. To see more about the contrast between Buckley's leadership style and those of his predecessors, see "Leading the Way" by Gerard Walter.

Another example of an alum who has taken on a significant role on campus is Gary Behm, who graduated from RIT's Electrical Engineering program in 1981. Behm took a job with IBM, and spent more than 20 years there before coming back to work at NTID. Since returning, he has taken on multiple roles relating to innovation, classroom learning, and access technology. All of these roles converged in his position as the head of the Center on Access Technology (CAT), an on-campus

Beam (SVP '81, '85). Fred has been leading efforts to revive the beloved performance group, Sunshine, Too!, in a new group called Sunshine 2.0. The group has been performing across the country over the past few months and continues the Sunshine tradition of entertaining at schools and within the community. Fred is making great strides in spreading NTID's name and tradition across the United States. For more information about the history of Sunshine at NTID, see "Finding a Home on Stage."

And another key area of NTID that must be mentioned is our alumni within the interpreting field, who play a vital role in NTID's history and continued success. NTID's interpreting history is mentioned in more detail in "How to Educate an Interpreter" by Linda Siple and T. Alan Hurwitz. The American Sign Language and Interpreting Education (ASLIE) program is headed by another alum who has returned to NTID to serve in a leadership role, Dr. Kim Kurz (SVP '88, '93, '95), who is the current department chairperson and has served in that role since 2010. She is also the co-author of the chapter "Signs of Change", along with Jeanne Behm, who is an alum as well.

The department employs several alumni who have come back to NTID to share their skills and teach the next batch of sterling students in the interpreting field. Richard "Smitty" Smith ('78, '08) is one of those alums, who graduated from the Basic Interpreter Training Program (BITP), as it was called back then. You can find more information about BITP, its alumni and the evolution of both interpreter training and access services in, "How to Educate an Interpreter" and "The Evolution of Access Services" by Richard Peterson and Stephen Nelson. Smitty began working at NTID soon after graduation, teaching in BITP, and dedicating four decades of his time and work to students here. Of those early days, he says, "there were approximately 40 of us full-time interpreters then. Interpreting Services was one small office in the basement of the Science Building. We were hourly employees who filled out actual time cards and data (log) sheets. Many of us would eat lunch in the SAU daily with Deaf students. The Cellar (the bar in the tunnels on the residential side of campus) was a great place to go. I was so fortunate to come at that time. The Deaf community (and interpreters) here welcomed me. They made me the interpreter I am today."[2]

These are some of the alumni who graduated, came back, and are continuing to work towards a better future for NTID. The Lyndon Baines Johnson building, now called LBJ Hall, and other buildings throughout campus, are full of similar alumni whose contributions are equally important. You will read about many others in this book.

Rick Postl (SVP '90, '95), Senior Associate Director of NTID's Admissions Office, who has been employed at NTID since 2008, comments on returning to work at his alma mater, "The National Technical Institute for the Deaf...is a niche institution of higher education, unlike anyplace else, and is a home to breakthroughs and great awakenings...I feel fortunate to have an outlet for my passion, working alongside the many pioneers and emerging leaders at NTID as I am a role model, in my ambassador capacity with the admissions team, for young students looking at life over the horizon."[3]

Seeding the World
Not only at RIT/NTID, but elsewhere in the world, NTID alumni are making their mark. From architects to artists, engineers to accountants, the programs that NTID has created to educate thousands of students have cast a wide net with their graduates. Many alumni have created their own places in the world and have met with great success.

We have alumni who have become teachers at schools all over the United States, as well as internationally. Entrepreneurs have built and launched their own companies. Alumni have played roles in politics at both the state and federal levels. The stage and screen have shone with alumni who have delighted audiences of all ages and walks of life with their performances, music, stories, and creative approaches to performing arts, as well as their work behind the scenes in theater.

NTID has championed alumni who have travelled the globe to reach out and help others, who are working in careers of service, and whose work impacts and improves the lives of citizens around the world. NTID graduates have worked for both Fortune 500 companies and for local businesses that do good work in their communities. Our alumni scientists are working on research that will have an impact on healthcare, accessibility, and technology in new ways. And our graduates have

Alumni gatherings through the years: These photos depict the 25th, 10th, and 45th anniversary reunions.

shown, in indisputable ways, that an RIT/NTID education is truly a stepping stone to success. Alumni can be found everywhere:

- in Europe as rising stars of the international art scene
- in Central Asia as founders of schools for the deaf in former Soviet republics
- on a plane over the Pacific between several countries in which their non-profits are funding educational programs
- in Redmond, Washington, as engineers for Microsoft
- in Cupertino, California, as programmers for Apple

- in Mumbai, India, as entrepreneurs
- as biologists studying water supplies in Western Africa

That's without mentioning all of the alumni who have stayed closer to home as teachers, scientists, inventors, lab technicians, artists, interpreters, and parents.

In short, our alumni have reached into many corners of the globe and are bringing their skills and knowledge, learned in the halls of RIT/NTID, to their own unique niches. Many of these alumni will be mentioned in chapters throughout this book. But with 9,000 alumni currently, it would be impossible to mention everyone. We have so many deserving alumni who have accomplished great things! And the list of successes will

only be added to as young students graduate and join fellow alumni in the exciting world of work.

Budding and Growth of Alumni Engagement

Although RIT had had an alumni office since 1912, it was not until much later that each college at RIT began to launch its own alumni engagement programs, and NTID quickly followed suit. When NTID Alumni Relations activities first began, the concept of alumni engagement was new. It was in the late '70s that Howard Mann ('74, '84) took on responsibility for alumni relations and functioned under the title of NTID Alumni Specialist, which was later changed to NTID Alumni Relations Coordinator. Mann, who held this position until 1981, worked to recognize more NTID Alumni

Clubs across the country, which later became our NTID Alumni Chapters. He began connecting alumni via the newsletters that were regularly sent from NTID. This innovative work set the stage for many things to come. Mann was also a pioneer in two other ways. He chaired the very first reunion, NTID's 10th in 1978, and during his time, the office began documenting and recognizing alumni successes and milestones in their lives.

Andrew Mayer ('75, '86, '96) then served officially as the first administrator in a newly established NTID Alumni Relations office. Andrew says of those early years that he saw his appointment "as a duty to serve the alumni community. [The] best moment was leaving a nationally recognized office with NTID and all the good things to be carried on, and a sense of unique pride among the alumni community. As for the future of the alumni community, the success lies within relations among the alumni, the Alumni Office, and the institute. Each one must do their part to keep the bonds that tie them together."[4]

It is clear that this was an exciting time, when alumni were beginning to be recognized, and the relationships between NTID and its graduates were being strengthened. Yet much remained to be done to engage our growing number of alumni.

Following Andrew, David Staehle (SVP '75, '78) was the next Alumni Relations Director. He brought the office to a new level by introducing alumni events across the United States, setting up an alumni donation program, and managing the very successful and well-remembered 25th Anniversary Reunion, which brought 1,500 alumni to campus. This was also when the office helped establish a new NTID Alumni Association, explained in more detail later.

David Strom (SVP '81, '86, '89, '92), Alumni Relations Director during the early 2000s, said that his time was an exciting and dynamic one, full of growing roughly 30+ active NTID alumni chapters across the United States and Canada and leading efforts for the NTID 35th Anniversary Reunion, which resulted in contributions that established the NTID Alumni Association Endowed Scholarship. This scholarship has supported countless NTID students over the years, and is still one of the largest funds that many alumni actively contribute to today. Thus, we see how our alumni continue to "pay it forward" and support future alumni in our current students.

When asked about what makes our NTID alumni so special and so closely tied with the NTID community, Strom had this to say: "Deaf/hard-of-hearing people are part of a unique culture and experience that's second to none...RIT/NTID is a place where individuals come from the world over and all walks of life to connect with one another and advance ourselves. With RIT being one of the leading higher education institutes in the country, if not the world, there is inherent pride in being a part of that identity."[5]

During the remainder of the 2000s, Erin Esposito ('96, '01) and then Matthew Driscoll (SVP '90, '94) served in the director role. Esposito proudly remembers "the

great strides that we (the NTID Alumni Relations office, the NTID Alumni Board of Directors, and the NTID Alumni Chapters) made in strengthening our collaboration with the RIT Alumni Relations office. For the first time in the history of NTID and RIT Alumni Relations, we participated in RIT Brick City Homecoming weekend with NTID alumni programs and events. The collaboration has continued to this day, and remains an extremely important and highly successful component of the alumni experience."[6]

Esposito had the unique distinction of going on to serve as NTID Alumni Association Vice Chair and then Chair following her time in the Alumni Relations office, which allowed her the advantage of seeing things from a different perspective.

During Driscoll's term, he continued to grow the Alumni Chapters in strength and spearheaded the NTID 40th Anniversary Reunion, which was a great celebration for the college. During the time that Driscoll was Alumni Relations director, and Esposito was leading the Alumni Association Board, the board was restructured and strengthened, recruiting new members and re-establishing its role in the alumni community.

When I began an interim role in 2012, the office was already well-established, with strong ties within the alumni community, and a good relationship with RIT peers across the university serving in Alumni Relation roles for each of RIT's colleges. NTID was truly seated on an equal playing field and as an important member of the Alumni Relations family at RIT.

During my interim role, NTID planned its 45th Anniversary Reunion, the first and only reunion held during the fall as part of RIT's Brick City Homecoming events. Alumni remarked that this reunion was different, as alumni could return to campus to see it during its active time—with students filling the classes and halls, favorite faculty available to visit and reminisce with, and a sold-out RIT Men's Hockey game in the Blue Cross Arena.

When I moved to a permanent role in 2014 and the position title was changed to Director of NTID Alumni and Constituent Relations, the role expanded to reach not only alumni, but other constituents such as staff, faculty, retirees, and current and past parents of students/alumni. This afforded opportunities to facilitate interaction between many of these groups. For example, parents of prospective students were able to meet alumni and learn from their first-hand accounts of living on campus, and retirees were able to stay in touch with their former students who are now employed and contributing members of the community themselves. Such interactions continue to be vital to NTID's growth and preserving its rich historical "story" to pass from generation to generation.

Growing Strong Roots: The NTID Alumni Association

No history of NTID alumni engagement would be complete without mentioning the NTID Alumni Association and its Board of Directors. The NTIDAABOD, as it's referred to, is NTID's strongest and most committed alumni group. The NTIDAA and board was created in the early '90s to fill a need to engage our alumni on a wider scale, involve them in volunteer opportunities, and obtain their support and direct assistance with needed projects that alumni themselves could foster and carry out. The NTIDAABOD meets twice a year on campus, membership is by nomination, and members have specific duties that must be carried out during their three-year term. The NTIDAA and board members fulfill a vital role, and NTID and the NTID Alumni Relations office would not be the same without this committed group of alumni.

NTID Alumni Relations representatives Andrew Mayer and David Staehle were involved with forming this group, along with then-members of the NTID administration. Alumni were excited to establish a formal alumni organization, recognizing their ability to contribute to their beloved alma mater and make a positive impact on current students. Robert Sidansky (SVP '72, '77), who was an original member of the first group that was formed, and has since come full circle to serve on the board again as a veteran member, said about those exciting pilot years for the NTIDAABOD,

Over the years, we were starting to see the growth of our proud history due to the success, achievements, innovative careers, and self-identity among alums. For instance, more NTID alumni were taking leadership roles within the Deaf community such as NAD and other professional organizations.

Alums had great success in networking through their friendships and professional contacts...Our alums have changed the lives of deaf and hard of hearing individuals all over the world![7]

The NTID Alumni Association and the NTIDAA Board of Directors have championed many outstanding projects over the years. They have encouraged fellow alumni to get involved, donate toward student scholarships and other efforts, and work to be shining examples to the alumni community. Current projects include a Summer Camperships scholarship, which supports students with financial need who want to attend an NTID summer camp; fundraising for, and providing feedback on, the planned NTID Alumni Museum; helping to manage the 30+ NTID Alumni Chapters across the United States and Canada; and strengthening relationships between alumni and current students to foster meaningful mentorships.

NTID recognizes and appreciates every alum who has served on the NTIDAA Board during its first 50 years, and thanks alumni who have given countless hours in volunteer work, and who have been thoughtful in sharing their skills, wealth, and talents toward support NTID's mission.

Distinguished Alumni of NTID

For 41 years, since 1976, NTID (along with the other colleges of RIT) has been honoring select alumni through a Distinguished Alumni Award program. This award is presented annually to alumni from an NTID or NTID-supported program who have shown success in their chosen fields, have given back to RIT/NTID in various ways, and are exemplary alumni whom NTID is proud to recognize. These alumni have important roles during their awarded year and beyond. Many of them have performed crucial tasks, such as coming to campus to share their skills and knowledge by presenting to current students, working with their employers to provide employment opportunities for students seeking co-op or permanent positions, giving to or establishing key scholarship programs that support student research and education, representing RIT/NTID to the outside world, guiding us to key relationships to further NTID's mission, and more.

Alumni are selected via a nomination process that

NTID is honored to showcase these Distinguished Alumni Awardees during its first 50 years:

2017 Sam and Barbara Ray Holcomb

2016 Barbara Jean "BJ" Wood

2015 David J. Nelson

2014 Andrew Jacobson

2013 Robert Rice

2012 Jerry Nelson

2011 Mark Feder

2010 Sharon L. Applegate

2009 Christopher Wagner

2008 Barbara M. Fallon

2007 Andrew Brenneman

2006 (no award given)

2005 Jelica B. Nuccio

2004 Gary W. Behm

2003 Susan (Wolf) Downes

2002 W. Scot Atkins

2001 David L. Binning

2000 Angela (Donnell) Officer

1999 Philip J. Jacob

1998 Colleen Daviton

1997 Robert J. and Sue (Mozzer) Mather

1996 David S. Rosenthal

1995 James F. Northcutt

1994 Sharaine (Rawlinson) Rice

1993 David H. Pierce

1992 Linda (Kessler) Nelson

1991 Fred R. Mangrubang

1990 Andrew D. Baker

1989 Gary J. Etkie

1988 Gerald M. Isobe

1987 (no award given)

1986 Darlene (Rhoads) Sarnouski

1985 Gerard J. Buckley

1984 Edward B. Lord

1983 George O. Kononenko

1982 Thomas R. Nedved

1981 Robert J. Green

1980 Carmella (Sinaguglia) Ramey

1979 Cynthia (Rohlin) Davidson

1978 William S. Mather

1977 Kevin J. Nolan

1976 Donald H. Stoops

includes the NTID Alumni Association and Board of Directors, the NTID Alumni Relations office, key constituents within NTID itself, and the NTID Office of the President. Awardees are recognized at a premier event with the RIT president, and deans from each of the RIT colleges, as well as friends, family and supporters of each awardee.

Looking Back: A Well-Planted Garden

As we march toward the summer of 2018, excitement grows. Many alumni have not been back on campus in several years—some not since their graduations in the '70s or '80s. Alums are excited to see firsthand the changes to campus, the transformation of the Rochester area, and former classmates. Although technology and social media keep us well-connected these days, there is nothing that can replace a good old-fashioned chat in person, and thousands of alumni plan to do just that when they return for the NTID 50th Anniversary Reunion in June 2018.

Plans are under way for the reunion, with a committee that includes alumni from all decades, geographic regions, and a wide variety of academic programs. And this time, due to the significance of this golden anniversary and the large number of alumni, faculty, staff, retirees, and friends of NTID who will be attending the celebration, the committee has an even more challenging charge to create something enjoyable for all.

Chris (SVP '86, '94) and Staci ('92) Wagner were approached by NTID to co-chair the reunion. As key leaders within the Deaf community for many years, Chris and Staci fit the role perfectly, and together as a team, they have provided strong leadership since the beginning stages of reunion planning. The reunion committee itself is made up of the co-chairs, NTID Alumni Relations Director, and two-person teams leading various areas (registration, lodging, marketing, entertainment, and so on). These two-person teams include an alum from within NTID and an alum from the larger community outside of NTID. This way, a wide variety of alumni are involved with the plans. Also tapped were individuals to serve in "ambassador" roles for each of the decades—'68-'69, '70s, '80s, '90s, 2000s, and 2010s. Ambassadors serving both ASLIE alumni and an NTID retirees group ensure that these unique groups are also included.

The NTID 50th Anniversary Reunion will truly honor our past, while looking to an exciting future.

Another way that the alumni, faculty, staff, and students of NTID are choosing to honor the history of the college is through this book. You may have noticed the references to other chapters in this book throughout this chapter. Because this is the chapter about alumni, that only serves to underscore just how important NTID's alumni community is to NTID's past, present, and future.

This book is meant to serve as a reflection and reconnection with NTID's history through a variety of stories. Some of the chapters that follow are chronicles, a straight telling of a chain of events, while others rely much more heavily on personal stories and the memories of the people who lived this history. Because of the personal influences you will see in the chapters of this book, it is more like a collection of short stories than a timeline; you don't need to start at the beginning and read to the end. You're free to pick and choose which chapters to read and when to read them.

It is important to note that, like NTID itself, the lives of the people mentioned in this book—their experiences, hopes, dreams, and successes—are surrounded and supported by a framework that has evolved over the past 50 years, and will continue to evolve onward into the future. This book is an effort to show how all of the various parts of NTID, along with its people, have grown and changed over the past 50 years.

With that, I wish you all a wonderful 50th anniversary celebration. Happy reading!

Loriann Macko is the Director of Alumni & Constituent Relations.

Notes

1. John Macko, personal communication, 2017.
2. Richard "Smitty" Smith, personal communication, 2017.
3. Rick Postl, personal communication, 2017.
4. Andrew Mayer, personal communication, 2017.
5. David Strom, personal communication, 2017.
6. Erin Esposito, personal communication, 2017.
7. Robert Sidansky, personal communication, 2017.

Signs of Change
ASL on Campus

Jeanne Behm and Dr. Kim B. Kurz

I moved to Rochester in 1979 and have been here for 38 years with a hiatus of four years in the early nineties. I worked at NTID for 23 years, teaching, directing plays, and acting in some of them with students. Therefore, I can dare to say that the use and acceptance of ASL has been going through a beautiful transformation as if it were a metamorphosis from a larva to a butterfly. Best of all, it has helped so many deaf and hard-of-hearing students to gain their true identities as well as their leadership skills. In addition, it has created skilled interpreters. That is our beautiful contribution to the world.

— Patrick Graybill[1]

NTID is a federally funded postsecondary institution that is widely recognized as the premier higher education institution producing deaf and hard-of-hearing graduates, and leading them to successful career opportunities. For many of those deaf and hard-of-hearing students, American Sign Language (ASL) plays a pivotal role in their experience at NTID. The same can be said about NTID faculty, staff, and alumni, who shared stories for this chapter about how ASL has shaped their identities and roles within the signing Deaf community at RIT. This chapter provides a brief history of the developmental path towards acceptance of ASL at NTID. The information mentioned in this chapter is much more rich and complex than can be explained in a few pages; thus this chapter should not be considered a comprehensive description of the cultural fabric of NTID.

Vestibule Programs and SVP Class Signs

As soon as NTID opened its doors in the late 1960s, deaf and hard-of-hearing students arriving for the Vestibule Program went through several days of testing related to their communication skills. Established by NTID in 1969, Vestibule started as a one-year general-education core (i.e., math, science, English, and social studies) that was required for all students. Vestibule was meant to prepare the wide range of deaf students coming from all over the U.S. for later studies toward a four-year degree at RIT.

In 1970, there was growing demand for NTID to increase certificate, diploma, and associate's degree programs, as well as to provide support services for students pursuing bachelor's degrees. For that reason, the original full-year run of the Vestibule Program became a shorter version offered in the summer time. It became known as the "Summer Vestibule Program" (SVP). For a few weeks each summer, this orientation would ease entering students' transition into college life. Faculty member Geoff Poor recalls how long lines would form outside his door so that he could advise students about which communication courses they would need to take in all majors. In those pre-computer days, Poor would look at data processing printouts of their scores in order to advise them.

The move to increased numbers of certificate, diploma, and associate-degree programs meant that entering students had a variety of programs from which to choose, and thus would be graduating at different

Sam Holcomb ('77) and Marguerite Carrillo (SVP '01, '12) demonstrate the SVP signs for 1985 and 2013, respectively.

times. Students identified strongly with their fellow SVP members, and they became creative in showing that identification. From that time on, each entering SVP cohort created its own distinctive vestibule sign for the cohort that would follow it. This established one of NTID's earliest traditions as a college.

There are three rules for the selection of each SVP class sign: (1) the sign must use the "V" handshape, (2) the sign must be unique and cannot duplicate any other SVP class sign, and (3) no inappropriate signs are allowed. The previous class would provide the new sign to the entering group based on their characteristics.

As Leslie Greer (SVP '75, '78) NTID alumna and current President of the Conference of Interpreter Trainers (CIT) says, "the best thing about NTID is its tradition of having a new SVP sign each year. There is no tradition related to ASL such as this anywhere else in the country, which makes NTID a unique and a very special place."[2]

Sign Language Classes for Students

NTID began to recognize the importance of offering sign language classes to deaf and hard-of-hearing students who do not yet know sign language. According to Baldev Kaur Khalsa, Associate Professor, "when these students arrive at RIT/NTID, they are introduced to a new cultural paradigm. They begin a new acculturation process. This is not easy for some students."[3]

In 1988, the college began hiring NTID students to teach ASL to other students. Keith Cagle was one of the early instructors who trained deaf students in teaching methods and strategies for teaching ASL. Additionally, in the 2000s, NTID offered non-signing deaf and hard-of-hearing students ASL I and ASL II (known as NASL) courses for credit.

In 2012, NTID implemented a new summer program known as the New Signers Program (NSP), which is designed to introduce non-signing deaf and hard-of-hearing students to ASL and Deaf culture. Lisa DeWindt-Sommer took the initial leadership role in the

implementation of this program until Marguerite Carrillo (SVP '01, '12) took over the role of coordinator in 2015. From 2012 to 2015, NSP was a week-long program; it was expanded to two weeks in 2016. There were 17 NSP participants in 2012, 16 participants in 2013, 21 participants in 2014, 30 participants in 2015, and 21 participants in the new two-week program in 2016. The college saw the value of this program in helping those deaf and hard-of-hearing students integrate into a signing environment at NTID. "This program allowed students to be comfortable with communicating in ASL and to gain the capability to communicate with a wide spectrum of people here at NTID," says Carrillo. "It is almost like opening the doors for them to interact with and become a part of a diverse Deaf community."[4]

To further support students' communication and language access, the NTID Committee on Equal Opportunity, Communication, and Access (CEOCA) was established by NTID President Dr. Gerard Buckley in 2016. The committee, which was composed of equal numbers of faculty, staff, and students, submitted a list of recommendations for ways to more strongly support the use of ASL and English, both in the classroom and throughout NTID. Dr. Buckley accepted most of the committee's recommendations; in fact, several of the recommended actions were already under way. Other recommendations will shape the strategic-planning process for years to come, deepening NTID's long-held commitment to access and diversity of communication preference.

Faculty and Staff
In 1968, for the first time, NTID offered a sign language class to faculty and staff prior to the Deaf and hard-of-hearing freshman students arriving at the RIT campus. In 1970, The Free University was established to offer courses in manual communication to RIT faculty, staff, and students. During that same year, the Faculty and Staff Sign Language Program (FSSL) was established. This was about the same time that the interpreter education training program started (see "How to Educate an

Interpreter" by Siple and Hurwitz).

In the late 1970s, the Division of Communication Programs offered sign language classes run by Dr. Gerard Walter. Sign communication specialists worked within four Communication Instruction Departments to provide instruction in English, Speech, Listening, and Signed Communication. In 1980, the Communication Division was reorganized into distinct discipline-focused departments, and Dr. William (Bill) Newell became the chairperson of the Department of Sign Communication.

The term "sign communication" was used because, in the 1970s, the term "ASL" was not as widely used. Poor was hired as a sign communication specialist, and part of his work involved teaching sign communication to new hires who had no prior experience with sign language. Over a three-course sequence relying on *Basic Sign Communication*, a book written by several NTID-based authors, Poor discovered "very real flaws; it was a PSE [Pidgin Signed English] book through and through, but [was] probably the best of them." Nevertheless, this emphasis on sign communication", instead of ASL, led to a fragmented student body. "It was horrendous," said Poor. As a result of the confusion, he was prompted to develop a course called ASL for Signed English Users.[5]

In the late 1970s, the sign communication specialists developed a new curriculum to instruct faculty and staff who were hired without the ability to communicate in sign language. The lingua franca of the institute during this point was simultaneous communication (speaking in English and using signs at the same time), also known as SimCom. The curriculum for instructing faculty and staff was developing along these lines; that is, to teach faculty and staff to communicate using simultaneous communication.

Because of the reliance on spoken English as well as sign language, the basis for the grammatical aspect of this curriculum was English. In fact, the first signed sentence taught to faculty/staff in the first class was "This is a pencil." The curriculum was being developed within the framework of Berlitz methodology and Direct Method (DM), which included pointing to objects and labelling them, as one of the first instructional tactics employed. There was no articulated speech used in instruction, but lip movements of English accompanied the production of this signed sentence.

Newell argued that we should teach a more natural form of signing, such as the way fluent users of sign language communicated. However, understanding ASL from a linguistic perspective was just emerging at this point into the consciousness of sign language instructors nationwide. The Green Books[6] had just been published. Newell took responsibility for the Department of Sign Communication in 1980 and the project direction for Basic Sign Communication.[7] The focus was shifted toward American Sign Language, although at the time it was probably closer to the more natural mixture of signing with English that communicators referred to at that time as Pidgin Signed English (PSE).

In 1992, RIT's Office of the Provost recognized the importance of exposure to sign language in the other colleges of RIT. The Provost Summer Intensive ASL & Deaf Culture Experience for RIT Faculty and Staff was implemented by Ellie Rosenfield and Keith Cagle. In 2006, Barbara Ray Holcomb took over this program. Carrillo became a teacher's assistant in 2003 and 2006 ,before she became coordinator of the program from 2007 to 2014. Heather Miller from the ASL Training & Evaluation Department took over in 2015 as the coordinator of this program.

Having NTID as part of the RIT family is truly a distinguishing feature for the university. I know of no other university that can pride itself on the wonderful interaction between hearing and deaf/hard-of-hearing students, faculty, and staff. With NTID comes many terrific features like the RIT ASL & Deaf Studies Community Center, which shares deaf culture with all of us at RIT. And it is gratifying to me to see so many of our hearing students take our ASL language courses. It says to me that NTID is truly integrated into the fabric of RIT.
— Jeremy Haefner, Provost and Senior Vice President for Academic Affairs[8]

In 1993, Dr. Albert Simone became the first RIT president to take formal ASL training. Sam Holcomb provided early morning private tutoring to prepare Dr. Simone to deliver part of his inaugural address, and Convocation and Commencement addresses, in sign language. Dr. William Destler, RIT's 9th president, took private ASL lessons from Sam Holcomb and continues the tradition of signing portions of his convocation and commencement addresses in sign language. RIT Provost Jeremy Haefner joined this new tradition as well, using ASL at Convocation and Commencement activities. Every year, a crowd of deaf people use hand waving as part of their visualized way of clapping after the president and provost sign in front of the entire audience.

Although the signing of these administrators does not perfectly represent ASL structure and they may be using some form of simultaneous communication. For many deaf people, this represents progress and shows that sign language is being recognized and accepted throughout the RIT community. Some deaf people would like to see future university administrators use only ASL without voicing and signing at the same time, so that they can incorporate more ASL features that are frequently missing when they use simultaneous communication.

ASL Curriculum Materials

In 1983, NTID instructors developed and published the first Basic Sign Communication curriculum. In 1991, the Department of Sign Communication was dissolved, and the department's responsibilities for instructing students, staff, and faculty in ASL use was merged with the Department of Interpreter Training. Five years later, the faculty from the Department of American Sign Language and Interpreting Education (ASLIE) were tasked with developing a new curriculum for teaching faculty and staff to communicate with students. This project resulted in the publication of *ASL at Work*.[9,10] NTID had come to a fuller acceptance of ASL and the use of the term "American Sign Language" in a publication issued by the college.

One summer day in the early 1990s, during a break,[11] a working interpreter from Chicago in the intensive ASL course in NTID's Summer Institute approached Poor, who was teaching at that time, and asked him if there was some "secret" part of ASL vocabulary that nobody was teaching in class. Poor gave her question a lot of thought, and in response, created *The ASL Video Dictionary and Inflection Guide,* which was first published on CD in 2002. Poor was the lead project director, along with Patrick Graybill and Dorothy

Wilkins on the core development team. The goal of this project was to create a dictionary that integrated ASL morphology as closely as possible into a sign's presentation in the dictionary. This project eventually became available online and through mobile apps on Android and iPhone platforms. The mobile apps have been downloaded in countries around the world, including Japan, Paraguay, and the United Arab Emirates.

The ASL faculty decided it was time to change their curriculum to better align with the STEAM (Science, Technology, Engineering, Arts and Mathematics) majors at RIT, as well as with national standards. With the increasing popularity—and standardization—of ASL teaching and learning, a new philosophy was adopted for the ASL curriculum; for both first- (L1) and second-language (L2) learners, the vision mandates the linguistic and cultural preparation of students in order to communicate successfully using ASL in the American Deaf community.

The design of the most recent curriculum was based on national ASL standards for language teaching and learning.[12] This curriculum is used as a model in the Standards for Foreign Language Learning from the American Council on the Teaching of Foreign Languages (ACTFL).

The National ASL Standards encompass five elements: Communication, Cultures, Connections, Comparisons, and Communities. The five Cs aim to teach students to "know how, when, and why to say what and to whom" (Standards for Foreign Language Learning in the 21st Century). To become competent in both cultural and linguistic aspects, students learn ASL as a language other than English, gain knowledge and understanding of Deaf culture, reinforce and use ASL in other disciplines and viewpoints, develop insights into the nature of ASL and Deaf culture, and participate in Deaf community events at home and around the world.

To meet the demands of a new age, the curriculum design is based on electronic media and is known as "e-curriculum." The ASL e-Curriculum provides innovative pedagogical approaches and student-centered measurable learning outcomes, and works as a robust and flexible tool for creation and customization. Many featured elements of the curriculum are based on online learning, which allows teachers and students to have access to curriculum-based content, which can include handouts, scholarly articles, e-books, images, videos, and additional ASL-related materials. Learning units are designed for context-specific learning with materials that can be altered and/or expanded, resulting in a flexible and evolving collection of resources to accomplish specific learning outcomes.

The e-Curriculum is versatile, flexible, and adaptable in order to provide authentic and holistic experiences in learning ASL and Deaf culture. In 2012, Paul Dudis, Chairperson of Gallaudet University's Department of Linguistics Chairperson,[13] also came to present about depiction in ASL to ASLIE faculty at the RIT ASL and Deaf Studies Community Center (RADSCC). As part of Dudis's in-service training, participants learned about the latest linguistic findings related to depicting verbs, use of space, and classifiers, all of which are part of the new ASL e-Curriculum.

Sign Language Assessment

At the same time that curricula were being designed and offered to faculty and staff who wanted to learn sign language, NTID recognized the need to measure their sign language skills as part of the requirements for tenure and promotion. Drs. Bill Newell and Frank Caccamise developed the Sign Language Proficiency Interview (SLPI).[14]

In the 1990s, when NTID decided to make sign language proficiency evaluation more formal, and start using it for tenure and promotion decisions, Donna Gustina eventually became the SLPI coordinator. In the 2000s, Poor took over the SLPI operation.

The Faculty and Staff Sign Language Program (FSSL) today is known as the Center of American Sign Language Training and Evaluation (ASLTE). NTID has recognized that documenting ASL competency requires multiple measures, so the college has committed effort, funds, and faculty to developing new state-of-the-art sign language proficiency measures.

To that end, NTID has recently invested in a new Sign Language Assessment Center, led by Drs. Peter Hauser and Kim Kurz, with the goal of creating and developing a variety of sign language assessments that are valid and reliable, instead of depending on only the SLPI. The NTID Sign Language Assessment Center is located at the Center of Cognition and Language in

Rosica Hall. Since the development of the SLPI at NTID, universities around the world have developed sign language measures to be used in educational, cognitive science, and psycholinguistics research. Most of these measures were developed to document the sign language skills of deaf children and adults. "Only recently, there have been efforts internationally to develop instruments to document the sign skills of adults who learn a sign language as their second language (L2)," said Hauser. "NTID is leading this effort through the Sign Language Laboratory at the NTID Center on Cognition and Language."[15]

ASL Classes for Hearing Students

Since RIT accepted the first class of deaf and hard-of-hearing students in 1968, hearing and deaf students have interacted in social and educational settings on the RIT campus. As with all instances where different cultures come together with a common goal, there are challenges in communication and understanding different cultural norms. Both deaf and hearing students, along with administration, staff, and faculty on campus, have embraced this challenge with varying degrees of success over the years.

During the first years of NTID at RIT, deaf and hard-of-hearing students were mainstreamed into RIT classes with the support of notetakers, interpreters, and tutors, many of whom were usually hearing classmates. NTID faculty also had offices in the different colleges of RIT. Deaf and hearing students were seen together in the library, dining halls, bookstore, labs and athletic events. Deaf and hearing students also lived in the same dorms on campus (Kate Gleason, Nathaniel Rochester, and Sol Heumann). There were fraternity and sorority houses on campus, and deaf students were also part of these organizations.

In 1974, the Lyndon Baines Johnson Building (LBJ), now LBJ Hall, was built on the east side of campus to house NTID programs. Mark Ellingson Hall, Peter Peterson Hall and Residence Hall D were also built with accessibility features for deaf and hard-of-hearing students, such as doorbell lights, flashing smoke alarms, and TTYs. Some hearing students and students in the internationally-known interpreting education program (also housed in LBJ) lived in the dorms with deaf students. Soon the east side of campus became the "deaf campus" where deaf students attended classes, deaf teachers taught, and faculty and staff took courses in American Sign Language. The "deaf campus" was ideal for deaf students, with all buildings being accessible, faculty, and staff communicating in sign language, and their own culture in the classroom.

Over the past 15 years, more and more deaf and hard-of-hearing students from mainstream educational settings and students with cochlear implants began applying to RIT with NTID support. With the passage of the Rehabilitation Act of 1973, the progenitor to the Individuals with Disabilities Education Act (IDEA) in 1975, and the Americans with Disabilities Act (ADA) of 1990, increasing numbers of deaf and hard-of-hearing students were mainstreamed into their local public schools. Schools for the Deaf in the United States began to dwindle in numbers; this led to a decline in NTID's enrollment of students from residential schools for the Deaf, which have traditionally been centers of Deaf culture.

With the increase in numbers of mainstreamed deaf and hard-of-hearing students taking RIT courses, there developed a renewed interest on the part of RIT administrators, staff, faculty, and students to learn more about American Sign Language, strategies for communicating with deaf and hard-of-hearing people, and Deaf culture. The burgeoning sense of "Deaf Pride" also encouraged deaf and hard-of-hearing students to be more active in their own advocacy for communication access at RIT and to learn more about their heritage. The pendulum was swinging back toward conditions that existed in the earlier years of NTID.

Under the leadership of Donna Gustina (2004–2009) and Dr. Kim Kurz (2010–present), the Department of American Sign Language and Interpreting Education (ASLIE) began offering more ASL courses on the west side of campus to make the classes more accessible to RIT faculty and staff. In the 2000s, the RIT Student Government petitioned for ASL courses to be offered to students for credit. Up to this point, non-credit ASL courses were offered as part of a training program for faculty and staff. The only programs where ASL was offered for credit were in the ASLIE's interpreting degree program and the Master of Science in Secondary Education of the Deaf (MSSE) program at NTID. ASL courses were closed to students outside these majors.

To increase access to ASL courses, ASLIE collaborated with the Department of Modern Languages and Cultures in RIT's College of Liberal Arts (COLA) in developing an ASL curriculum approved by RIT's Institute Curriculum Committee (ICC) and the Office of the Provost. In the 2000s, the first ASL classes for language credit as part of second-language requirements in different degree programs at RIT were offered and taught by faculty in the ASLIE Department. These courses became very popular. As of this writing, more than ten sections of three levels of ASL are currently offered, covering Beginning, Intermediate, and Advanced ASL skills. A minor and an immersion in ASL/Deaf Studies are also offered to RIT bachelor's degree students. Approximately 500 students at RIT take ASL classes every year.[16]

Additionally, history shows that sign language and Deaf culture were already popular with RIT hearing students as early as the 1970s. Mary Lou Basile helped implement an orientation program for hearing RIT students called Deaf Deaf World, which was led by Barbara Ray Holcomb for many years, until Carrillo took the reins of the orientation program in the 2000s. No Voice Zone (NVZ) is another popular event at RIT that has recently been established. In the NVZ program, both hearing and deaf students meet, interact, and sign with each other without using their voices for a specific time frame every week. It has been a very successful student activity with high attendance numbers.

RIT ASL & Deaf Studies Community Center (RADSCC)

The RIT American Sign Language and Deaf Studies Community Center is guided by a strong commitment to sharing information, resources, talents and knowledge regarding American Sign Language and Deaf culture. The center supports diversity on the campus by providing a comfortable and creative environment for collegial and social interaction among Deaf and hearing people. It supports preservation of American Sign Language. The center is a resource for community, national and international outreach activities that enrich and celebrate achievements of the Deaf community and support

RIT President Dr. William Destler stands at the podium as onlookers cheer during the opening ceremony for the RADSCC.

advocacy and education among Deaf, hard of hearing and hearing colleagues.

— RADSCC's Mission Statement[17]

Three factors led to the establishment of the RADSCC. First, hearing RIT students made clear their interest in learning ASL and learning more about Deaf culture. Second, the administration of RIT was open to supporting cultural diversity. Third, deaf and hard-of-hearing students were more confident and knowledgeable about ASL and their heritage.

In response to these events and trends, a feasibility study was presented to, and accepted by, the administration of RIT in 2006.[18] The vision was for a "drop-in" place where Deaf and hearing people could to learn ASL and Deaf culture, practice their ASL skills, participate in cultural events, and interact with their fellow students. The administrations of RIT and NTID worked together to help make the center possible.

Visits to other Deaf Cultural Centers in the United States and Canada provided committee members with some ideas and collaborative contacts. The mezzanine area on the second floor of the Student Alumni Union (SAU) was determined to be central to most activities and events on campus. Work on the space was completed

in 2010, and Jeanne Behm (SVP '76, '81) was appointed as the center's coordinator in November of 2010. An opening celebration took place on January 19, 2011.

The opening celebration took place in the Fireside Lounge of the Student Alumni Union, which was below the new center on the second floor. Among those who gave remarks were Dr. Gerard Buckley as the new president of NTID, RIT President Dr. William Destler, RIT Provost Dr. Jeremy Haefner, ASLIE Chair Dr. Kim Kurz, and RIT Student Government President Greg Pollock.

In Buckley's introduction,[19] he said that "[This center is] designed to be a resource that enriches and celebrates the achievements of the Deaf community, and supports advocacy and education among deaf, hard-of-hearing and hearing colleagues. But more than that, this center is a gateway, both physically and symbolically, of true cross-cultural collaboration."

After the ribbon-cutting ceremony, the celebration moved to the new RADSCC area in the SAU with a performance from Luane Davis Haggerty's Masquers Drama Club (MDC) students. RADSCC souvenirs (e.g., RADSCC mugs and Post-It cubes) were also given out.

In fall 2013, the center was moved to the first floor at The Wallace Center, which also houses RIT's library, and began offering ASL classes to faculty and staff. Since part of RADSCC's mission is to "support diversity on the campus by providing a comfortable and creative environment for collegial and social interaction among Deaf and hearing people," the new location was a perfect fit, allowing the center to be within an area where resources are more centralized within RIT.

The creation of the RADSCC had a huge impact on the RIT community. The center became a place for students taking ASL courses in the College of Liberal Arts to practice their ASL with deaf people, and it began hosting interpreting courses in the ASLIE program. ASL at Lunch is a popular midday program where people bring their lunches and practice conversing in ASL in the lounge area just outside the center's classroom. RADSCC also sponsors student events where deaf and hearing students are involved in planning and implementation. ASL and Deaf culture presentations, such as the long-running ASL Lecture Series, also take place in the center, which was transferred to the RADSCC soon after the center's relocation to the Wallace Center.

The classroom at RADSCC also houses pieces of art created by Deaf artists. Some are loaned out to the Dyer Arts Center, and others are exchanged for other pieces of art stored in the Deaf Studies Archive. The use of artwork in the RADSCC's classroom helps lend a mini-gallery appeal to the center.

ASL Lecture Series

NTID has always been home to many well-known and respected deaf and hard-of-hearing individuals. When people shared their concerns with former NTID President William Castle during his tenure in the 1980s about the lack of recognition for the use of sign language at NTID, Dr. Castle decided to establish a special program and allocate a budget for workshops and training opportunities related to sign language. This helped fund the ASL Lecture Series,[20] starting in 1985 and continuing to the present day. The series was helmed by Barbara Ray Holcomb until her retirement in 2013, when Jeanne Behm took over the leadership role as coordinator of the RADSCC.

Judy Kegel had the honor of being the first distinguished speaker in the series, hosting a workshop titled Narrative and Discourse Structure in 1985. Ever since, NTID has hosted many well-respected scholars of Deaf culture, ASL, and history. (See the end of this chapter for a full list of past presenters.)

ASL Literature Conferences

Members of the Deaf community collaborated to present the first ASL Literature Conference October 10–13, 1991.[21] Hosted in Rochester, the conference was sponsored by NTID and funded by a grant to the Flying Words Project through the New York State Council of the Arts. Laurie Brewer, Karen Christie, Patti Durr, and Kenny Lerner coordinated the event, which featured performers Clayton Valli, the Flying Words Project (Peter Cook and Kenny Lerner), Sam Supalla, Bruce Hlibok, and Ben Bahan, among many others. The performers also led artistic-analysis sessions to discuss their works.

In addition to the performances and analyses, Bernard Bragg and Gil Eastman led some workshops on signlore and storytelling, language and culture, sign language metaphors, ASL poetry, and ASL literature

It would have not been possible to successfully implement the heart of ASL and Deaf Culture at RIT without the support of the following individuals.

The RIT and NTID administrators who were actively involved in the implementation of RADSCC and provided support included RIT Presidents Dr. Albert Simone and Dr. William Destler; RIT Provosts Dr. Stanley McKenzie and Dr. Jeremy Haefner; RIT Student Affairs Vice President Dr. Mary Beth Cooper; NTID Interim President Dr. James DeCaro; NTID President Dr. T. Alan Hurwitz; NTID Associate Vice President of Academic Affairs Dr. Laurie Brewer, NTID Associate Dean of Student Affairs Dr. Rob Adams; and ASL and Interpreting Education Chair Dr. Kim Kurz.

The RADCC Steering Committee included Donna Gustina, NTID ASL and Interpreting Education Chair; Barbara Ray Holcomb, American Sign Language and Interpreting Education; Cynthia Sanders, American Sign Language and Interpreting Education; Jeanne Behm, American Sign Language and Interpreting Education; Pamela Kincheloe, College of Liberal Arts; Doney Oatman, RIT Interpreting Services; Aaron Kelstone, Department of Cultural and Creative Studies; Joan Naturale, Wallace Research Librarian, RIT/NTID; Fredda Bishop, College of Engineering Student Services; Bryan Fitzgerald, student in College of Liberal Arts and ASL courses; Jillian Darden, student in College of Liberal Arts and ASL courses; Randall Jackson, NTID Student Government; and Greg Pollock, RIT Student Government President.

It was necessary for the steering committee to work with the RIT and NTID Facilities staff to determine available space for the center, design, and build the future RADSCC. These Facilities Committee members were Carol Reed, RIT; Karey Pine, NTID; Al Smith, NTID; William Priess, RIT; and Quent Rhodes, RIT.

Attendees dine and converse at the 2016 Deaf-Mute banquet, hosted in the Dyer Arts Center.

in education. Although this conference did not have a theme, it was designed to expand the previous 1987 ASL Poetry Conference in order to include a greater representation of ASL literary works beyond poetry, as well as more recent scholarly analysis.

The Second National ASL Literature Conference, sponsored by NTID and the University of Rochester, took place on March 28–31, 1996. Karen Christie, Deirdre Schlehofer and Dorothy Wilkins coordinated the conference, which had a similar format to the 1991 conference.

Performances by Juliana Fjeld, a production of *Hear No Scream* from Lights On! Deaf Theater, and NTID student Isaiah Eaton (and company) were featured at this conference. Additionally, performances from students at NTID (including Rosa Lee Gallimore (SVP '95, '00), who would later become Rosa Lee Timm, the well-known ASL performer), the Rochester School for the Deaf, and the Lexington School for the Deaf— where Peter Cook (SVP '81, '86) was an artist in residence—entertained the audience.

The main goal of the second conference was to focus more on education and how to teach ASL literature in the classroom, as well as giving the stage to young performers. "Additionally, we wished to reach beyond the NTID campus and coordinate a conference that included the University of Rochester, the Rochester School for the Deaf, and the Rochester community theatre of LIGHTSON Deaf Theatre," says Christie.

Deaf-Mute Banquets

Deaf people used to gather and celebrate various occasions by having their own banquets, often referred to as "Deaf-Mute Banquets." Although this term is currently viewed as insulting, it originally recognized the values of sign language, Deaf culture, and the importance of gathering as a close-knit community. In the early 1800s, three Deaf educators, Jean-Ferdinand Berthier, Claudius Forestier, and Alphonse Lenoir, established an annual banquet to honor the anniversary of the birth of Abbé de l'Épée, the founder of the first permanent Deaf school to use sign language. Because of the importance of this event, this first banquet has been described as the "birth of the Deaf-Mute nation"[22] and a "first step in developing a conscious Deaf history."[23]

On November 9, 2012, RADSCC hosted a community-wide Deaf-Mute Banquet, mirroring historical dinners of French society circa 1834, to celebrate the 300th anniversary of de l'Épée's birth, and a new NTID tradition was begun. Students, as characters representing Veditz and other notable figures of his time, circulated among the dinner guests. On November 22, 2013, RADSCC hosted the second annual Deaf-Mute banquet in honor of the 100th anniversary of George Veditz and his film, *Preservation of Sign Language,* with a screening and discussion at the Panara Theatre afterwards. The RADSCC has held banquets every year since, and in November 2016, RADSCC hosted its fifth annual historic Deaf-Mute banquet, celebrating its tradition of gathering students, faculty, staff and community members from far and near. The theme for this celebration of de l'Épée's 304th birthday centered around the 200-year history of ASL, since Thomas H. Gallaudet and Laurent Clerc's arrival. Ben Bahan of Gallaudet University was the guest lecturer.

NTID's Legacy of ASL Role Models

There have been many well-respected ASL instructors who have had a huge impact on students, faculty, and staff over the years, and have left their legacy at NTID. It is impossible to identify and recognize every ASL instructor in this chapter. However, several names are the ones you see frequently when NTID alumni, faculty, and staff discuss their experience of learning sign language. Those people are Keith Cagle, Colleen Evenstad, Donna Gustina, Patrick Graybill, Leslie Greer, Barbara Ray Holcomb, Sam Holcomb, Tom Holcomb, and Robert Panara. Panara was recently immortalized on a stamp issued by the United States Postal Service. We are proud to have him represent us and be a reminder of the importance of communicating in ASL.

In closing, NTID alumnus Keith Cagle (SVP '77, '82) summarizes the overall history of ASL at NTID nicely:

> I have seen a great change in how NTID viewed and adopted ASL. In the past, ASL was an underground language. Today, ASL is a star-shining language. NTID has contributed to [the ASL] movement in several ways. First, its Sign Language Proficiency Interview (SLPI): ASL is widely adopted and used in many schools for the deaf and other services for the deaf and hard of hearing. Next, NTID...played a big role in revitalizing Sign Instructors Guidance Network (SIGN) which later was renamed to American Sign Language Teachers

Association (ASLTA). NTID's significant contribution in the 1980–1990s has made the continuance of SIGN-ASLTA possible to today. NTID's support for ASL is valuable.

— Keith Cagle, (SVP '77, '82)[24]

Jeanne Behm is the Coordinator of the RIT/NTID ASL & Deaf Studies Community Center. **Dr. Kimberly Kurz** *is the chairperson of the ASL & Interpreter Education program at NTID.*

2017	Roslyn Rosen	LEAD-K: Getting Kids Kindergarten-Ready
2017	Storm Smith	The Naked Truth: Reclaim the Power of Self
2017	Marie Coppola	The Effects of Language Experience on the Development of Number Representations in Deaf, Hard-of-Hearing and Hearing Children
2017	Nancy Hlibok Amann	The Value of Deaf Elders
2016	Ben Bahan	The Value of ASL Literature
2016	Robert Sirvage	From Stimulus to Shared Representation: Non-representational Convergence as a Foundation
2016	Kathleen Brockway	Wakening Deaf Culture & Bringing Values Back to the Deaf Community
2016	Raychelle Harris	ASL in Academics: Citing and Referencing Bilingually
2016	Trudy Suggs	Deaf Disempowerment and Today's Interpreter
2016	Takiyah Harris	Black Deaf View/Image Art
2015	Debra Russell	Tapping into the Cognitive Processes: Use of Think Aloud Protocols with Educational Interpreters
2015	Khadijat Rashid	Deaf Citizens: Perspectives from Sub-Saharan Africa
2015	Isaac Agboola	Andrew Foster: The Courageous Life of a Black Missionary, Educator, Mentor, and Advocate
2015	Dr. Kim Kurz and Dr. Jason Listman	Resilience of Deaf Students in Postsecondary Education
2015	Dr. Flavia S. Fleischer	America's Constructed Image of Deaf People as Drawn from Newspaper Articles on Cochlear Implant
2014	Paddy Ladd	A Long Strange Journey: More Than A Decade of Deafhood
2014	Arnaud Balard	Deaf Union Flag and Vexillology
2014	Braam Jordaan	The Animated Life of Filmmaker and Animator Braam Jordaan
2014	Dr. Curt Radford	Exploring the Efficiency of Teaching ASL Online
2014	Melissa Malzkuhn	The Science of ASL Storytelling
2014	Dr. Liisa Kauppinen	World Federation of the Deaf and Language Rights
2014	Scott Farrell	A Deaf Athlete's Success Through Obstacles and the Legacy of Dummy Hoy
2013	Chris Kurz and Albert Hlibok	Laurent Clerc's Perspectives of Sign Language
2013	Thomas K. Holcomb	Introduction to American Deaf Culture
2013	Joseph C. Hill	Black ASL: Its History and Structure
2012	Harlan Lane	The People of the Eye – Deaf Ethnicity and Ancestry
2011	Louise Stern and Oliver Pouliot	Chattering – A Collaborative Performance
2011	Nancy Rourke and Warren Miller	Deaf Introspective
2011	Mark Zaurov	Deaf Jewish Life in Germany and Eastern Europe during the 1940s
2011	Dr. John Bosco Conama	Equality of Condition and Deafhood
2011	Dirksen Bauman	The New Normal: Deaf-Gain and Biocultural Diversity

2011	Newby Ely	Deaf Japanese Americans' incarceration in USA concentration camps, 1942–1946
2011	Dr. Keith M. Cagle	Are Some ASL Signs 1000 Years Old?
2010	Anne Marie Baer	Topicalization in ASL: Usage and Teaching
2010	Dr. Peter Hauser	Why Culture is Important: Role of Community Cultural Wealth in Deaf Education
2010	Dr. Anita Small and Joanne Cripps	Deaf Culture Centre: Vision to Reality
2010	Dr. Harry G. Lang	Edmund Booth–Renaissance Man
2008	Dr. Jordan Eickman	Tracing Deafhood: Exploring the Origins and Spread of Deaf Cultural Identity
2007	Dr. Peter Hauser	Signing in the Public Space
2007	Newby Ely	Deaf Nikkei (Japanese-Americans) Incarceration in U.S. Concentration camps in WWII
2006	Guy Wonder	Storytelling through Art
2006	Dr. Carol Padden	Inside Deaf Culture
2006	Dr. Simon Carmel	Genre of Deaf Cartoons and Their Hidden Meanings
2005	Dr. Thomas Holcomb	A Sign of Respect
2004	Dr. Thomas Holcomb	See What I Mean?
2004	Dr. Deborah Sonnenstrahl	Deaf Artists in America
2004	Dr. Paddy Ladd	Understanding Deaf Culture: In Search of Deafhood
2003	Dr. Karen Emmorey	Language, Cognition, and the Brain: Insights from Sign Language Research
2003	Dr. Peter Hauser	Psycholinguistics of Deaf Readers
2003	Dr. David Quinto-Pozos	Contact between Mexican Sign Language and American Sign Language along the U.S. – Mexico border
2002	Vicki Hurwitz	Deaf Women History Resources
2002	Pamela Lloyd and Martina Moore-Reid	Sounds like home: Growing up Black and Deaf in the South
2002	Patti Durr	Crying Hands: Eugenics and Deaf People in Nazi Germany
2002	Paula Grcevic and Patti Durr	De'VIA
2001	Sam Holcomb	Deaf Culture Our Way: Anecdotes from the Deaf Community
2001	Harry Lang and Bonnie Meath-Lang	Deaf Persons in the Arts and Sciences
2000	Dr. Barbara Kannapell	The Forgotten People: Deaf People's Contributions During World War II
2000	Dr. Dirksen Bauman	Line/Shot/Montages: Cinematic Techniques in ASL Poetry
2000	Cindy Campbell	A Semiotics Analysis of ASL Poetry
2000	Dr. Simon Carmel	Deaf Folklore: Identity and Culture
2000	Brenda Schertz	What is De'VIA?
2000	Patti Durr and Paula Grcevic	Affirmation and Resistance Art Within De'VIA: Two Deaf Women's View
1999	Dr. Laurene Gallimore	Diversity: The Change of Heart

1998	Don Bangs	Moving Pictures, Moving Hands
1998	Dr. Marty Taylor	Interrelatedness of ASL, Interpretation, and Message Equivalency
1998	Dr. Douglas C. Baynton	Savages and Deaf Mutes: Evolution Culture and the Campaign Against American Sign Language
1998	Dr. Karen Christie and Dorothy Wilkins	Opening Eyes: Literature and Literacy Studies
1998	Dr. Harry Lang	Deaf Scientists: The Invisible Roles in the History of ASL and Deaf Community
1997	Byron Bridges	Importance of Non-Manual Signals in ASL
1997	Dr. Elizabeth Winston	Spatial Mapping in ASL Discourse
1997	Dr. Christine Monikowski	Assessing L2 Proficiency in ASL with a Cloze Test
1997	Dr. Ted Supalla	Reconstructing the History of ASL
1997	Patrick Graybill	Translation: Challenges and Opportunities
1996	Dr. William Stokoe	Evolution of Human Language
1996	Deirdre Schlehofer	ASL in Society: A Sociolinguist looks at ASL
1996	Dr. Marina McIntire	How Deaf People Become So Expressive?
1996	Charles Katz	The Power and Promise of Deaf Studies
1996	Dr. Susan Fischer	Critical Periods
1996	Dr. Linda Siple	Use of Addition in Sign Language Transliteration
1995	Shanny Mow	Quasimodo, Johnny Belinda and Children of a Lesser God
1995	Willy Conley	Thoughts from a Playwright: Building Plays with ASL and English
1995	Dr. Thomas K Holcomb	ASL in Educational Settings: Exclusive or Inclusive?
1995	Dr. Karen Petronio	Tactile ASL Used by Deaf-Blind People
1995	Matthew Moore	Read English, Think ASL: The Story of Deaf Life
1994	Dr. Susan Mather	Building Bridges: Facilitating Communication in the Deaf Classroom
1994	Raymond Luczak	Discovering ASL and Myself After a Life of Obedience
1994	Marlon Kuntze and Ed Bosso	Developing ASL and English Literacy
1994	Stephen M. Nover	The Politics of ASL in Deaf Education
1994	Carolyn McCaskill-Emerson	Deaf People of Color: What are the Real Issues?
1994	Anthony Aramburo	ASL and the African-American Deaf Identity
1994	F.R. Gomez	ASL in the Context of Hispanic Culture
1994	Yutaka Osugi	ASL is Beautiful; JSL is Also Beautiful
1993	Marie Jean Phillip	I vs. We
1993	Dr. Brenda Schick	Learners and Teachers: Who Teaches Whom?
1993	Peggy Hlibok	ASL as a Second Language in Public Education
1993	Dr. Lawrence Fleischer	Great Discoveries in Deaf Studies: The Coming End of Follies, Foibles, and Fallacies

1992	Dr. Harvey Goodstein	ASL Requirements for Gallaudet University Faculty
1992	Keith Cagle	The ASL Civil Wars
1992	Barry White	ASL Through the Camera Lens
1992	Evelyn Zola	The Art of Deaf Humor
1991	Bruce Hlibok	Deaf Theater: Fact or Fraud?
1991	Patrick Graybill	Original Poetry in ASL
1991	Ben Bahan	ASL in the Arts or the Arts in ASL
1991	Clayton Valli	Self-Discovery of a Deaf Adult
1991	Aaron Brace	On Becoming Real
1991	Barbara Jean Wood	You Speak So Well- Why Aren't You Using Your Voice?
1991	Emory Dively	Keeping Ownership of Deaf Culture in a Hearing World
1991	Robert Cagle	Integration of English and ASL in My Life
1990	Mike Lamitola	Acting with ASL
1990	Dr. Harlan Lane	Deaf Advocacy, Oppression, and Social Change
1990	Dr. Sam Supalla	Language Access as it Relates to Education
1990	Dr. Elissa Newport	Critical Periods and Creolization: The Effects of Input and Age on the Acquisition of ASL
1990	Bill Newell	ASL Is Not A Four-Letter Word: Education Can Dance With Boogieman
1989	Marjoriebell (Mabs) Holcomb	Sign Language Across the Generations: A Personal History
1989	Gary Mowl	The Laurent Clerc Story
1989	Dr. Nancy Frishberg	Historical Change in ASL Structure
1989	Dr. Sherman Wilcox	American Sign Language in Schools: The Status of ASL as a Foreign Language
1989	Dr. Robert Johnson	Unlocking the Curriculum
1989	Dr. C. Tane Akamatsu	Educating Teachers for Deaf Children: A Model Preparation and Demonstration Program
1988	Brenda Liebman Aron	Historical Sketch of Sign Language
1986	Dr. Susan Fischer	Showing Cause in ASL
1985	Dr. Judy Shepherd-Kegel	Narrative and Discourse Structure

Notes

1. Patrick Graybill, personal communication, 2016.

2. Leslie Greer, personal communication, 2016.

3. Baldev Kaur Khalsa, personal communication, 2016.

4. Marguerite Carrillo, personal communication, 2016.

5. Geoff Poor, personal communication, 2016.

6. Charlotte Baker-Shenk and Dennis Cokely, *American Sign Language: A Teacher's Resource Text on Grammar and Culture* (Washington, D.C.: Gallaudet University Press, 1991).

7. William Newell, Frank Caccamise, Keitha Boardman, and Barbara Ray Holcomb, "Adaptation of the Language Proficiency Interview (LPI) for Assessing Sign Communicative Competence," *Sign Language Studies 41* (1983): 311–343.

8. Jeremy Haefner, personal communication, 2016.

9. William Newell, Cynthia A. Sanders, Barbara Ray Holcomb, Samuel K. Holcomb, Frank Caccamise, and Richard Peterson, *ASL at Work: Teacher's Manual* (San Diego, CA: Dawn Sign Press, 2010).

10. William Newell, Cynthia A. Sanders, Barbara Ray Holcomb, Samuel K. Holcomb, Frank Caccamise, and Richard Peterson, *ASL at Work: Student Text* (San Diego, CA: Dawn Sign Press, 2010).

11. Geoff Poor, personal communication, 2016.

12. Glenna Ashton, Keith Cagle, Kim B. Kurz, William Newell, Richard Peterson, and Jason E. Zinza, *Standards for Learning American Sign Language: A Project of the American Sign Language Teachers Association.*

13. Mr. Dudis gave a workshop presentation to the ASLIE Department on April 26–28, 2012.

14. Newell et al., "Adaptation of the Language Proficiency Interview."

15. Peter Hauser, personal communication, 2016.

16. Enrollment information is based upon a yearly average calculated through the RIT Student Enrollment System (SIS).

17. Found in the history of RADSCC planning report prior to ribbon cutting ceremony on January 19, 2011.

18. Donna Giustina, personal communication with J. DeCaro, 2006.

19. Ribbon cutting ceremony (script) available on YouTube, 1/19/2011.

20. Conference materials can be located in the RIT Archive entitled ASL Lit Conference, 1991.

21. Karen Christie, personal communication, 2016.

22. Bernard Mottez, "The Deaf-Mute Banquets and the Birth of the Deaf Movement," in *Looking Back: A Reader on the History of Deaf Communities and their Sign Languages,* eds. 16. Renate Fischer and Harlan Lane (Washington, D.C.: Gallaudet University Press, 1993): 143–156.

23. Anne Quartararo, "The Life and Times of the French Deaf Leader Ferdinand Berthier: An Analysis of His Early Career," *Sign Language Studies* 2, no. 2 (2002): 183–196.

24. Keith Cagle, personal communication, 2016.

Finding a Home on Stage
The History of Performing Arts at NTID

Dr. Bonnie Meath-Lang, Dr. Aaron Kelstone, and Jim Orr

It was like someone unzipped a body suit and I jumped out...I was finally able to express myself. The Performing Arts department became my second home...

— Camille Jeter, former artistic director,
National Theatre of the Deaf[1]

Camille Jeter (SVP '78), Peter Cook (SVP '81, '86), Adrian Blue, CJ Jones, Mike Lamitola (SVP '74, '80), Chuck Baird ('74), Wayne Betts Jr. (SVP '00), Sean Forbes (SVP '00, '04, '08), Debbie Rennie (SVP '76, '80, '86) and Rosa Lee Timm (SVP '95, '00) are a few of the alumni artists who found a home on stage in the Performing Arts programs of the National Technical Institute for the Deaf at RIT. Hundreds of other Deaf professional and civic community leaders and artists are also members of this extended and extensive theater family. For the past 50 years, the performing arts at NTID have addressed the strengths, aspirations, and needs of Deaf, hard-of-hearing and hearing students eager to "jump out" into the world—to express themselves, create new, imaginative work and explore universal human questions.

Whether for their own personal growth or in preparation for a career in the arts, RIT/NTID students have continually participated in a comprehensive variety of theater courses and productions—main stage, laboratory, touring, classic drama, comedy, dance, performance art, visual theater, musicals, workshops and new work. Production seasons have included work by professional and student playwrights and choreographers.

More importantly, students and alumni have found community—nurtured by the emphasis on collaboration, ensemble work and responsibility to the team that is fundamental to theater. For many, the theater has also been a place where identity has emerged and been clarified. The translation process, the creation of work in American Sign Language (ASL) and the production of multicultural, multi-ethnic work have involved a rich diversity of students, many of whom previously found the theater an unwelcoming and inaccessible place. The Performing Arts program has also included hearing students and community members, where, working in partnership, Deaf and hearing students have formed life-long friendships.[2]

Another feature of a true home is the presence of wise guidance and support. The Performing Arts program at NTID has a long history of strong student, alumni and faculty/staff relationships. There is rarely an evening or weekend where a faculty or staff member cannot be found in the halls of the Panara Theatre, the backstage shops, the Dance Lab or the Laboratory Theatre. The mentorship that happens in theater is particularly productive: students and faculty/staff work together to create something bigger than any individual contribution, and at the same time develop an appreciation for each individual's unique strengths.

The program has also welcomed pioneering Deaf theater artists and important hearing performer/teachers, many of whom have served on the faculty, or as artists-in-residence and guest artists: Michelle Banks,

Most of NTID's productions have included the talents of voice actors. Hundreds of RIT students and community members have participated. It is impossible to list all, but a few who have been in multiple productions and served as voice coaches are Ed Alletto, Tom Bohrer, Kathy Buechel, Steve Cena, Peter Elliott, Joanne DeRoller Everts, Chris Felo, Samantha Geffen, Ed McDonald, Gus Navarrete-Guastella, Fred Nuernberg, Linda Siple and Ed Wing.

Fred Michael Beam, Elena Blue, Bernard Bragg, Willy Conley, Garth Fagan, Phyllis Frelich, Patrick Graybill, Monique Holt, JJ Jones, Richard Kalinoski, Aaron Weir Kelstone, Claude Kipnis, Raymond Luczak, Sean McLeod, Shanny Mow, Freda Norman, Howie Seago, Iosef Schneidermann, Mary Vreeland, Nat Wilson and William Warfield are a few. Students have worked shoulder-to-shoulder with these and other professionals, and learned firsthand their perspectives on acting, directing, play creating, scenic art and other aspects of theater. In addition to benefiting from the experience of such pioneers in the field, Performing Arts students and alumni develop an understanding of their own place in the world of theater and in the overall history of NTID.

To understand how the theater at NTID came to be home for so many students, it is helpful to see its range of over 200 productions and the building of Performing Arts' history and home decade by decade.

The Early Days: Home Under Construction (1968–1980)

I'm so happy to be coming back to perform [in the Panara Theatre production *Equus*, 2009]…And I'm so happy to see NTID Theatre is going well and has built a strong program. It makes me feel good.
— Kevin Nolan ('71),
founding Masquers Drama Club member

NTID's commitment to the performing arts began even before the arrival of Deaf students on the RIT campus.

The founding director of NTID, Dr. D. Robert Frisina, in his request for funding of the Lyndon Baines Johnson academic building, specified that a full, state-of-the-art theater be constructed as part of it, cautioning that it not be an auditorium, or a "cafeteria with a platform."[3] He envisioned the theater as a welcoming place where Deaf and hearing students and faculty could come together on the RIT campus. Frisina also saw theater as a way for students to develop self-confidence, learn literature and history and showcase their art to the wider community.

He was very much influenced by his colleague and friend, Gallaudet College English and drama Professor Robert F. Panara. In addition to his teaching and writing, Panara had served on the National Advisory Board that selected RIT as the resident campus for NTID and developed the guidelines for its mission. Panara was a charismatic teacher, whose creative signing in literature classes and in performance was cited by William Stokoe as an inspiration for his early research on ASL as a language. Frisina was determined to bring Panara in as NTID's first Deaf faculty member, citing his ability to teach and advise both Deaf and hearing students. Panara enjoyed his work at his alma mater, Gallaudet, but he was ready for a change and a new adventure. Frisina recalled his own strategy in piquing and persuading his friend: "In wooing Bob to NTID, I indicated that he would be the 'Laurent Clerc' of this new college[4]."

Panara came to RIT in 1967, in advance of the first NTID class. He taught language and literature classes in the then-RIT College of General Studies (now Liberal Arts), and met with hearing students regularly to discuss the profound cultural change that would come to RIT with the presence of NTID. He also worked with Frisina on the proposals for the new academic building and its theater. In 1968, with the arrival of the first students, Panara headed the English program, and began a series of sign language and drama workshops. In the 1969–70 academic year, with the popularity of the workshops and a visit from the famed Deaf actor Bernard Bragg in the fall, momentum built for the establishment of a drama club.

That winter, on a snowy night where students had to trek a quarter mile to the Webb Auditorium to vote, the Masquers Drama Club was established[5]. Among its early leaders were Guy Wonder ('71), Chuck Baird ('74), Fred Gravatt (VP '70), Farid Bozorgi ('76), Kevin Nolan,

Ray Kenney (VP '69) and Ron Trumble ('77, '79).[6] Its first production, at RIT's Booth Auditorium, was called *Footlight Fever*, a revue that included haiku, skits, songs and a one-act play, "The Marriage Proposal." In May, the group performed in another collection of literary works, *The Silent Stage*.

At about the same time NTID was being established, the National Theatre of the Deaf (NTD) was founded. The company was acclaimed internationally as unique in its vision and interpretation of the performing arts. NTD also began a summer professional institute at the Eugene O'Neill Memorial Theatre in Waterford, Connecticut. In summer 1970, Robert Panara was on the NTD institute faculty, and six students attended. In the next four decades, many NTID students and alumni attended the institute and would later become members of the National Theatre of the Deaf, including Chuck Baird, Dennis Webster (SVP '80, '87), Robert DeMayo, Chaz Struppman (SVP '71, '75), Ruthie Jordan (SVP '97, '02, '08), Beth Applebaum (SVP '05, '10), Christina Cogswell (SVP '05, '09, '14) and many others.

As the Drama Club was expanding to involve more and more members of the NTID student community, the new Experimental Educational Theatre (EET) was nearing completion[7]. As Bob Panara put it, "The 'home of our own' became official..."[8] The first EET production was timed to coincide with the dedication of NTID's Lyndon Baines Johnson Building (now Lyndon Baines Johnson Hall).

In October 1974, *The Taming of the Shrew*, attended by dignitaries from around the nation, was directed by David Hagans, and starred Paul Johnston, Betty Bonni, Janis Cole, Ricky Smith, Barbara Ray (Holcomb) and Linda Siple. And as fully staged productions were now possible, new faculty and staff in theater were hired to include professionals in acting, design, directing, movement and technical direction. This led to the development of credit-bearing courses and the development of a theater curriculum to satisfy General Education requirements as well as production work.

The newly formed department took full advantage of its new space and its potential, mounting a series of memorable productions through the decade. *Joseph and the Amazing Technicolor Dreamcoat* (1975) directed by Marj Pratt, was one of the first American productions

of the Andrew Lloyd Weber/Tim Rice musical. Faculty member Jerome Cushman's love of and connections to Japanese culture led to a residence by the classical dance artist Sahomi Tachibana and the Kabuki-style production, *Tormented Pathway* (1976). Movement was an essential part of the program, taught by Cushman and a new, upcoming choreographer named Garth Fagan.

Other productions spanned an impressive range of genres and styles, including *Lysistrata, Dark of the Moon* (with a residency by the playwright Howard Richardson), *Alice in Wonderland, A Streetcar Named Desire, Wenebojo, A Funny Thing Happened on the Way to the Forum, Romeo and Juliet* and *The Fantasticks*. At the time of NTID's 10th anniversary celebrations in 1978, the renowned Deaf actor Bernard Bragg starred in a production of Molière's *The Bourgeois Gentleman*, directed by Jerome Cushman, in the EET. Bragg has referred to NTID's theater as "being at home away from home" during his many visits through the years.

By the close of the decade, the new program was winning regional and national awards, such as Best Supporting Actor (Jim Orr) and Best Play (*Alice in Wonderland*) at the New York State Theatre Festival in 1978, and two regional finalist achievements in 1977 and 1979 at the American College Theatre Festival—the first, for *Alice in Wonderland* and the latter, the Irene Ryan Acting Award for Matthew Moore's performance in *The Fantasticks*. The theater was now a home for nearly half of NTID's students, and its presence was firmly established on the landscape of the university.

Following Bob Panara's leadership as Drama Club (Masquers) advisor, the leadership of the Performing Arts Department included Chairs David Hagans, Jerry Argetsinger, Paul Thayn, Bruce Halverson, Richard Nichols, Bruce Halverson, (second term), James Graves and Kelly Morgan. The department then became a program of the multidisciplinary Department of Cultural and Creative Studies in 1997-98, with Joe Bochner as chair, and added an artistic director, Bonnie Meath-Lang, and later a program director, Aaron Kelstone.

Alice in Wonderland, 1978 (Kathy Buechel, Jim Orr, Bill Barber).

The Second Decade: Building Additions (1981–1990)

So, I'm playing basketball in the gym one afternoon...and there's this guy staring at me—strangely,
I thought—he's watching me closely...I started to
leave, nervously. He followed me out and introduced himself as Jerome Cushman, and said,
"You're a dancer!" I said no way, especially after
seeing tights...but he planted a seed...
— Fred Michael Beam (SVP '81, '85), professional
dancer and choreographer, Director of Sunshine 2.0

As happens with homes, the theater family and its activities soon called for additions to support the massive
amount of creative energy coming out of the program
and its students, and the multiple requests of its expanding audiences.

Distinguished Deaf artists continued to play an
important role in the life of the department. During
this period, Howie Seago and Patrick Graybill taught as
artists-in-residence. Graybill starred as Prospero in *The
Tempest* (1981) and was honored by making the cover of
The Smithsonian Magazine in costume. He also would
play an elderly lady neighbor opposite alumna—and
later professional actor—Mary Beth Barber (Mothersell)
in *Porch*, directed by Seago.

The theater expanded to become an integral part
of the General Education curriculum, adding courses
in mime, dramatic literature, dance and costume. The
Experimental Educational Theatre also began to partner

with RIT's complementary education and physical education programs. The complementary education program evolved to establish a funding unit, RIT Creative Arts, where students and faculty could write proposals for new endeavors in the performing, visual and industrial arts. Several student lab productions at NTID were funded through Creative Arts, and this program was key in supporting a comprehensive dance program at NTID.

The RIT Dance Company (now RIT/NTID Dance Company) was first directed by artists-in-residence Pat Frawley, Stefa Zawerucha and Susan Galligan. Later, the company was established formally as part of Creative Arts in 1987. The theater program hired the internationally respected Deaf dancer, Michael Thomas, to lead the productions and expand dance course options. The classes were available to NTID students for General Education or physical education credit, and to RIT students for physical education credit. Ballet, modern, jazz, choreography and dance history courses were developed. Among the first dance productions were *Rhythm Nation, Gravity's Angels, Tiananmen Square*, and other dance concerts showcasing a variety of styles.

Through the 1980s, a wide range of productions continued to be performed on the main stage, including *Oklahoma, The Threepenny Opera, The Adding Machine, The Caucasian Chalk Circle, The Odd Couple, Everyman*, and an innovative visual theater production of *Macbeth*, directed by Jerome Cushman, and a finalist in the American College Theatre Festival in 1986.

Perhaps the most notable addition to the theater home during this period was the establishment of a performing arts outreach company, Sunshine Too. The troupe, consisting of three Deaf and three hearing professional staff, evolved from a group of faculty and staff (first known as Sunshine and Company), who performed poetry and songs for the community, and for educational conferences such as the National Registry of Interpreters for the Deaf and the Convention of American Instructors of the Deaf.[9]

The popularity of these performances was quickly noted by institutional leaders such as dean/director William Castle and department chair Bruce Halverson. The decision was made to seize the opportunity to have a group of young actors travel and perform as the face of NTID nationally and internationally. Timothy

Patrick Graybill as Prospero and Peter Cook as Caliban (with Jim Murphy, Andy Corvo and Jim Peinkhoper) in Shakespeare's *The Tempest*.

Toothman was the first outreach coordinator and manager of Sunshine Too (1980), and Jim Orr, who had been an actor in early NTID plays, succeeded him in 1984.

The group presented full-length and short theater productions, and conducted workshops in ASL and voice at K–12 schools, universities, community events, fundraisers and media outlets. These shows and workshops centered on Deaf awareness, community and culture, sign language and social issues, such as bullying. By the end of the decade, Sunshine Too had appeared in live performances before 75,000 audience members, and received numerous accolades, including a special recognition for promoting environmental awareness and sustainability by the Environmental Protection Agency.

During the 1980s, with increased awareness of Deaf performers and actors on stage and in films such as *Children of a Lesser God*, NTID theater students and alumni began to appear professionally before a wider national audience. A notable example was the award-winning McDonald's commercial featuring Beth Ann Bull and Andrew Rubin, one of the first national commercials in ASL. Helen Hayes Award-winning alumna Mary Vreeland appeared on Broadway and in national play tours (She won that award for the her role as Katrin in the John F. Kennedy Center's production of *Mother Courage*), and television programs such as *Hunter* and the CBS Afternoon Specials. Mary Beth Barber guest starred in the "Silent World" episode of *MacGyver* in 1986.

The Performing Arts program had already used music in several of its productions, but with support from Creative Arts, a music program was also established. Robert Mowers and Diane Habeeb taught Deaf and hearing students a variety of instruments, formed a combo, and organized pit orchestras for theater productions. The Laboratory Theatre was used for music rehearsals, but also for experimental, often multimedia productions and workshops. Some of these were original student work, such as *C'est Autre Chose*, written and directed by Matthew Moore and Tom Connor.

With the addition of dance, music, outreach, multimedia and expanded stagecraft course options, the Experimental Education Theatre was re-named the Department of Performing Arts. And the theater at the heart of it would also be re-named during the decade.

On May 18, 1988, Dean Castle invited Bob and Shirley Panara to a student-faculty awards ceremony, asking Bob to recite his award-winning poem, "On His Deafness" as part of the event. Bill Castle was known for his love of theater and his own dramatic flair. When the unsuspecting Panara turned to leave the stage, Castle called him back, and announced to the audience: "This plaque commemorates the renaming of the NTID theater in honor of Bob. By vote of RIT/NTID, it will henceforth be named the Robert F. Panara Theatre!" He then led the astonished Panaras out to the reception in the front lobby. Previously hidden from view, the foot-high letters reading ROBERT F. PANARA THEATRE were already emblazoned at the entrance.

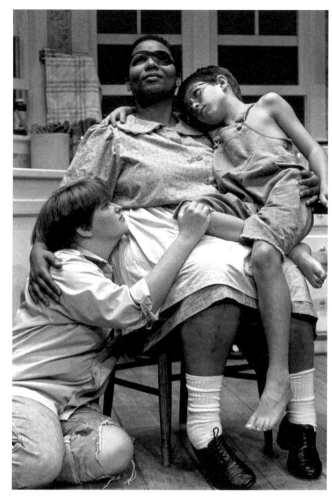

Tracy Washington performs in *The Member of the Wedding*, 1994 (with Sara Lawson and Davin Searls).

The Third Decade: Renovations (1991–2000)

When I auditioned for *Cabaret*, I was still reeling with grief over the devastating loss of my mother two years earlier. I felt so vulnerable and needed to find a safe space for my heavy heart somewhere at NTID. During one of Michael Thomas's dance rehearsals for *Cabaret*, I started to smile again for the first time in two years. Thanks to Michael and his generous spirit, I found myself in the middle of many wonderful conversations with Bob and Shirley Panara, Patrick Graybill, Patti Durr and many other gregarious and brilliant faculty and staff. Little did I know how strongly these meaningful connections would persist to this very day!

In addition, the NTID theater program provided me with such valuable experience with acting, costumes, publicity and everything else connected with the arts world, and it continues to stoke my creative fires even now—so much so that I still call the Panara Theatre my second home!

       — Stacy Lawrence (SVP '88, '93)

The 1990s at NTID began with a major strategic planning effort focused on organizational and curriculum changes intended to bring the college into the new millennium. A Humanities and Social Sciences Task Force was formed on the recommendation of the central Strategic Planning Committee, and Bonnie Meath-Lang and Michael Thomas represented performing arts on that task force. As a result, the curriculum was expanded and revised to give more prominence to script analysis, creative translation in ASL and technical theater. There were also courses intended to give more attention to student leadership in the arts, such as stage management and choreography. A formal agreement with RIT's School of Film and Animation led to NTID Performing Arts courses being transferable to that program, and work was begun on a Certificate in Performing Arts, similar to a minor, being offered by the program.

At the same time as this substantial curricular work was being done, the NTID theater worked toward increasing sophistication in its use of technology on stage. Various types of captioning were tested for select productions. Intelligent lighting (*Pollack, The Spirit and the Man*), all-ASL productions with original environmental sound (*Picnic*, directed by the visual theater expert Rebecca Holderness), star drops (*Cinderella*), and other special effects characterized the atmosphere of experimentation in the '90s.

There was also conscious effort to bring the work of Deaf writers, actors and directors to the curriculum and the production seasons. *Meta* (1993), written by Patti Durr and directed by Dennis Webster, was a collaboration between the program and the Deaf community theater LightsOn!, highlighting the intersecting issues of Deaf and African-American oppression and anti-Semitism. The first and second American Deaf Play Creators' Festivals (1996, 1998), sponsored by a gift from the Nathan Cummings Foundation and co-produced

Cinderella, 1995 (Amy Flowers and Torrie Armour).

by the Performing Arts program and Matthew Moore's MSM Productions, brought in leading Deaf actors, directors, and playwrights—Phyllis Frelich, Shanny Mow, Raymond Luczak, Howie Seago, Susan Jackson, Nat Wilson, Megg Masterjohn, Elena Blue and Chuck Baird—to create original work. The actors were joined by students Mel Westlake, Matt Hochkeppel and Dennis Smith. Other students also had the opportunity to attend workshops and observe the creative process of these artists, while working on the productions as colleagues[10].

The first BFA students began the process of pursuing the new track in Performance/Stagecraft in NTID Performing Arts' collaboration with RIT's School of Film and Animation. Julie Stewart, who as a student intern in 1997 became Sunshine Too's first Deaf road and stage manager, directed John Guare's surrealistic *The General of Hot Desire* as the first BFA junior project in the Laboratory Theatre. Josh Liller began the program and stage-managed the extraordinarily difficult *West Side Story*, directed by Bonnie Meath-Lang and choreographed by Thomas Warfield, with 100 students (and hundreds more cues for him to execute)—as a sophomore.

Other productions from 1991–2000 included *The Miser, Steel Magnolias, The Grapes of Wrath* (with its full-size replica of a 1930s truck on stage, built in the scene shop), *The Importance of Being Earnest* (with Patrick Graybill as Lady Bracknell), a futuristic *Antigone*, *Extremities*, and *A Sailor's Daughter*, directed by Ray Fleming, about the life of the Deaf playwright Marie Leneru during WWI. *The Tempest*, directed by Luane Davis Haggerty, was performed for two weeks at the West Side Dance Theatre in New York City. That production was featured in *The Chronicle of Higher Education*, discussing the process of collaboration between Deaf and hearing actors, and its implications for diverse partnerships in other colleges and universities.[11]

Sunshine Too continued its ambitious travel schedule, giving hundreds of performances around the United States. And in 1995, Sunshine Too was the only American company selected to perform at the International Deaf Theatre Festival in Helsinki, Finland.

From the 1990s to the present, about 500 students have called the NTID theater a home each year[12]. However, as with all homes and families, the program has experienced loss. Michael Thomas's untimely death brought the RIT/NTID and larger Rochester dance community together in the tribute *The Spirit and the Man*, directed by Bonnie Meath-Lang. In addition to the RIT/NTID Dance Company, dancers from the Rochester City Ballet were featured, many of whom have gone on to work in major companies all over the world. Shortly after this sad time, however, another door opened, and internationally respected dancer and musician Thomas Warfield was hired to make NTID Performing Arts his home, and help bring the dance company into the next decade.

The Fourth Decade: At Home in the Community (2001–10)

I learned so much with you all—My time at NTID Performing Arts with the NTID theatre family absolutely played a huge part in this journey!
— Michael Sauder (SVP '98, '03), upon announcing his hire as a production/stage manager for New York's Radio City Music Hall/Rockefeller Center, 2016

On Tuesday, September 11, 2001, the Performing Arts program was preparing for its annual Fall Open House, a time new and returning students were traditionally invited to meet faculty and staff, sign up for courses and auditions, and get information about the program, other RIT drama and music groups, and regional accessible community theater.

The first plane hit the World Trade Center at 8:46, just as faculty and staff were setting up tables along the street level in front of the Panara Theatre and bringing in food. Immediately, projection screens on the stage were pulled down to air multiple news broadcasts, the food was offered to anxious students and the theater was a community center all day for grieving faculty, staff and students[13]. Thus, the decade began with the Performing Arts program continuing to be a heart, home and haven for the RIT community.

Later, that 2001–2002 academic year would host two sell-out Panara productions that dealt with the challenges of coming of age in a turbulent world: *The Diary of Anne Frank*, directed by Bonnie Meath-Lang, hauntingly relevant seven weeks after 9/11; and in the spring, the soaring, joyous *Peter Pan*. Directed by Jim Orr, the latter play was notable for many reasons, including the return of alumnus Matthew Moore to the Panara Theatre stage as Captain Hook, and the use of sophisticated flying techniques under the supervision of Fly by Foy, one of the premier flying companies in the business (*Cirque du Soleil* has been their client).

Funding issues put Sunshine Too on hiatus early in the decade, although outreach requests continued to come in to the program at a brisk rate. This was addressed by the shoulder-to-shoulder collaboration of students and staff. They created programs with student actors and dancers to go to schools, ASL classes, campus special events, other colleges and universities, vocational rehabilitation and interpreter conferences, and commemorative events, such as World AIDS Day.

In summer 2001, Luane Davis Haggerty directed another play taken to New York City with its cast and crew. In spring 2002, *The Emperor Jones*, starring Troy Chapman, Antilla Zulkifl (now performance artist Antie Z), Michael Spady, Chris Coles, and others won the OOBR Best Play Production Award from the *Off-Off-Broadway Review*, a critics' magazine. The play, about a man's estrangement and isolation from his community, was one of many productions that decade that confronted social issues, and addressed the students' desire

Peter Pan, 2002 (Jenamarie Daviton-Sciandra, Holly Schroeder, Thomas Minch, John Feeney).

to grapple with questions of identity and belonging.

The Laramie Project, directed by Bonnie Meath-Lang, and designed by alumnus Ethan Sinnott and Damita Peace, was the first Deaf production of the account of the tragic murder of gay college student Matthew Shephard and its impact on the community of Laramie, Wyoming[14]. *Beast on the Moon,* directed by Aaron Kelstone, examined the damage done to victims of persecution and displacement, specifically during the Armenian genocide of 1915. Playwright Richard Kalinoski came for a residency to discuss his process and his research with students and staff, and pronounced himself fascinated by seeing the play—which has been performed in multiple countries and languages—produced with Deaf actors in American Sign Language. Other productions addressing the complex web of culture and community in this decade were *Tales from a Clubroom, A Raisin in the Sun, The Deaf Woman Project, The Shape of Things, Like Totally Weird, Walls, The Crucible,* and *The Boys Next Door*[15].

Naturally, classic plays—*Lysistrata, Macbeth, Tartuffe, The Bungler, A Midsummer Night's Dream, Romeo and Juliet,* and *Inherit the Wind*—continued to be part of every season; new interpretations were expanded as production values were intensified. The RIT/NTID Dance Company, led by Thomas Warfield, took advantage of innovative lighting and special effects in its dance concerts and productions such as *Oz.* Student choreographers were empowered as well—Nicole Hood, Andrea Mariani, Kelli Benjamin, Sarah

Joe Hamilton, technical director, in front of the set of *Frankenstein*, 2005.

Clarke, Joe Fox and others brought new dance styles to the program and reinvented classic ones.

Handamation, directed by Aaron Kelstone, Luane Davis Haggerty, Thomas Warfield, and Duane Palyka, a professor from RIT's School of Film and Animation, combined ASL poetry, dance and animation, and traveled to the International Visual Theatre Conference in Maryland. Jim Orr directed the horror classics *The Passion of Dracula* and *Frankenstein*. With the latter show, the construction of a massive platform on which the monster was raised and lowered 30 feet was one of the more interesting career challenges for alumnus-turned-technical director, Joe Hamilton[16]. Another production, *Equus*, directed by Jerry Argetsinger, was commended for its innovative design and choreography in incorporating voice actors as the horses in an American College Theatre Festival review.

The partnership with RIT's School of Film and Animation produced BFA projects in the Laboratory Theatre that were invariably creative and well-attended. Original playwriting and choreography were conceived and directed by Deaf BFA students Beth Applebaum, Daniel Brucker, Ruthie Jordan and Peter Trzesniewski. Directing and design projects were also presented by Phetsakone Peter Bounsanga, JW Guido, Roger Phipps

and Jeff Pratt. Among the BFA productions were *Deathtrap*, *The Deaf Woman Project*, *A Soldier's Play*, *Rumplestiltskin*, *Naomi in the Living Room*, *The Lottery*, and *The Red Shoes*. Josh Liller's senior project was the lighting design for *The Diary of Anne Frank*.

Other students from the 2000s continue to work or have worked in professional theater, television and film in addition to the BFA graduates, including Luke Adams, Martina Bell, Chris Bradley, Chrissy Cogswell, Jeret Hackbarth, Amanda Montgomery, Jeremy Rosete, Michael Sauder, Michelle Schaefer, Holly Schroeder, Michael Spady, Darren Therriault, Amber Zion and Antie Z. Several of these students auditioned and were selected for Deaf West Theatre's first summer institute.

Another successful collaboration also began in the fourth decade. Modeled on programs in medical and law schools, which employ professional actors to interact with students in mock/simulated trials and crisis situations, the NTID Master's degree program in secondary education (MSSE) and the Performing Arts program created a similar program for teachers-in-training. Select NTID Performing Arts scholarship student-actors are given scripts and coached to improvise critical incidents and behavioral issues in a simulated classroom. The student teachers, who will be going out to high schools in the next term, teach their practice lessons to the actors. The actors play a range of the typical challenging behaviors and disruptions documented in educational research. Then the actors, education professors, and fellow student teachers give feedback and discuss problem-solving strategies. The program is widely praised as an innovative way to build confidence in new educators.

In 2009, alumnus James Cooley and Bonnie Meath-Lang were invited by the National Endowment for the Arts, U.S. Department of Labor, and the John F. Kennedy Center for the Performing Arts to be delegates at the National Summit on Careers in the Arts for People with Disabilities. Cooley performed part of his one-man show there, a monologue from NTID alumnus, playwright, and professor Willy Conley's play, *Broken Spokes*, which had been produced at NTID and in New York, and directed by J. Matt Searls, the previous year.

The decade ended with even more activity, as RIT announced its decision to change from the quarter to

Dack Virnig and Maya Ariel perform in *Guys and Dolls*, 2011.

the semester system. Major course revisions were under way as faculty, staff and students worked together to create a future in a new time frame.

The Fifth Decade: Creating a Future at Home (2011–present)

Time to focus on my play. Blocking ideas. I can't wait!!! Check off my theatre list...DIRECTOR!!! I have done everything except directing a big show. I have been...an assistant director, actor liaison, stage manager, tour manager, assistant stage manager, dancer, actor in drama, comedy, and musical plays, sound and light operator, spot light follower, prop sound effect crew (the gun sound from the blank firing gun...the BEST), backstage crew, and directing a student club with Dr. Luane Davis Haggerty. I'm glad I took lots of theatre courses when I was a student in college...You guys are my theatre angels. Thank you for teaching me about theatre. Now, THEATRE IS MY LIFE AND PASSION!

— Joe Fox (SVP '01, '06), theater production assistant, NTID Performing Arts

Predictably, the beginning of a semester-based curriculum in the early 2010s offered challenges to all academic programs, including Performing Arts. The quarter system contained 26 different course offerings; however, the reduction in the general education requirement to 12 credits, and the need to merge courses, reduced the number of course offerings to 14. Opportunities were also present within the new semester system where expanded time for planning allowed for multiple creative projects to cross college boundaries at RIT. For example, the NTID Performing Arts program and the RIT College of Liberal Arts collaborated on such productions as *Almost, Maine, The Rocky Horror Picture Show,* and *The Royal Hunt of the Sun.* Interactions with the RIT Players allowed the program to mount *Hairspray* and *Godspell.*

Interdisciplinary opportunities also became possible with the dance production *AstroDance,* creating a visual, multimedia show blending science, art and ASL, and was performed in New York City as well as on the RIT campus. The idea of *AstroDance* was developed by Thomas Warfield, who later directed and choreographed the production, and was additionally supported by multimedia and set design by Erin Auble. This collaboration was based on conceptual work by astrophysicist Manuela Campanelli, and scientist Hans-Peter Bischof of RIT's College of Science. The production was sponsored by a National Science Foundation grant. Performing Arts continues to be a regular presence at the annual Imagine RIT and Rochester Fringe Festivals.

Joseph (Joey) Ausanio ('13) directed the comedy *Dog Sees God* as his senior BFA project in the transfer agreement between NTID Performing Arts and the RIT College of Imaging Arts and Sciences' School of Film and Animation. He continues to work in and produce independent films, Web television series, and professional theater productions, notably playing the character Billy in *Tribes* in regional theaters across the United States. Michelle Schaefer also played Billy professionally numerous times, as well as the role of Sarah Norman in *Children of a Lesser God.*

Graduate "theater rats" continue to have an impact on the national stage. Julie Mason founded and leads the Deaf Talent Network, a platform for sharing information and opportunities for Deaf individuals in the arts and related fields. In the 2010s, alumni performers Amber Zion and Kriston Lee (Pumphrey) signed the National Anthem and America the Beautiful at Super Bowls XLVII and LI, respectively (Angela Laguardia performed at Super Bowl XL in 2006). Beth Applebaum and JW Guido, current artistic director, direct and act for New York Deaf Theatre as well as other regional theaters.

Over time, the number of events sponsored in the Panara Theatre has become a significant part of its season activities. This has made it challenging to coordinate events and productions each season within the Panara space. To respond to the intense demand for event and production space, efforts have been made to renovate the 1510 Experimental Lab Theater, the Dance Studio and the Green Room to expand the potential performance spaces within LBJ Hall. Matthew Moore, serving as the chairperson of the Performing Arts Advisory Group has provided significant leadership to spearhead the efforts for renovation and expansion of the theater spaces within LBJ Hall.

Fifty-year-old homes beg for continued maintenance and remodeling. In addition to major sound, light and equipment upgrades, this decade, former students from the program led in the design and reconfiguration of the front of house outside the Panara Theatre. Christopher Brucker, with his rich background in theater, architecture and industrial design, worked with technical director Joe Hamilton and program director Aaron Kelstone to make the greeting areas more accessible, harmonious with the Dyer Gallery across the lobby, and state-of-the-art. This served to complement a wide variety of productions in this decade, including *Hairspray, Arsenic and Old Lace, Charlie and the Chocolate Factory,* and *The Crucifer of Blood. Godspell,* directed by Luane Davis Haggerty, originally performed in the 1510 Laboratory Theatre space was later performed at Geva's Nextstage Theatre, establishing a new working relationship with the Rochester theater community. This production also toured to New York City. Recently, *Pippin* was produced with the Multi-use Community Cultural Center (MUCCC) further expanding the program's community presence in Rochester.

A particularly exciting development in this decade was a "reboot" of the Sunshine Too concept for this era. Through the urging of Matthew Moore and others, NTID President Gerry Buckley provided supporting funds, and charged Performing Arts Program Director Aaron Kelstone, Cultural and Creative Studies Chair Joe Bochner, and Performing Arts Program Advisory Group Chair Matthew Moore to re-establish a new outreach touring company. Temporarily named Sunshine

2.0, the company hired professional dancer and alumnus Fred Michael Beam as director and choreographer, as well as energetic and charismatic performers Ronnie Bradley and Katie Mueller. A very active touring season was initiated during 2016–2017.

Conclusion

> Home isn't where you're from, it's where you find light when all is dark.
>
> — Pierce Brown[17]

In the Robert F. Panara Theatre, as in theaters around the world, the centuries-old tradition of the ghost light is strictly observed. After rehearsals and performances, or simply any time the theater goes dark, a pole lamp with one bare bulb is lit center stage. The practical reason is to prevent falls, of course, but there have been a number of more romantic and fanciful explanations. One is that the ghosts of the people who have walked that stage are never really far away, and the memory of wonderful performances that happened there will draw them back; their way should be lit.

The Performing Arts courses, productions and outreach at NTID have touched thousands of lives—students, alumni, faculty, staff, audiences, the RIT community and the world community. Its history has produced actors, dancers, designers, filmmakers, civic and professional leaders. New creative work has been produced in ASL, English and pure movement, and classic work has been revitalized and re-visualized. As the great Deaf actor Phyllis Frelich said in a workshop at the American Deaf Play Creators' Festival, hosted by NTID in 1996, "We're here to give people their eyes back."

The Performing Arts program, while looking back, also has an eye on the future. But students, former students, and their teachers, in action and memory, will always have enough light to find their way home.

Dr. Bonnie Meath-Lang is Professor Emerita and former artistic director of the NTID Performing Arts program. James Orr, retired, is the former Outreach Director for the NTID Performing Arts program. Dr. Aaron Kelstone is a faculty member in NTID's Department of Cultural and Creative Studies.

Notes

1. Kathleen S. Smith, "NTID's Performing Arts department celebrates 20 years of entertainment." *FOCUS Magazine* (Fall, 1995): 17.

2. Halverson, Bruce. "Deaf and Hearing Together." in *Perspectives: A handbook in drama and theatre by, with, and for handicapped individuals*, eds. Ann M. Shaw, Wendy Perks, and C.J. Stevens (New York: American Theatre Association, 1981).

3. Harry G. Lang, *Teaching from the heart and soul: The Robert F. Panara story.* (Washington, DC: Gallaudet University Press, 2007): 159.

4. Harry G. Lang and Karen C. Conner, *From dream to reality: The National Technical for the Deaf.* (Rochester, NY: Rochester Institute of Technology, 2001): 38.

5. Greg Livadas, "Curtain going up: Performing Arts at NTID provide extraordinary experiences for students and audiences." *RIT: The University Magazine* (Spring, 2010): 19.

6. Livadas, "Curtain going up."

7. Gerald S. Argetsinger, "Experimental educational theatre as a tool for living the good life." Paper presented at the NTID Mini-Convention, Rochester, New York, June 1978.

8. Livadas, "Curtain going up."

9. Kathy A. Johncox, "A rich creative history." *FOCUS Magazine* (Fall/Winter, 2012): 10–11.

10. Bonnie Meath-Lang, "Dramatic interactions: Theater work and the formation of learning communities." *American annals of the deaf* 142, no. 2 (1997): 99–101.

11. Zoe Ingalls. "On Prospero's island, deaf and hearing students learn to act together." *Chronicle of Higher Education* (July 14, 2000).

12. Livadas, "Curtain going up."

13. Bonnie Meath-Lang, "Embodying curriculum in an age of terror: Theatre work to challenge boundaries and confound perceptions." Paper presented at the Conference on Curriculum Theory and Classroom Practice, Dayton, Ohio, October, 2005.

14. James McCarthy, "The Laramie Project." *NTID's The View* (Fall 2002): 7.

15. Joe McLaughlin, "All in this together: The deaf, the hearing, and the NTID Performing Arts." *Reporter Magazine* 57, no. 26 (2008): 16–19.

16. Kathy A. Johncox, "It's alive! Technology rules in NTID Performing Arts." *FOCUS Magazine* (Spring/Summer, 2004): 12–13.

17. Pierce Brown, *Golden son.* (New York: Del Rey, 2015).

The Kitchen Light of NTID

Miriam Lerner

It is often noted that great events are a concurrence of great people, great ideas, and the right time and place for the perfect fusion of energy to explode into a supernova of enlightenment. It can be difficult to find specific times and locations when great changes and shifts in attitude occur, as they usually follow a more geologic model of slow and almost imperceptible change over time. However, when considering ASL poetry and literature, the importance of NTID and specifically the Panara Theatre housed in LBJ Hall cannot be overstated. The right people, and—of paramount importance—the right environment, were ready to come together for the unleashing of new forms of ASL performance art. This chapter documents that story from a mix of firsthand experience and information gained in the process of making the film, *The Heart of the Hydrogen Jukebox*.[1]

In 1982, a hearing poet named Jim Cohn was traveling around the United States, honing his craft and ruminating on different modalities of poetry and literature. He became interested in the idea of American Sign Language, and what poetry—a word-based representation of images—would look like in a language that essentially consists of images. He found his way to NTID, was accepted into the Interpreter Training Program, and set about learning what ASL poetry might look like.

While at NTID, Cohn sought out the Deaf poet Robert Panara, perhaps the greatest 20th century Deaf scholar of Deaf literature. With Panara acting as Cohn's cultural informant, they discussed similarities and differences between Deaf and hearing poetry. Cohn studied all of Panara's writing on Deaf poetry and its history. Taking this ethnographic approach, Cohn became convinced that, not only was Deaf poetry a literary genre that survived outside the American literary canon, but also that American Sign Language poetry was a living, breathing American poetic form—its own literary space.

Cohn confronted a perplexing challenge during his quest: the Deaf people he encountered who were creative signers eschewed the notion that what they were producing could or should be called "poetry." In their minds, poetry belonged to written and spoken languages, and they had no templates for the existence of ASL poetry. Their experiences of poetry were, for the most part, that of being compelled to memorize sound-based poems in English classes, thus instilling in them the notion that only spoken language with rhyme and meter could lay claim to producing poetry. The notion that ASL was a true language was getting traction in the late '70s and early '80s, so the time was ripe for a paradigm shift in terms of ASL literature genres.

If this chapter were a river, we would now have side channels to wander, as there are two concurrent stories that meet again further downstream.

One story also takes place in the early 1980s, when a small group of extremely creative Deaf students at NTID began having parties in their rooms and playing translation games. They would read a story or a comic book, look at illustrated magazine or album covers (this was before CDs, iPods, or personal computers), and attempt to "translate" and perform the images in ASL. They played with the language and stretched their imaginations in ways they had not attempted before, but the aggregate synergy of their inner visions pushed them in surprising ways. Other students heard about the fun, and the rooms were soon so crowded that another venue had to be found to accommodate their fans and to carry on their experimentation.

At the time, there was a bar called The Cellar located in the tunnels underneath the dorms at NTID. The sign-play parties migrated there, and soon students were taking turns performing on a makeshift stage for any and all who showed up. One of those students was Peter Cook, who would later go on to become an accomplished ASL poet and storyteller, as well as a respected interpreter trainer, ASL and Deaf Studies professor, and chair of the ASL department at Columbia College Chicago.

It was Cook who came up with the idea of naming these weekly performances at the Cellar "The Birdsbrain Society," after seeing a poem by Allen Ginsberg of the same name. Cook was also the person responsible for organizing these first poetry "readings" in ASL by Deaf students. It was during this time that Cohn first interviewed Cook about ASL poetry and began publishing his poetry in *ACTION*, a magazine of poetry and poets based in the Rochester community.

Meanwhile, in our second story, Cohn was hot on the trail of what ASL poetry might look like. Along with becoming involved in the Rochester hearing poetry community, especially at the literary center Writers & Books, he attended the The Cellar gatherings with great interest and was intrigued by what he was witnessing. Cohn had studied under and served as a teaching assistant to the famous American Beat poet, Allen Ginsberg, in Boulder, Colorado. Cohn invited Ginsberg to come to NTID and provide a workshop/discussion group to students, NTID professors, and invited guests, on February 1, 1984. Dr. Robert Panara was the co-presenter, and together with Ginsberg explored the various ways poetry functions in language and culture, attempting a cross-linguistic, bi-cultural understanding of meaning, translation, and aesthetic.

At one point Ginsberg read from his famous poem, "Howl". He stopped at one of his favorite images

in the beginning of the poem, "...listening to the crack of doom on the hydrogen jukebox." He asked if there was a way to render that phrase adequately in ASL, or if it would be impossible to translate. Patrick Graybill, a founding member of the National Theater of the Deaf, had years of experience translating English texts into ASL for performances. Much to his chagrin, Graybill was "volunteered" by other members of the audience to attempt an ad-hoc rendition in front of the group. It is, indeed, fortunate that we have video footage of the event, because Graybill's spontaneous and brilliant offering astonished and delighted all present, including Ginsberg, who exclaimed, "That looks like it!" That moment changed Graybill's understanding of his own work, and also proved to be an epiphany for a young deaf student who was in attendance that day, Peter Cook.

And now these two river channels come together, producing a current as swift and resolute as the Yukon River. Cohn had seen Cook's work in The Cellar and was impressed with his pieces, as well as those performed by Debbie Rennie and Patrick Graybill. He set about convincing these talented authors that what they were doing *was* poetry, and to open up their work to the hearing community of writers in Rochester. To accomplish this, the Deaf poets would need someone to use their voices to translate the work and perform it with them. Cohn had a friend, Kenny Lerner, a hearing teacher who signed ASL and worked in the English Learning Center (ELC) at NTID at the time. Cohn intuited that Lerner and Cook would be a good fit, and even though Lerner wasn't an interpreter, Cohn introduced them to each other. They did, indeed, connect in an artistic way, became good friends and performance partners, and eventually formed the partnership, The Flying Words Project. Lerner also worked in the creation and translation of pieces by Rennie, who later worked with hearing interpreter Donna Kachites. Graybill wrote his own English translations for his poems, and would rehearse with any interpreter assigned to work with him in performances.

A small group of Rochester interpreters were interested in exploring this new enterprise of interpreting poetry from English to ASL and from ASL to English, and began serving as translators and voice interpreters for much of the work that was being performed at this time. Writers & Books provided a stage [obscured] Jazzberry's, a small vegetarian restaurant i[obscured] town Rochester. Cohn initiated a poetry series [obscured] cross-fertilization of poetry began to occur among Deaf and hearing poets.

In September 1987, Cohn organized and executed the First National ASL Poetry Conference, sponsored and hosted by NTID. For three days, lectures, panels, and performances were held in the Panara Theatre. Showcased during this event were five major Deaf poets of whom Cohn was aware at the time: Cook, Graybill, Rennie, Ella Mae Lentz, and Clayton Valli. Voice interpreters were assigned to all events. A complete video record of the conference is housed in the Deaf Archives section of the RIT Library. The documentary film, *The Heart of the Hydrogen Jukebox*, also in the RIT Library on DVD, as well as posted in its entirety on YouTube, includes interviews and footage from the conference. It was the first time a full conference had been convened specifically for the purpose of exploring and elevating ASL poetry as a distinct art form.

Although there was no follow-up symposium that focused solely on ASL poetry, in 1991, The Flying Words Project (Cook and Lerner) used money awarded by a New York State Council on the Arts grant, in collaboration with NTID, to sponsor an ASL Literature Conference. It was held primarily in Panara Theatre, as well as various classrooms in NTID's Lyndon Baines Johnson Hall. This conference investigated not only ASL poetry, but also storytelling and theater. A second literature conference was held in 1993 at NTID, as well, with Panara Theatre serving as the focal point and meeting place for all of the major performances, lectures, and panels.

As awareness, acknowledgement, and respect for ASL literature in all of its various manifestations has grown, NTID has served as a cultural and linguistic petri dish, growing generations of talented performers and scholars. In a sense, Panara Theatre has become the epitome of the Deaf kitchen: a place for people to congregate, connect, discuss, learn, and grow together beneath the bright light of community. Its stage has hosted numerous performances of plays, poetry, lectures, and discussions, as well as serving as a laboratory for Deaf performance artists to hone their craft and follow their creative muses in an exciting, nurturing environment. The history that has transpired in that auditorium is full and rich, spanning generations of Deaf students who have been fortunate enough to call NTID their temporary home.

To borrow a hearing phrase and change it up a bit: "Oh, if those walls could only sign!"

Miriam Lerner is a current RIT/NTID interpreter.

Notes

1. *The Heart of the Hydrogen Jukebox*, directed by Miriam Nathan Lerner and Don Feigel (Rochester, N.Y.: Rochester Institute of Technology, 2009), DVD.

Empowerment
The Importance of Deaf Cultural Studies

Patti Durr

The founding of NTID was first called for by Peter N. Peterson, a Deaf vocational teacher who noted the lack of technical and vocational secondary education for Deaf youth. As stated on a plaque in Peterson Hall, this Deaf visionary wrote back in 1930, "A national technical institute for the deaf, located at the center of population in a large manufacturing city, is what deaf young America needs more than anything else. A dream you say, a wild, fancy fantastic dream! Perhaps so. But more fantastic dreams than this have come true."

So we see that NTID originated from a Deaf vision, and throughout its history, it has had Deaf visionaries leading the way. Deaf Cultural Studies was infused into literature courses at NTID's inception by Deaf professor Robert Panara. *The Washington* Post reported that "beginning in the 1970s, Mr. Panara wrote articles and books that helped establish deaf studies as a formal line of academic inquiry."[1]

Robert Panara's Influence

Panara was not only the first Deaf professor that many RIT/NTID students met; he was also the first person to introduce them to the lives and creative expressions of people like them. In 2017, the U.S. Post Office issued a stamp in recognition of Panara's gift as a teacher and a pioneer of Deaf Studies. The stamp features a photograph by NTID's Mark Benjamin of Robert Panara signing the word "respect." The photo came from a campaign at NTID to encourage faculty and staff to use ASL in open spaces so that Deaf students, faculty, and staff would have equal access to everyday conversation. Panara was a strong supporter of ASL, Deaf culture, and Deaf rights, both inside and outside the classroom for all the years of his life.

I took Deafness & American Culture and Deaf Studies in Literature with Bob Panara. Bob's great storytelling of famous people like William Hoy, Laurent Clerc, and Thomas Gallaudet, as well as others enhanced my awareness of success among deaf individuals and that the sky was the limit.
— J.T. Reid, NTID Alumnus and NTID Senior Admissions Counselor[2]

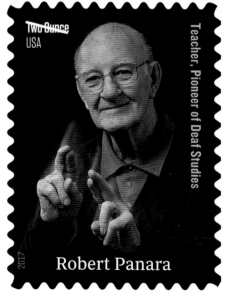

Two Ounce
USA

Teacher, Pioneer of Deaf Studies

2017

Robert Panara

Panara smiles at the head of the class.

Vicki Hurwitz, faculty member, poses with her Deaf Women's Studies students.

I once took a class under Robert Panara called "Deaf Characters in Literature and Film"…We were told to be on the lookout for the "Deaf experience," and analyze the authenticity of it in each story or movie. Then, we were given a creative writing assignment where we would write about a personal experience of ours that involved a deaf experience. I received an "A" on my paper with encouragement to submit it to RIT's literary magazine. I ended up getting my first published story with a byline, and this led to an ongoing love for creative writing.

— Willy Conley,
Gallaudet Professor of Theatre Arts[3]

Dr. Karen Christie, Patricia Kenney, and Pamela Conley have continued this legacy of Deaf literature courses at RIT/NTID. Even in the early days, when there were only a few Deaf professors teaching Deaf Cultural Studies courses like Panara and Greg Emerton's "Deaf Culture in America", other professors made an effort to incorporate Deaf Cultural Studies into their course work. Alumna Nancy Rourke recalls such an experience in a general education course:

The assignment was about putting your life into a sketchbook and to focus on Deaf Culture, and what we saw each day. She told us we could do however we wanted in a sketchbook. So, I made sketches and notes and I used them for my art classes. And by the end of the quarter, sketchbooks were turned in for final grades. The professor went one by one, and then it was my turn, she told me my sketchbook was good and to keep making notes and sketches "because you'll never know what you wrote there and some day they become so important to you."
She was right.

— Nancy Rourke, alumna and Internationally recognized full time De'VIA artist[4]

The Evolution of Deaf Cultural Studies

Over time, other Deaf professors would develop and teach new and innovative Deaf Cultural Studies courses, such as Vicki Hurwitz's "Deaf Women's Studies", Paula Grcevic and Barbara Fox's "Deaf Art/Deaf Artists", and Patti Durr's "Deaf People and World War II" and "Civil Rights and Deaf People". The World War II course led to Durr conducting some visual-history interviews with Deaf Holocaust survivors and producing a few short documentaries, such as *Worry* and *Exodus*. These courses, along with other Deaf Cultural Studies courses, have grown and evolved over time. Currently, through the Department of Cultural and Creative Studies (DCCS), NTID offers a certificate in Deaf Cultural Studies and, with RIT's College of Liberal Arts, an immersion and minor in Deaf Cultural Studies and ASL.

In addition to unique and evolving course offerings, RIT/NTID has also been instrumental in gathering materials and creating attractive, visual, and user-friendly Deaf Cultural Studies-based websites. These are created as a collaboration among Web developers Simon Ting and Cathy Clark, author Patti Durr, and librarian/copyright specialist Joan Naturale. The websites are accessed by Deaf Cultural Studies' students, faculty, and the public at large from all over the globe. They cover topics including Deaf art,[5] Deaf people, and World War II,[6] and Deaf theatre.[7]

Patti Durr, faculty member, works with students in a classroom activity.

From Teaching to Doing

In addition to teaching Deaf Cultural Studies courses and coordinating that program and Performing Arts respectively, Drs. J. Matt Searls and Aaron Kelstone have directed original Deaf plays for the NTID Performing Arts program or community organizations.

Dr. Karen Christie has taught ASL literature courses at RIT/NTID. She has published articles in this area and, along with Patti Durr, created and edited *The HeART of Deaf Culture: Literary and Artistic Expressions of Deafhood*, which is used as a visual textbook in Deaf Cultural Studies and ASL classes at a variety of colleges and universities.

Christie and Durr also created the *US Deaf History* website, which houses a wealth of primary documents.[8] They have also worked diligently on the Deaf View/Image Art (De'VIA) curriculum, along with teaching

artists from across the country. Additionally, Christie and Durr have made short films contributing to Deaf Cultural Studies and exhibited their artwork at shows.

Drs. Harry Lang and Bonnie Meath-Lang researched and published several books showcasing the contributions of Deaf people and thus have contributed significantly to the field of Deaf Cultural Studies. Much of the rest of this book cites one Lang or the other.

Deaf Cultural Studies faculty and students have been instrumental in coordinating and hosting many major conferences and events, such as the National ASL Literature Conference (I and II), the Deaf Rochester Film Festivals and Viva De'VIA – 25th Anniversary of De'VIA Festival. Faculty and students have also performed and contributed to the annual Deaf-Mute Banquets hosted by the RIT ASL Deaf Studies Community Center (RADSCC).

In addition to Deaf Cultural Studies courses, the RIT Deaf Studies Archives was established in 2006, and houses many valuable collections and artifacts that are used by students and scholars across the world.

From Learning to Advocacy

Many Deaf and hearing students remark on the importance of Deaf Cultural Studies in their academic experience and personal lives. An important part of the field is learning to be change agents who bring about positive social change and work for social justice. The Deaf Cultural Studies program has invited numerous scholars and leaders to campus to engage the students and faculty. Faculty don't preach when they teach. They engage, empower, and act.

Even students who have not taken any Deaf Cultural Studies courses report on how RIT/NTID's rich Deaf culture environment has positively impacted their self-worth, growth, and identity formation. The Student Life Team has played a huge and vital role in the life and spirit of student development at NTID, and it has kept Deaf culture at the heart of their work.

> While I was a student at RIT/NTID, being true to myself, I constantly stood up, sharing experiences, encouraging others to share their experience, in the hope that others will comprehend our experiences. I also provoked their thoughts, to see how they react, and even played devil's advocate at times....I hope that when they leave RIT/NTID, they will remember all of our discussions. I noticed some students who have taken Deaf Cultural Studies classes, at first were skeptical or even resistant to using sign language, but at the end of semester, many of them found their identity, started using sign language, and at last, are proud of being Deaf.

> It is a great feeling seeing the students change their perspectives about being Deaf and to see them being proud of who they are after they take any Deaf Cultural Studies classes here at RIT/NTID.
>
> — Sara Smania[9]

Continuing to Grow

The Deaf Cultural Studies program and the Deaf Culture environment at RIT/NTID ensure that ASL, Deaf culture, and Deaf people are valued and respected as an important part of RIT's multicultural identity. As our society evolves and many individuals experience intersectionality and oppression, our Deaf Cultural Studies program continues to grow, engage, and renew.

"A dream you say, a wild, fancy fantastic dream!" lives on.

Patti Durr is a faculty member in NTID's Department of Cultural and Creative Studies.

Notes

1. Robert Panara, writer, poet, professor and pioneer of deaf studies, dies at 94. https://www.washingtonpost.com/national/robert-f-panara-writer-poet-professor-and-pioneer-of-deaf-studies-dies-at-94/2014/07/23/725ab652-1273-11e4-9285-4243a40ddc97_story.html?utm_term=.9435c6e5bc6a

2. J.T. Reid, personal communication, 2017.

3. Willy Conley, personal communication, 2017.

4. Nancy Rourke, personal communication, 2017.

5. Deaf Art / Deaf Artists. http://www.rit.edu/ntid/dccs/dada/dada.htm

6. Deaf People and World War II. http://www.rit.edu/ntid/ccs/deafww2/

7. Deaf Theatre. https://www.rit.edu/ntid/deaftheatre/

8. US Deaf history. https://usdeafhistory.com

9. Sara Smania, personal communication, 2017.

Dyer Arts Center
A New Home for Deaf Artists

Tabitha Jacques and Robert Baker

Introduction

Deaf artists have existed for centuries, but there have been limited resources for documenting and preserving the history of deaf-related art. That began to change when Gallaudet University was founded; after forming their Archives unit, efforts were set in motion to collect art by deaf artists and document information about their biographies, techniques, and processes.

As more attention began to be paid to deaf-related art, other organizations that began to contribute to this collection and the preservation efforts included residential schools for the deaf, the National Association of the Deaf (NAD), and the Alexander Graham Bell Association for the Deaf (AGBAD).[1]

In cases where deaf-related art was not actively collected or documented, environments where the general networking of artists could take place continued to grow. In the late 1980s, the Deaf Way I Conference sparked the movement of Deaf View/Image Art (De'VIA), where a group of artists came together and drafted a manifesto that shaped their art.[2] This was probably the first group of deaf and hard-of-hearing artists that started a movement. Although the Deaf Art Movement of the 1970s emerged earlier, it was powered mainly by a single artist named Ann Silver (and possibly a few other artists), but the movement did not become as widely recognized as De'VIA is.[3]

At the same time that deaf-related art and the movements surrounding it were beginning to coalesce into what could be termed a "school" or a "philosophy",

NTID was founded in 1968. Applied Arts was one of the first academic programs. Many of the De'VIA founding artists were NTID alumni and graduates from the program, such as Guy Wonder ('71) (one of the first students to enroll at NTID), Chuck Baird, and Paul Johnston.[4] Nancy Rourke, also a graduate of NTID, spearheaded the second wave of De'VIA in 2009.[5] Many other previous graduates also identify with the second wave of De'VIA and participate heavily in the De'VIA Central Facebook page that has over 4,000 members.

In 1976, upon the completion of NTID's Lyndon Baines Johnson (LBJ) Hall, C. Tim Fergerson, a professor in the Applied Arts, founded the NTID Art Gallery in the reception space for the office of the Director of NTID.[6] Very little information is recorded, but it is assumed that 1976 was the same year that NTID started to collect art by deaf or hard-of-hearing people, at first drawing from the work of NTID students and art faculty. In this way, NTID became the second institution to actively collect and preserve deaf-related art. In 1984, the NTID Art Gallery expanded, and it was designated as the Mary E. Switzer Gallery.[7]

In 2000, NTID received over $2.5 million from the Dyer family, and a matching federal grant to focus on collecting, preserving, and displaying art by deaf and hard-of-hearing people.[8] A beautiful 7,000-square-foot gallery was built and named the Joseph C. and Helen F. Dyer Arts Center. To date, the Dyer Arts Center houses approximately 1,000 pieces of artwork, and the collection is growing every year. The artists represented in

Rainbow by Chuck Baird, 2004.

the Permanent Collection are mostly deaf or hard-of-hearing. Those who are hearing are affiliated with RIT or with the deaf community in some way. If not already, the Dyer Arts Center is expected to become a leader in collecting and displaying all types of artworks made by deaf or hard-of-hearing artists, including those who are affiliated with De'VIA, who identify themselves with a specific type of hearing loss, a particular movement, or identity/identities.

NTID Art Gallery

The objective of the NTID Art Gallery was to expose students to the world of art, and to ensure their technical background was complemented by the arts. NTID Director Dr. D. Robert Frisina and Dean William E. Castle enthusiastically endorsed the arts as an integral complement to a technical education.[9] Gallery shows, consisting mostly of work by professional hearing artists, were held on a monthly basis.[10] A student honors show by student artists from the NTID Applied Arts

program was held every spring, and would remain on display all summer.[11] Approximately two or three deaf or hard-of-hearing professional artists or faculty members would have their own show per year.[12]

In 1981, Bob Baker, who assisted Mr. Fergerson with exhibits and was an events specialist in the Public Information Office (now known as Communications, Marketing, and Multimedia Services) took over the NTID Art Gallery. Baker was active in collecting art by deaf and hard-of-hearing artists.[13] After an exhibit, Baker would purchase a few pieces, or ask the artist to make a donation to the NTID Permanent Collection. One example is Chuck Baird's *Rainbow* piece. [14]

Because federal funding guidelines of NTID restricted the use of funds to supporting direct instructional needs, artwork could only be purchased using privately raised donations.[15] Approximately 100 art pieces were collected before 1984, and most were displayed in LBJ's hallways and offices.[16]

In 1984, when the Gallery was renamed to the

Mary E. Switzer Art Gallery, more exhibits by deaf and hard-of-hearing artists began to be staged.[17] The space was also used for special events, such as conferences, welcome receptions, and university-related events.[18] With the construction of the Dyer Arts Center, the current-day Switzer Gallery has evolved into a conference room.

The Dyer Arts Center

When the Dyers made their gift in 2000, the planners determined that the center would be located in the open-air courtyard near the front entrance of LBJ, renowned among NTID students—now alumni—as a smoking area that featured "the metal dandelion sculptures" by Harry Bertoia.[19] The dandelions were created for Eastman Kodak's Pavilion in the 1964 World's Fair, and donated to NTID by the company.

With the funds from the Dyer family, NTID hired contractors to enclose the courtyard and convert the existing space into an arts center.[20] The space contains three galleries, two storage spaces, and a kitchen. The main gallery is named the Elizabeth W. Williams Gallery. The smaller gallery upstairs is named the Milton H. and Ray B. Ohringer Gallery. They donated $500,000 and $300,000, respectively, to complete the renovation.[21] A small third gallery, as yet unnamed, is accessed through the main Williams Gallery. The smaller gallery is known as The Glass Room by current students, faculty, and staff.

When NTID celebrated the opening of the Joseph F. and Helen C. Dyer Arts Center on October 26, 2001, Baker planned an inaugural exhibit showcasing works by deaf and hard-of-hearing artists, along with honorary curator Chuck Baird.[22] Artists included were Baird himself, Rita Straubhaar, Paula Grcevic, Ron Trumble, Morris Broderson, Carl Zollo, and Charles Wildbank.[23] Joseph Dyer was able to see the opening of the Dyer Arts Center. Helen, however, had passed away one month before the opening.[24] Along with the monetary donation, Dyer also decided to donate his wife's paintings and sketchbooks.[25]

While Baker was at the helm, he was able to secure more than 800 pieces of art using individual or in-kind donations.[26] Some examples are paintings and drawings from Morris Broderson's estate, pieces made by RIT/NTID professors and staff, paintings by Frances

Top: The main Williams Gallery, with the Ohringer Gallery visible upstairs. Bottom: The 'glass room.'

Carlberg King, Paul Johnston, Chuck Baird, Nancy Rourke, Mary Rapazzo, Jeremy Quiroga, Uzi Buzgalo, Susan Dupor, and Sander Blondeel.[27] Baker also worked with major donors, such as Renate Alpert, who donated many of Jean Hanau's artworks.[28]

Baker also successfully organized a variety of exhibits during his tenure.[29] These exhibits included *Mythology Images,* an exhibit by Deaf women, curated by Paula Grcevic; a showcase of Russian Deaf artists in an exchange with NTID students; a collection of international Deaf artists in collaboration with Postsecondary Education Network (PEN) International; displays of historic deaf and hard-of-hearing photographers; a retrospective of the Allen Sisters; and exhibits by De'VIA founders, such as Betty Miller.[30]

Baker retired in 2013, and two interim directors, Jenamarie Bacot and Stacy Lawrence, were appointed.[31] During their time, they exhibited Tate Tullier's photography, Jeremy Quiroga's *Read My Lips* (acquired by NTID in 2008), and *Viva, De'VIA: Celebrating 25*

Years of the Deaf View/Image Arts, among a number of others.[32] Bacot and Lawrence were able to acquire some significant pieces, such as Tate Tullier's photos and David Call's woodblock prints. [33]

Tabitha Jacques took over as director in 2015 and implemented a new acquisitions system for managing the Permanent Collection. A number of exhibits have been featured in the Dyer Arts Center, such as the first-ever exhibit specific to Black/African-American artists, a collection of works by artists with disabilities on loan from the John F. Kennedy Center for the Performing Arts, and Jose Saldana's seminal series of photographs of cultures inhabiting the mountain ranges of the world.

In addition, Jacques brought with her a new drive to collaborate with institutions in the City of Rochester, bringing artwork from the Dyer Permanent Collection to First Friday events and developing relationships with local deaf and hard-of-hearing artists. This drive also includes welcoming the community to the Dyer Arts Center, with events attracting both NTID-affiliated attendees and attendees from the community. Jacques has also been able to acquire art pieces by Takiyah Harris, Fred Beam, Susan Dupor, Eddie Swayze, and Warren Miller.

Stand for Justice by Nancy Rourke, 2011.

Artist Highlights

As mentioned earlier, many of the founders of De'VIA were students at NTID. For example, Guy Wonder, renowned for his mixed-media sculptures, was one of the first students to enroll at NTID in 1968.[34] He studied weaving/textile arts and took numerous other art courses.[35] He was also heavily involved with theater and was the first president of the drama club founded at NTID.[36] After graduation, he moved to New York City, where he pursued a BFA degree in Interior Design.[37] While he was in New York City, he was involved with a citywide project to make museums accessible to people with disabilities, and he led tours in American Sign Language at the Metropolitan Museum of Art and the Museum of Modern Art (MoMA).[38]

Before he became involved with De'VIA, he had spent several years creating collage-based art about gay men.[39] Because of the AIDS epidemic, his target audience became discouraged, and Wonder started losing buyers.[40] He decided to shift his focus to deaf art.

Early on, he noticed many of his deaf-related art works included people with large eyes, little ears, and physical contact. However, it was not until 1989 that his work gained national attention after Deaf Way I.[41] Currently, the Dyer Arts center owns three of his pieces in its Permanent Collection.

Chuck Baird, also a member of the De'VIA movement, was a prolific artist and a graduate of RIT/NTID. He happened to be Guy Wonder's roommate during his first year of college, and like Wonder, he was heavily involved with theater at NTID.[42] He graduated with a BFA in Studio Painting in 1974 and went on to be part of numerous exhibits at RIT/NTID as an alumnus. The Dyer Arts Center is fortunate to own more than 15 pieces by Baird, especially from his early period. Baird did mostly paintings, but also ventured into mixed media later in his life, before his death in 2012.

Nancy Rourke, an artist who propelled the second wave of De'VIA, combining art and activism, graduated from RIT/NTID. She received her BFA in

Dr. Ernest Hairston Appeared from the Popcorn Can by Takiyah Harris, 2015.

Finding the Rosicas, Leon Lim.

graphic design and painting in 1982 and continued her education with a master's degree in computer graphic design and painting in 1986.[43] Rourke, also a prolific artist, has painted and sold numerous pieces. She is currently one of the administrators of De'VIA Central Facebook page. She also hosts the annual De'VIA 28-day challenges, in which artists from all around the world participate in a 28-day challenge to create artworks based on a motif each day. The Dyer Arts Center owns nine pieces of Rourke's work.

Takiyah Harris graduated from RIT/NTID in 1999 and is a member of the second wave of the De'VIA movement. Her preferred media are primarily haptic/collage art and fine-arts photography.[44] Themes of her work range from her experience as a Deaf person to her experience as a Black person, and often a combination of both.[45] She researches Black Deaf history, and her works are heavily influenced by art history.[46]

Leon Lim, born in Malaysia, graduated from RIT/NTID in 2005. He was commissioned by NTID to do

two large sculptural/mixed media installations. The first one was *3(656)*, a sculptural installation of three panels made of wood. Bars of Plexiglass-encased lights are carefully crafted into the wood panels, giving the installation a permanent glow. The second commissioned piece is *Finding the Rosicas*, a photographic composition of more than 600 family photographs. *Finding the Rosicas* is hung in Sebastian and Lenore Rosica Hall.

Persons of Distinction

The Dyer Arts Center would not exist if not for the following key players in the existence and reputation of the center, nearly all of whom were also artists or were affiliated with an artist.

The Dyer family, as mentioned earlier, donated a large sum of money to the foundation of the arts center. However, it's important to recognize that Helen Dyer was an artist herself. The center is fortunate to house her paintings and sketchbooks. Dyer was part of a circle of friends that included Elizabeth "Cookie" Williams,

Frances Carlberg King, and Florence Ohringer. Those women, also artists, supported each other in continuing the development of their artistic skills and exhibiting their work.

The Williams Gallery was named after Elizabeth "Cookie" Williams; the Dyer Arts Center also has several pieces of her work. Similarly, the Ohringer Gallery was named after Milton and Ray Ohringer, who also donated two works by the late Florence Ohringer, Milton's first wife, to the Permanent Collection. Frances Carlberg King did not have a gallery named after her, but she established a scholarship. The Drew and Frances King Endowment Fund supports RIT/NTID students majoring in art. King also donated a large amount of her artwork to the Dyer Arts Center.

Although the following donors were not artists, they had family members who are renowned in the Deaf community. Dr. James and Pat DeCaro donated a large number of works to the Permanent Collection—thanks to Pat DeCaro's father, David Mudgett, who was an artist, and was closely connected to other deaf and hard-of-hearing artists, such as David Bloch, during his time.

Joan Ankrum, owner of Los Angeles's Ankrum Gallery and Morris Broderson's aunt, donated many pieces by Broderson to the Dyer Arts Center. Ankrum first loaned Broderson's works for an exhibit at the Mary E. Switzer Gallery in 1984, and a relationship formed amongst Anrkum, Thomas Raco, and Bob Baker.[47] Raco, an NTID faculty member, approached Ankrum with an exhibit proposal that showcased works by NTID graduates.[48] Two years later, *Heart/Eye/Hand: Works by Twelve Deaf Artists* opened on May 27, 1986, at her gallery.[49] Ankrum was the driving force behind Broderson's success. She and her son donated many pieces of Broderson's works to the Dyer Arts Center from 1984 to 2011.

Alumni Memories

Over the decades, the art gallery/center has evolved. Alumni and current students have shared these recollections of the arts center during their time.

Sound of Flowers by Morris Broderson, 1958.

The Dyer Arts Center is a professional art gallery for deaf and hard-of-hearing artists. Bob Baker (director at that time) was great to work with. He treated me like royalty, making sure I was satisfied with my exhibit. The layout was beautiful and well-done, [and] the reception was wonderful. Rochester's *City Newspaper* even wrote a great article about my exhibit.
— Dr. Paul Johnston, alumnus (SVP '72, '78)[50]

When the Dyer Arts Center was first proposed, some folks were opposed to it because it would enclose the open courtyard that a lot of people smoked in, like a glass cage. Once it was completed, some folks said it would become a white elephant, but thankfully Bob Baker, Jenamarie Bacot, and Tabitha Jacques have been committed to making the Dyer Arts Center a beautiful, communal, inviting, and vibrant space. I have attended many outstanding exhibits, Deaf-Mute banquets, presentations, performances, discussions, paint parties, and activities in the Dyer Arts Center. Not only is it a great gallery space and collection, it is also a wonderful cultural center. So grateful to the Dyers, Williams and Ohringers for making this space possible.

— Patti Durr, NTID faculty member[51]

In 2010, I saw a painting of a bird on blue. I immediately understood that the wings were represented by human fingers, but I couldn't figure out what the body meant. It was shaped in a mysterious white oval. I came back to the Dyer Arts Center the next Sunday. To see the bird again came as luck, the feathered friend still hovering a day after its take-down date. Suddenly, I could make out the white oval as a pair of eyes. The painting is gone now. Traveling airborne, I think, but how unlike the bird to never vanish from sight, hands that fly.

— Eric Epstein, NTID student[52]

So many art shows that happened at the Switzer Gallery and bloomed into the Williams Gallery, I can sense all of the appreciation…coming from the deceased Deaf artists. There is no other place, but the Dyer Arts Center, where you'll find me.

— Nancy Rourke, alumna[53]

I remember when I was a student from 1986 to 1991, that courtyard was very drab and dark. No one went outside because it was just a dark hole in the middle of NTID. When NTID was granted the funds to develop the gallery, it truly transformed the space from a dingy negative space to a brightly lit gallery that consistently showcases outstanding artwork. Before the gallery, people would avoid that space, and after the gallery was established, it became a place for many social and professional gatherings. In other words, this gallery helped elevate De'VIA to solidify its rightful place in the art world.

— Rita Straubhaar, alumna[54]

The Dyer Arts Center allows people to cherish and appreciate artworks, just as we cherish the deaf culture.

— Perseus McDaniel, NTID student[55]

Highlighted exhibits at the Switzer Gallery that I remember the most were Brenda Schertz's touring *Deaf Culture* art exhibition, Morris Broderson's paintings, and the Deaf Russian art show. We actually got to meet some of the Deaf Russian artists! Most of the artists who showed their artwork were hearing, from RIT and the Rochester area. Once in a while, they would have the NTID Applied Art faculty show. Bob Baker was a very kind person. He was supportive, always smiling and helpful. I thank him for encouraging more Deaf artists to be included in the Switzer Gallery and Dyer Arts Center. It was a transition phase from showcasing hearing artist to Deaf artists. I really liked the mediating natural light coming from the large windows at Switzer, and can see the trees and field at front of LBJ. I think there was the dean's secretary or receptionist's desk in the Gallery, too. Then came along Tabitha Jacques, who turned the volume up.

— Susan Dupor, alumna[56]

Collections

The Dyer Arts Center boasts more than 1,000 pieces in its collection. Artists collected by the Dyer Arts Center include Paul Johnston, Sander Blondeel, Morris Broderson, Jean Hanau, Cadwallader Washburn, Susan Dupor, Gary Mayers, David Bloch, and many other deaf and hard-of-hearing artists.

The following pieces are selections from the Dyer Arts Center's Permanent Collection that may interest the reader. They represent an important piece of history or are noteworthy in some way in the art world. This list is not comprehensive, and it does not imply that the other pieces in the collection are less important.

To begin with, Dr. Paul Johnston has created many beautiful pieces of work. One of his most famous is *Deaf*

Deaf Education Pinball by Paul Johnston, 2008.

Reception Deception by David Bloch, date unknown.

Education Pinball. The print shows a pinball machine with various symbols from Deaf culture and/or representations of Deaf education. The print is a powerful commentary on Deaf education and is a favorite of visitors when they ask for a tour of the Dyer Arts Center collections.

Commissioned pieces by Sander Blondeel are hung throughout LBJ. Blondeel works specifically with stained glass and creates stunning pieces that tell a story. While the Dyer Arts Center owns a number of pieces by Blondeel, two in particular are hung permanently in LBJ. The first is called *Education and Technology*, created in 1998. The second is called *Establishment of NTID*, created in 2002. The second piece includes important figures instrumental in the founding of NTID, such as President Lyndon Baines Johnson, Dr. D. Robert Frisina, Mary E. Switzer, and Governor Hugh L. Carey.

David Bloch, a Holocaust survivor, created pieces that recalled his time at Dachau. The Dyer Arts Center owns two bodies of work by Bloch. The first body is of

his woodcut prints that portray the melancholy, desolation, and horror of the Holocaust. *Reception Deception* is a familiar art piece for many visitors. The second body of work is his boxcar series that also document the tragedy of the Holocaust. The boxcar series measures 13 inches high by 48 inches wide. The work is largely depicted in blue-gray tones.

Hanging from the ceiling of the main staircase in Rosica Hall are three large metal sculptures, *Three Sisters*, created by Gary Mayers. He specializes in sculpture and uses a wide range of materials, such as wood, marble, metal, and stone to create his organic pieces. Rather than creating representational forms, he seeks to create conceptual sculptures that evolve during his artmaking process. Many of his sculptures have been purchased by museums and galleries internationally. The Dyer Arts Center has several of his sculptures, plus many on loan by Mayers himself.

Morris Broderson, as mentioned earlier, became a very successful artist, thanks to his aunt's persistence

Three Sisters by Gary Mayers, 2013.

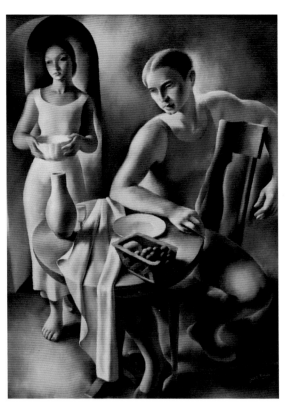

Male and Female Circus Performers by Jean Hanau, 1934.

and connections.[57] Broderson exhibited his first show in his late 20s, and continued to exhibit his works at numerous museums and galleries.[58] His artworks have clearly evolved from one style to another. He originally created works that were semi-realistic: human bodies that did not necessarily look accurately human, placed in dream worlds. However, his style changed in the 1980s to focus more on realism, portrayals of people, still life, or intricate details of a cloth or a flower.

The Dyer Arts Center's oldest pieces date back to the 1930s. One is an etching of an elderly woman by Cadwallader Lincoln Washburn, who is renowned for his drypoint etching. Washburn studied with famous artists of his time, such as William Merritt Chase, Joaquin Sorolla, and Albert Besnard. He was known as The Silent Artist amongst his hearing peers.[59] Washburn had a long and illustrious career as an artist, and had numerous exhibits that showcased his works.[60] The Washburn Arts Building at Gallaudet University was named after him in 1969.[61]

Jean Hanau's artworks also date back to the 1930s. Most memorable are his large-scale oil paintings of circus performers as his subject matter. Hanau is a French-American artist who is known for working in Art Nouveau and Art Deco styles. He became an American citizen in 1942.[62] He was an active member of the Merry Go-Rounders group in New York City.[63] This group promoted the use of oralism as a communication method. It is, in fact, possible that Helen Dyer, Frances Carlberg King, and Elizabeth Williams were members of the same club.[64] Like Washburn, Hanau has had a number of exhibits showcasing many of his works. Thanks to a donation by Renate K. Alpert, the Dyer Arts Center has a large collection of Hanau's works that represent the breadth of his artistic capabilities.[65]

On the opposite spectrum of subject matter, the Dyer Arts Center has a number of pieces made by Susan Dupor. Dupor creates beautiful, and sometimes heart-wrenching, paintings about the Deaf experience. Many of her artworks capture sign language, portray

Hard Winter's Fall by Susan Dupor, diptych, 2004.

the beauty of being part of Deaf culture, and illustrate the common experience of oppression in the lives of Deaf people. Dupor is still active as an artist and was commissioned to do a triptych to celebrate NTID's 50th anniversary in 2018.[66]

The Dyer Arts Center is also fortunate to be the recipient of Leo Villareal's *Coded Spectrum* installation, located in Rosica Hall. Villareal, who is hearing, is an internationally renowned contemporary artist with art installations at the Smithsonian and the National Gallery of Art. The piece was purchased thanks to a grant from Sprint Relay and a donation from Dr. James DeCaro and Patricia Mudgett-DeCaro.[67]

Conclusion

Thanks to efforts in collecting and documenting deaf art, NTID has gained national and international attention for its collection and preservation of deaf-related art. Thanks to endowment funds, social media, support from NTID administrators, and loyal patrons, the Dyer

Arts Center has been able to expand from collecting, preserving, and exhibiting arts to hosting art events, artist lectures, and events that celebrate the arts.

What does the future hold for the Dyer Arts Center? For starters, there is a considerable amount of potential to expand into an art museum, especially when the amount of artwork being collected increases over the years. This would require a separate facility dedicated to storage, exhibit spaces, and an activity center. Currently, there is no museum that focuses on deaf-related art. This gives the Dyer Arts Center the opportunity to become a hub for deaf art, which may naturally lead into becoming a museum. Visitors to Rochester will want to add this museum to the list of places to visit.

The center is looking into best practices for how to preserve and exhibit artworks, as well as how to best operate the center to benefit NTID and the deaf community. Eventually, the center hopes to become a research center on deaf artists, art, and art history. To that end,

Coded Spectrum by Leo Villareal, 2012.

center staff members have begun collecting news articles on artists, creating artist folders, developing profiles, and updating the art center's database. Additionally, the center's online presence has become a powerful tool for reaching out to the general public, especially to the deaf community.

The Dyer Arts Center website could become a centralized place to learn more about deaf art, to view artworks from afar, to read various articles and blogposts on artists and/or events in the Dyer, and to document exhibits and interviews with artists. Future plans include making certain parts of the database available to the public for research and centralizing artist information, so that the Dyer Arts Center becomes a one-stop shop for research.

Beyond that, because the face of deaf and public education is changing so quickly and programming is being cut, the Dyer Arts Center wants to be accessible to schools for free arts education. This includes providing an arts curriculum designed specifically for

deaf children, art activities for local schools with deaf children, and opportunities to nurture young would-be artists in their talents. In this way, the Dyer Arts Center hopes to not only catalog the past, but also help to shape the future.

Tabitha Jacques is the current Director of the Dyer Arts Center. Robert Baker is the former Director of the Dyer Arts Center.

Notes

1. Deborah Sonnenstrahl, *Deaf Artists in America* (San Diego, CA: DawnSignPress, 2000): xxii.
2. Betty G. Miller, "De'VIA (Deaf View/Image Art)," in *The Deaf Way: Perspectives from the International Conference on Deaf Culture*, ed. Carol Erting (Washington, DC: Gallaudet University Press, 1994), 770.
3. Ann Silver, personal communication, April 2017.
4. Miller, "De'VIA."
5. Nancy Rourke, personal communication, February 2017.

6. Emily Leamon, "The NTID Art Gallery." *FOCUS Magazine* (Winter 1981): 26.

7. "Mary E. Switzer Gallery Dedicated." *FOCUS Magazine* (Fall 1984): 32.

8. Robert Davila, "Supporting the Arts." *FOCUS Magazine* (Spring 2000): 2.

9. Leamon, "The NTID Art Gallery."

10. Ibid.

11. Robert Baker, personal communication, February 2017.

12. Leamon, "The NTID Art Gallery."

13. Robert Baker, personal communication, February 2017.

14. Ibid.

15. Ibid.

16. Ibid.

17. "Mary E. Switzer Gallery Dedicated."

18. Ibid.

19. Davila, "Supporting the Arts."

20. Robert Baker, personal communication, February 2017.

21. Karen E. Black, "Celebrating Creativity, Community and Culture: The Joseph F. and Helen C. Dyer Arts Center." *FOCUS Magazine* (Fall 2001): 13.

22. Ibid.

23. Ibid.

24. Ibid.

25. Robert Baker, personal communication, February 2017.

26. Ibid.

27. Ibid.

28. Ibid.

29. Ibid.

30. Ibid.

31. Ibid.

32. Jenamarie Bacot, personal communication, March 2017.

33. Ibid.

34. "Roster Truly Nationwide." *FOCUS Magazine* (November 1968): 2.

35. Guy Wonder, personal communication, January 2017.

36. Ibid.

37. Ibid.

38. Ibid.

39. Ibid.

40. Ibid.

41. Ibid.

42. Ibid.

43. Nancy Rourke, personal communication, February 2017.

44. Takiyah Harris, personal communication, January 2017.

45. Ibid.

46. Ibid.

47. Emily Andreano, "Portraits of Success." *FOCUS Magazine* (Fall 1986): 15.

48. Ibid.

49. Ibid.

50. Paul Johnston, personal communication, January 2017.

51. Patti Durr, personal communication, January 2017.

52. Eric Epstein, personal communication, February 2017.

53. Nancy Rourke, personal communication, February 2017.

54. Rita Straubhaar, personal communication, January 2017.

55. Perseus McDaniel, personal communication, February 2017.

56. Susan Dupor, personal communication, March 2017.

57. Andreano, "Portraits of Success."

58. Ibid.

59. Sonnenstrahl, *Deaf Artists*, 103–109.

60. Ibid.

61. Ibid.

62. Sonnenstrahl, *Deaf Artists*, 165–169.

63. Ibid.

64. Robert Baker, personal communication, February 2017.

65. Ibid.

66. Susan Dupor, personal communication, March 2017.

67. Robert Baker, personal communication, February 2017.

Developing Leaders
The NTID Student Congress and Student Organizations

Greg Pollock, Yvette Chirenje, and Roxann Richards

NSC Overview

The NTID Student Congress (NSC) is the largest deaf and hard-of-hearing student organization at Rochester Institute of Technology. Formed in 1971 in order to represent deaf and hard-of-hearing students and numerous deaf organizations in RIT's Student Government (SG), NSC's mission is:

1. To create awareness of issues among all members of the community.
2. To provide a platform of expression for the deaf and hard-of-hearing majority and minority communities of Rochester Institute of Technology.
3. To encourage union, interaction, and understanding among all NTID and cross-registered students who converge at Rochester Institute of Technology.
4. To provide leadership and facilitate communication, cooperation, networking, and mutual support among its affiliates.
5. To advocate and encourage NTID and cross-registered students' personal growth and the advancement of NTID and cross-registered students within RIT as a whole and individually.

This chapter will investigate the founding of the NSC, its evolution over the decades, and the defining moments of its history. One common thread that emerges through the study of NSC's history is that of advocacy and activism. From its early days, the student officers of NSC were working to improve their conditions and those of others in the community.

The Founding of NSC

Prior to NSC's founding, NTID students were represented by the NTID Student Association, an affiliate organization of RIT's Student Association (RITSA, now known as Student Government). In the late 1960s, RITSA began rolling out a system that allowed affiliate organizations to serve independently of the governing body. Attracted to this new approach, NTID students convened to develop a proposal that called for an entity that existed independently of RITSA.

The proposal was met with controversy. A significant percentage of students stood by the notion that NTID's student leadership needed to continue to operate under RITSA, while another group of students felt that NTID student affairs needed a separate identity. After some debate, it was decided that dialogue would be given a chance. According to Jerry Nelson ('74), "[The shift to NSC] was really all about forming our own identity and reducing the necessity to comply with SG."

In spring 1971, NTID Dean Dr. William E. Castle appointed a group of students to look into the formation of a government body, the development of bylaws, and the use of parliamentary procedures.[1, 2] A separate account exists indicating that a separate group of student leaders created their own task force. This task force drafted the bylaws and proposal that was ultimately pitched to RITSA.

The first elected officers of the NTID Student Congress (1972–1973). [Clockwise from left] Mark Feder, vice president; Miriam DeVincenzo (nee Sotomayor) ('72), secretary; Jerry Nelson, president; John Swan (SVP '70, '74, '76), treasurer.

The proposal was successful. RIT's Student Affairs approved the NSC's formation as a student organization by an affirmative vote of two-thirds of the total voting membership of RITSA, and the resulting entity was recognized as the NTID Student Congress.

The Founding Officers

The founding of NSC led to the immediate dissolution of the NTID Student Association. The NSC held its first election in January 1972, in which Jerry Nelson ('74) and Mark Feder (SVP '71, '74, '76) were the first president and vice president to be elected. At the time, the NSC office was located in a cage in the basement tunnels between Nathaniel Rochester Hall and Sol Heumann Hall. The office was later moved to Ellingson Hall (Tower A) upon its construction. Due to the lack of an existing budget, NSC was largely dependent on fundraising and donations.

One of the first key issues to be addressed by the NSC was the removal of speech therapy requirements.

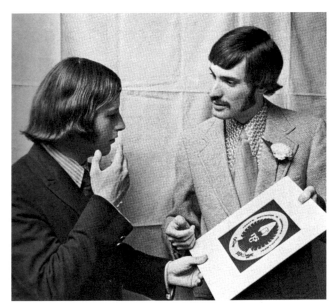

Steve Weikart (SVP '70, '73) (left) discusses his award-winning design with NSC President Mark Feder.

NTID students were required at the time to take speech classes. Audiological training was also a requirement for all NTID students. The NSC appealed this policy, citing concerns that it distracted from students' academic pursuits and belittled their postsecondary experience. The requirement was later revoked by Dr. Castle.

The NSC Eagle

In 1973, the NSC found it necessary to build a lasting identity within the NTID community. Its leaders sought to build the NSC's reputation and strengthen its identity as a governing organization. As part of a trust-building initiative, NSC leaders held a contest to determine the formal insignia that would be used in official communications and documents. At the end of the contest, NSC President Mark Feder was presented with the award-winning design of the NSC Eagle by Steve Weikart.

Once the contest result had been announced, James Grigsby, a student woodworker, committed a year to the design of a wooden sculpture of the NSC emblem. The emblem was gifted to NSC in 1974 and hangs in the NSC office today.

In addition to strengthening its presence as a young community governance organization, the NSC began participating in regular debates hosted by Gallaudet University. These debates were the early stages of what later became the RIT/Gallaudet Sports Weekend.

RIT/Gallaudet Weekend

The RIT/Gallaudet Weekend (currently known as Brickfest or Rockfest) is an annual competitive sports tradition that originated in the mid-1970s as a relationship-building initiative between the two institutions. The first event was hosted at Gallaudet University, and then NTID and Gallaudet took turns hosting the event. The purpose of this annual event was to foster a spirit of sportsmanship, competition, and cultural experience.

In 1977, disagreements arose between the two institutions on whether or not interpreting students were eligible to participate in the competition. NSC stood by the belief that interpreting students were NTID students as well and should be permitted to participate. This viewpoint ultimately won out, albeit not without several boycotts by Gallaudet student-athletes

James Grigsby, Robert Sidansky and Farid Bozorgi stand next to the newly-created emblem at NSC's 4th annual banquet in 1974.

in the intervening years.

The name of this event evolved from RIT/Gallaudet Weekend to Brickfest when held at RIT or Rockfest when held at Gallaudet, a transition formalized by the NSC in 2011. However, the intercollegiate sports weekend has not been hosted since 2015 for reasons that will be discussed later in this chapter.

Defining Issues of the Early NSC

In the late 1970s, the NSC held open-captioned movie nights every Friday, and since broadcast television programming was not yet captioned, most students would attend these events. The NSC took advantage of these opportunities to host debates about the hot issues of the day during the intermissions of these captioned movies.[3]

Among these discussions, prominent issues affecting the community began to form the basis of NSC's advocacy: pressure for an improved English system, accessibility at RIT/NTID for Deaf students, and improved interpreting skills.[4] In the early 1980s, NSC

---

board minutes describe the push to improve the criteria used for hiring instructors and faculty, requesting a minimum level of sign-language proficiency. This push was ultimately successful, and subsequent years have seen a tightening of those requirements for new faculty.

The NSC's advocacy extended off campus as well. Former NSC President Robert Sidansky (SVP '72, '77), undertook a letter-writing campaign to local television stations in 1974.[5] At the time, local stations open-captioned only the 11 p.m. newscast, citing fears that hearing viewers would be annoyed by the text appearing onscreen.[6] Sidansky argued that 11 p.m. was too late, that Rochester's deaf community would benefit more from an earlier captioned newscast and that using interpreters onscreen was not as helpful as captioning.[7]

Though Sidansky's efforts were not entirely successful, local news broadcasters, perhaps mindful of his campaign, were among the first to adopt closed-captioning technology when it emerged in the 1980s.

An Early Push for Reform

On May 18, 1979, RIT Student Affairs suspended the NSC for its failure to formulate a valid constitution in accordance with a newly adopted RITSA policy applicable to all student organizations. [8]

This led to a series of student protests (and quick alterations to the submitted constitution), which resulted in NSC's reaffirmation in 1980.[9] The NSC constitution was reformed in 1982 in order to clarify the appropriate use of NSC funds; outline NSC's goals and purpose as an organization; and redefine NSC's relationship with incoming SVP classes, other NTID student organizations, and affiliated entities.[10]

The constitutional reform of 1982 began to lay the foundation for NSC's transformation into a significant organization with an impact felt all over campus.

NSC: Major Student Organization

In spring quarter 1983, NSC leaders drafted a proposal to redefine NSC as a Major Student Organization (MSO) under the auspices of the RIT Student Directorate (now Student Government), as the representative entity for a college of RIT. The Student Directorate approved the proposal, formally recognizing NSC as an MSO. The changes that resulted from this proposal defined the

relationship that exists today between the NSC and SG. It also became possible for NSC to work in a closer capacity with SG and the other MSOs that make up the campus today, such as the Residence Hall Association, the College Activities Board, and Global Union.[11]

MSOs receive significant operating budgets from RIT SG, which allow them to implement programs and/or services for their respective constituents. While the financial model has changed over time, NSC originally had responsibility for the allocation and management of the budgets for its affiliate clubs and organizations. Today, RIT SG is responsible for the determination and allocation of club/organization funds as a consequence of the reorganization of the late 1990s, which is discussed later in this chapter.

Ebony Club

In 1985, the Ebony Club was founded by Larry Smith, Fred Beam (SVP '81, '85), Eva Faison ('92), and Jeff Pecot (SVP '82, '93), after Smith expressed concern that there was no space for black deaf students on campus. A student organization focused on developing a community of black deaf students, the Ebony Club sought to develop opportunities for its members to learn more about black history and culture. This focus on pulling together led to the motto eventually adopted by the Ebony Club, "One family, one love".[12]

Although the original purpose of the Ebony Club was to offer a space for black deaf students, the organization evolved over the years to develop a stronger focus on leadership, whether through hosting annual events like Phatsgiving, Sweetheart Day, and an annual end-of-the-year barbecue, or through working with the Black Awareness Coordinating Committee to increase knowledge of the issues facing the black deaf community, both on campus and nationwide. NTID alumni who are past members of Ebony Club often continue to lead after graduation. Many former members have gone on to work for National Black Deaf Advocates and the National Association of the Deaf, among other organizations.[13]

As of this writing, the Ebony Club continues to be among the oldest surviving student organizations at NTID, having operated continuously for more than three decades. It also represents one of the first indications that NTID students identified increasingly with communities beyond simply deaf or hard of hearing.

Other Cultural Student Organizations

The Ebony Club served as the spark that enabled other student groups to found their own organizations based on the communities with which they most identified. The following information is courtesy of the 2017 memberships of each club listed, unless otherwise indicated.

Asian Deaf Club

Founded in 1988, the Asian Deaf Club (ADC) followed closely on the heels of the Ebony Club. The founders, Richard Lin (SVP '85, '91, '98) and Rickey Tom (SVP '87, '91, '94), saw that the numbers of Asian deaf students had begun to increase considerably and decided that there needed to be a student organization that would work in their best interests.[14]

Although for much of its history the ADC was generally composed of students of Asian descent—specifically, those with Chinese, Japanese, Korean and Southeast-Asian heritage—it has recently become "a lot more inclusive...allowing non-Asians to feel more comfortable in joining," according to Alicia Wooten ('11), former president of the organization.[15]

The ADC continues to be active today, 28 years after its founding, with an annual banquet for members, community events for non-members and—famously—sushi during NSC's Pulse Happy Hour.[16]

Latin American Deaf Club

Founded in 1995 as the Hispanic Deaf Club, the Latin American Deaf Club (LADC) was the product of "Jaime Mariona (SVP '94, '00) with a small group of deaf Latino students who wanted to get together and share their challenges and accomplishments," said Jeannette Vargas, long-standing advisor of LADC and Senior Staff Specialist in NTID's Development and Alumni & Constituent Relations Office.[17]

"Throughout the years, LADC has developed into an organization that not only supports deaf Latino students in their academic and social transition into college, but all students," Vargas continued.[18] Given that the segment of the population of Latino heritage is one of the fastest-growing demographics in the United States, it seems appropriate that the group has grown, as well. Their major cultural events include the annual Hispanic Deaf Week celebration, the Day of the Dead, and the Three Kings.[19]

Spectrum

Originally named Deaf GLO, Spectrum is NTID's organization focused on LGBTQIA students and their allies. It originally started as an informal gathering in the mid-1990s and lasted for a few years before going on hiatus until spring quarter 2002. It was renamed Spectrum in 2009.[20]

Formally speaking, Spectrum's goals include "providing education, advocacy, networking, and support for Deaf GLBT students in order to create a safe and thriving community for GLBT students and their allies," said Bryan Lloyd, Spectrum advisor and Assistant Director of Counseling and Academic Advising Services.[21]

One of the most significant developments in Spectrum's history was the creation of the ColorFest Conference in 2007.[22] A multi-day conference focused on leadership development, advocacy, and community-building designed specifically for LGBTQIA students at NTID and Gallaudet, the conference is student-run and is considered part of the leadership-development experience for Spectrum members.[23]

WOLK Deaf Jewish Culture Club

Originally established through a gift from the Louis S. and Molly B. Wolk Foundation in 1998, WOLK goes by either "WOLK" or "RIT/NTID Deaf Hillel."[24] This organization offers a community on campus for deaf Jewish students to observe the traditions of Judaism and to share Jewish cultures and histories.

WOLK focuses on bringing guest speakers to campus to increase awareness of the issues faced by the Jewish community around the world, and the organization strives to be open to all students, whether or not they practice the Jewish faith.[25] WOLK is also involved with RIT's Hillel House, which is maintained by the main campus Hillel organization, and works closely with NSC to support the group's activities.[26]

Deaf International Students Association

The youngest of the cultural student clubs, Deaf International Students Association (DISA) was founded in 2003 as the Deaf International Student Club.[27] Given that NTID was not permitted to accept international students until 1990,[28] it is no wonder that it took some time for the international student community to achieve the critical mass necessary to form an organization.

"DISA was established because the members didn't find a 'home' among the available clubs, such as Asian Deaf Club or Ebony Club," said Abdul Yussif, a student from Ghana and current leader of DISA, as of this writing.[29] The cultures and values held by many international students didn't quite fit with the already established student organizations, so in 2003, Nashiru Abdulai (SVP '00, '05) and Minoru Yoshida ('04, '08) established an organization with a broad enough mission to account for the pluralism represented by the international student body.[30]

As a result of this diversity, DISA has partnered with Global Union for nearly its entire history and is well-known among the student body for their Diwali and World as One celebrations. Unfortunately, due to declines in international student admissions, DISA's membership has also declined over the past few years.[31]

Deaf President Now

In 1988, Gallaudet University made international waves when the outcome of the university's presidential search process was met with student protests known as the Deaf President Now movement, or DPN.

Administrative staff at NTID were concerned about the impact of the protests, according to Bruce Beston (SVP '84, '93) and Angela Officer (SVP '83, '88), NSC President and Vice President, respectively, in the 1987–1988 academic year.[32]

"We clearly and professionally explained to the NTID administration, through Ellie Rosenfield when she worked in Academic Affairs, that the NTID student community had no desire or cause for a protest," recalls Beston.[33] Instead, Beston and Officer worked with the NTID administration to provide support to protesters at Gallaudet, renting buses for NTID students who wanted to join the protest.[34] "The administration agreed and worked with us on this. We also did fundraising to support the DPN movement," says Officer.[35]

Thirty years later, as of this writing, Officer looks back on that period as a fundamentally formative experience. "[The] Gallaudet DPN movement was a defining moment for the NSC Board and NTID student community," she says.[36] "It taught us to speak up for our civil rights. We learned so much. We had to work with different leaders…We had to really think and ensure we were doing the right thing."[37] In fact, the 1987–1988 NSC Board is also known for its revisions of the NSC bylaws according to Robert's Rules of Order and the closing of several procedural loopholes.[38]

Along with parliamentary procedures, the leadership skills developed while working with such a diverse group of constituencies during DPN also improved matters for the NTID student community in general. Officer says that "the NSC Board were very proud that we implemented the Chess Club and the Asian Deaf Club based on student input."[39]

Equal Access Now

In October and November 1991, chants of "Equal access now!" erupted as hundreds of students rallied on campus to bring attention to the cultural and communication needs of RIT's deaf and hard-of-hearing population, as well as to the importance of making RIT a fully accessible learning environment.[40]

This campaign was led by Anthony DiGiovanni III ('94), then a third-year accounting student and the 1991–92 president of the NSC.[41] After the fall rallies, DiGiovanni met regularly with administrators to address student concerns with the Campaign for Accessibility Now (CAN), a highly publicized weeklong series of rallies, meetings with university administrators, and presentations to NTID's National Advisory Group and RIT's Board of Trustees.[42] The outcome of this movement was greater accessibility for deaf and hard-of-hearing students to both services and safety measures on campus.

Dean-Student Leadership Advisory Group

In 1994, a Dean-Student Leadership Advisory Group (DSLAG) was formed by Dr. James J. DeCaro, then Dean of NTID, and Dr. T. Alan Hurwitz, then Associate Dean for Student Affairs, for the purpose of improving

The newly-constructed CSD Student Development Center.

relations among students, faculty, and NTID administration.[43] DSLAG met regularly, with an emphasis on following up on the needs that CAN articulated. CAN led to the establishment of numerous access improvements and to the formation of the Provost's Deaf Access Committee.[44] In 2011, Dr. Gerard Buckley (SVP '74, '78), who had since become president of NTID, renamed DSLAG the NTID Student Leadership Advisory Group.

NTID Student Assembly

In 1997, under the leadership of NSC President Debbye Byrne (SVP '93, '01) and Vice President Sean Furman (SVP '93, '06), NSC-affiliated clubs and organizations were given an opportunity to re-evaluate the role of NSC governance in the community. There were calls for the decentralization of NSC's club budget. After numerous conversations, NSC's affiliate organizations restructured their funding mechanisms in order to receive their operating budgets directly from RIT SG.[45]

With the partnership between NSC and its affiliate organizations thus strengthened, the voices of affiliate leaders became increasingly important to NSC's overall mission.[46] To drive collaboration, community leaders developed the framework of the NTID Student Assembly (NSA), a forum to serve as a check on, and as a balance to, the NSC. The NSA would hold NSC accountable for prudent budget allocation, advise officers in key decisions impacting the community, and serve as a sounding board on community issues. With the formation of NSA, student engagement skyrocketed, and the foundation of NSC as we know it today began to form.

An NSC for the 21st Century

Under the leadership of Mark Sullivan, NSC president for the 1999–2000 academic year, both NSC and NSA grew and changed.[47] NSC relocated from its long-standing dormitory basement office and meeting spaces into new multi-room headquarters located on the first floor of NTID's Shumway Dining Commons.[48] The NSC's new location included a large-group meeting room, a computer lab, and spacious offices. According to Sullivan, this new visibility for NSC brought greater cohesion to the RIT/NTID community.[49]

In the early 2000s, NSC advocated for a commons area that would strengthen students' ties to NTID, foster interaction with faculty and staff, and become a hub of campus activity, thus supporting students' academic and personal success. With the support of Ellie Rosenfield, then Associate Dean of Student Affairs, and years of NSC advocacy, the dream of a Student Development Center (SDC) became a reality.

Recognizing the critical need for students to feel connected and for the institution to provide learning that goes beyond the classroom, Communication Services for the Deaf (CSD), a private non-profit telecommunications and human-services organization, gifted NTID a sum of money to address these needs. It was this gift that led to the construction of the CSD Student Development Center, which opened to the campus community on November 9, 2006.

The new facility featured a coffee/tea shop, large multi-purpose meeting/conference center, study center, and informal spaces to facilitate interaction and socializing. The SDC is now home to NSC and several of its affiliated organizations.

RIT's Student Government Gets Its First Deaf President

In 2006, Elizabeth "Lizzie" Sorkin (SVP '99, '07), a student in RIT's Film/Video and Animation program, was elected as president of RIT SG, following an unopposed campaign.[50] This election made Sorkin the first deaf student government president at a U.S. college with a mostly-hearing student population.[51]

Sorkin is also the first former NSC officer to hold the highest office in SG. She and her vice president, Daniel Arscott, a Boston, Massachusetts, native who is hearing, campaigned around their slogan "Identify."[52] Sorkin and her cabinet members worked to provide students with bus route maps posted at each stop, an earlier exam schedule, and SGTV, a station dedicated to programming for RIT students. In her 2007 Commencement Address, Sorkin remarked, "We don't just talk about diversity on this campus, we live it every day in so many ways."[53]

NTID Cross-Registered Senators

When NTID was established in 1968, its first class had around 70 deaf and hard-of-hearing students. At the time, there was no such thing as a "cross-registered" student, a term used to refer to deaf and hard-of-hearing students who are enrolled in four-year programs at RIT with support from NTID.

When the NSC was founded, it was designed to serve as the sole governing entity of the NTID student body. By 2001, the number of students had skyrocketed to more than 1,000. At the same time, there was a growing population of deaf and hard-of-hearing students enrolled in bachelor's degree programs in RIT's other colleges. The number of cross-registered students had grown to approximately 40% of the deaf and hard-of-hearing population of RIT/NTID.[54]

No one was prepared for this sudden surge in bachelor's degree enrollment, and it created an additional burden for NSC, long thought to be the sole backbone of the entire NTID student body. The organization struggled to support students academically in nine different colleges, with widely varying language and accessibility needs, and at the same time provide programming events to meet the needs of all deaf and hard-of-hearing students.[55]

In October of 2009, following a Senate meeting, SG President Matt Danna approached NSC President Greg Pollock ('12) with the idea of creating a new Cross-Registered Senator position. Following a lengthy discussion, they agreed that the new position was necessary.[56]

As part of the process of shifting the involvement of deaf and hard-of-hearing students in the broader campus community, Pollock and NSC Vice President Randal "Randy" Jackson ('11) developed a plan that would essentially end NSC's involvement in academics. This withdrawal turned out to be temporary. The NSC Executive Board began deliberating the proposal that would eventually create the position of Cross-Registered Senator.[57]

NSC's stance was that its withdrawal from academic matters was necessary in order to balance its responsibility to the community by allowing senators to focus on the academic aspects of RIT/NTID.[58] By January 2010, NSC relieved itself of all academic obligations. The responsibilities previously held by academic

Elizabeth Sorkin presents at Commencement in 2007.

Either way, NSC had one last opportunity to make its appeal for a cross-registered senator. So Randy and I enlisted the assistance of an old friend. Erin Esposito, former Assistant Director of the Student Life Team and former Vice President of NSC, gave a compelling case in favor of the proposition. Her unparalleled rhetoric led to the 18–3 vote in favor of a new senate seat.

Consequently, Alicia Wooten (2010–2011) and Jonathan MacDonald (2011–2012) have been the first two Cross-Registered Senators at RIT, and have pioneered new ways to connect with and represent the needs of deaf and hard-of-hearing students in RIT colleges beyond NTID."

— Greg Pollock[61]

The cross-registered senator position within SG went into effect in April 2010. It is classified as a community senator.

Bridging the Gap

In the early 2010s, the NSC turned its attention to bridging the gap between the NTID community and the RIT community. Since the formation of NSC, both communities had operated as mutually exclusive with separate Greek organizations, clubs, governance systems, and programs. As a response to the distance felt between both sides of campus, NSC presidents throughout the 2010s ran on platforms that centered on bringing the two communities closer together.[62]

In April 2010, Pollock, a student in RIT's Professional & Technical Communication program, was elected the second deaf president of RIT SG, and the first to win a second term. Pollock and Vice President Phil Amsler, a hearing ASL user, ran under the campaign slogan "Dream Big."

Pollock's "Dream Team" accomplished many changes that can still be seen at RIT today: Shuttles between RIT and Rochester, televised RIT hockey games, and 24-hour access to the library.[63,64,65] His team also started the planning that led to SG's Rideshare (orange bike rental) program.[66] Under his leadership, student clubs, Greek organizations, and MSOs that were historically composed of hearing students became increasingly accessible for deaf and hard-of-hearing students.

affairs roles within NSC were transferred to the Student Government role of NTID Senator.[59]

All that remained was to pitch the proposed Cross-Registered Senator position to the RIT SG Senate. At the time, the SG Senate was gridlocked in a landmark issue, the "Quarters vs. Semesters" debate that ultimately led to the conversion of RIT's calendar from quarters to semesters. Due to competing priorities, and hostile relations between some members of the Senate, the proposal turned into a three-month debate shadowed by the semester conversion disputes.[60]

The proposal, led by Pollock and Jackson, reached its final vote in spring 2010, following a compelling pitch on the topic by past NSC Vice President Erin Esposito ('96, '01). The motion passed with only three votes opposed.

A number of SG senators were vocally opposed to [the proposal]. But fortunately for us, there were also great forces at work in its favor. SG President Matt Danna, SG Advisors Karey Pine and Heath Boice-Pardee, and several MSO presidents lined themselves up behind NSC. In late March, the final vote was set to take place. At this point, we had no idea which way the vote would go.

On the Field of Play
NTID Athletics

Sean "Skip" Flanagan

In virtually every year since NTID's founding in 1968, RIT's intercollegiate athletic programs have sported deaf or hard-of-hearing athletes. As NTID has grown over the past 50 years, so has the number of deaf or hard-of-hearing athletes in intercollegiate sports. Currently, the number of athletic alumni stands at around 450 and growing.

At some point in the past 50 years, nearly every sport at RIT has had deaf or hard-of-hearing students competing alongside, or against, their hearing peers. Some of those students performed at such high levels that they were recognized in RIT's Hall of Fame. This chapter discusses those athletes. This is not to exclude every other RIT/NTID student-athlete, but to recognize their efforts as represented by the outstanding athletes described below.

This chapter concludes with a few words on a newly established program that will help support future student-athletes and—we expect—future inductees in the RIT Hall of Fame.

Hall of Fame Inductees

Albert "Al" Walla (SVP '70) started his career with a quick adjustment. A native of Stamford, Connecticut, Walla stepped onto campus as a freshman as one of the RIT swimming program's top swimmers. He had goals, he was focused on winning, and he had been used to working on his own. This approach paid off, placing Walla fourth in total team points by coming in first and second 11 times each, while finishing third twice.

Albert "Al" Walla (right)

Although he certainly did well in the pool, his greatest success came in the form of teamwork in a predominantly individual sport. He became a part of the swim team that was recently immortalized in the RIT Hall of Fame for having the only undefeated season in its history, registering an unblemished 16–0 win-loss record. Walla's head coach, John Buckholtz, applauded Walla and his deaf teammates for their rapid development as a team. "In the beginning the deaf swimmers didn't seem to relate well to team concepts," said Buckholtz

Marie Benson (McKee)

Gregory "Greg" Coughlan

Marie Benson ('80) had a career to remember as a member of the RIT women's tennis program, compiling a 29–2 record. Then known as Maria McKee, Benson lost one match her freshman year, then another one her sophomore year, and then something incredible happened. She stopped losing.[13] Benson owns the records for most wins in a season with 11, in a career with 29, and consecutively after registering 15 straight victories. Because of her stellar performance, she was named the RIT Senior Female Athlete of the Year, NTID Female Athlete of the Year, and a finalist for the Rochester College Athlete of the Year Award. She was inducted into the RIT Athletic Hall of Fame in 2008.

Gregory "Greg" Coughlan ('93) left a long-running legacy as a student-athlete at RIT, running his way

out of Massachusetts into four NCAA championship berths, the Deaflympics, RIT's prestigious Hall of Fame, and great success in the workplace. "I was just a small-town boy from Massachusetts," Coughlan recalls.[14] Coughlan's coach attributed his academic success (winning the Ellingson Award for Academic Excellence as an athlete), athletic success (three-time All-American and Senior Male Athlete of the Year at RIT) to one thing: "an unbelievable amount of hard work."[15] Coughlan's success and name in the record books still stand to this day. He was named to the Hall of Fame in 2000.

Bring up Kristine Gray ('94) to any NTID student in the know, and you'll see all of them shake their heads in disbelief. Considered one of the greatest athletes to ever grace the RIT/NTID campus, Gray excelled in not

Kristine "Kris" Gray

Matthew "Matt" Hamill

one, but two sports.[16] In softball, Gray owns 25 pitching records—most of which still stand today, more than 20 years later—and had a 27-game hitting streak at the plate.[17] On the volleyball court, Gray was a three-time All-American and New York State Women's Collegiate Athletic Association All-Tournament honoree.

"Hammer! Hammer! Hammer!" the crowd roared for Matthew "Matt" Hamill ('99) as he became an NCAA Division III national champion on the wrestling mat. Hamill's legacy is as one of the finest athletes in RIT history, garnering honors as a three-time All-American, New York State Champion, and the RIT Invitational Champion.[18] His 89-3 record landed him in the Hall of Fame, netted him an award-winning movie about his life, and prompted a music video about his legacy.[19]

After three years at RIT (having transferred from Purdue after his first year), Hamill graduated and climbed up the Ultimate Fighting Championship ranks as a professional fighter. He still holds the all-time record for most tournament wins at RIT.

Anthony "Tony" Wallace ('03) was a tough competitor. Growing up in the face of adversity, Wallace dominated his opponents on the wrestling mat. The four-time collegiate state placer and three-time NCAA All-American battled injuries to finish with a 108–27 career record, the second most in RIT history. "People said that I couldn't go to college because I was deaf," Wallace said, "and that I couldn't finish my wrestling career because I was injured. I proved to them, and to myself, that I could do both."[20] Wallace graduated with a degree in business

Anthony "Tony" Wallace

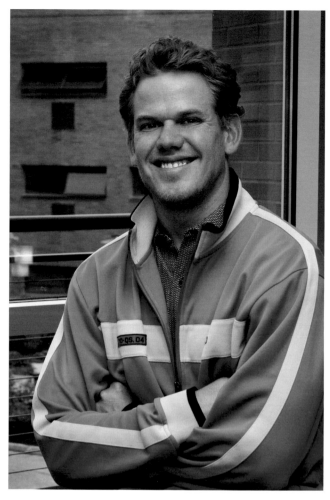

Michael "Mike" Lawson

administration and served as an assistant coach for the RIT wrestling program from 2003 to 2005 while moonlighting as a Public Safety officer on campus.[21] He moved to Alaska to become a law enforcement officer and was killed in the line of duty in 2010.[22] Wallace was inducted into the Hall of Fame in 2008.

Michael "Mike" Lawson ('07) started his career with an absolute bang and would end it the same way a few years later. In his Hall-of-Fame career, Lawson garnered the Empire 8 Athletic Conference Rookie of the Year award, then completed his last two years of collegiate soccer with Player of the Year honors.[23] A three-year captain playing center-midfielder, Lawson led his team to two league titles and an NCAA tournament berth. His success in the classroom is equally impressive,

posting a 3.64 grade point average as an undergraduate, and then a 3.90 in graduate school.[24] His success comes from a strong support system of coaches and teammates. "I have a great relationship with Coach Garno and the players on the team who are learning how to communicate with me," Lawson said. "It makes me feel comfortable and helps me play my best."[25] He entered the RIT Hall of Fame in 2012.

For more than 20 years, until the early 2010s, at any athletic event on campus, you could reliably find a blonde woman on the field of play, interpreting for deaf and hard-of-hearing student-athletes.[26] A West Virginia native, Meredith Ray has been involved with intercollegiate athletics and recreation ever since she came to RIT/NTID.[27] She was the coordinator of RIT

Meredith Ray

NTID Athlete Development Program

In recognition of the achievements of past student-athletes, as well as the increasing importance of athletics and physical fitness to university life around the country, the NTID Athlete Development Program was established in 2016. The mission of this program is to maximize the potential of deaf and hard-of-hearing student-athletes in the classroom, on the field, and as members of the community. The program offers a range of services, including academic support, educational workshops, personal mentoring, leadership development, and technology development.

The program begins before a student has graduated from high school. Program staff connect with high-school student-athletes who are interested in competing for the Tigers by showing them around the athletic facilities when they visit campus and arranging meetings with the coaches. Program staff also facilitate communication between NTID Admissions and the Athletic Department.

Once a prospective student becomes an enrolled student-athlete, the NTID Athlete Development Program staff maintain communication with the student, coaching staff, and their teammates to foster an inclusive environment for the deaf and hard-of-hearing athletes. Although RIT Athletics has historically been one of the most inclusive programs in the country, program staff stop by practices and games to see how the coaches, teammates, and interpreters are working with deaf and hard-of-hearing student-athletes.

As the year goes on, program staff develop strong working relationships with each student-athlete, often providing mentoring and guidance. It can often be a challenge for student-athletes to find a balance between their schoolwork, the requirements of their sport, and their personal lives. In addition to mentoring, the program now offers a four-year leadership-development program called Relentless Tiger Leadership. The goal is to form the student-athletes into better athletes, better people, and better leaders.

Aside from mentoring, program staff also make sure that student-athletes are aware of the various academic resources available on campus, whether it involves encouraging them to visit tutoring centers, to see their academic advisors, or to meet with their department

interpreting services for students involved with intercollegiate athletics, physical education, intramurals, recreation, and wellness.[28] She interpreted for almost all 24 of RIT's varsity athletic programs. For her involvement in sports and her excellent performance, she was awarded the Coaches' Appreciation Award, Outstanding Interpreting Award, and the Jan Strine Memorial Award. Louis Spiotti, Jr., the RIT Executive Director of Intercollegiate Athletics, sang her praises. "Meredith is more than an interpreter. She has brought the hearing and deaf communities together through her enthusiasm and support of both deaf and hearing students. She has our respect and admiration."[29] Ray was named to the Hall of Fame in 2004.

chairs to seek necessary help for a specific course or track. The NTID Athlete Development Program also offers educational workshops. The program has worked with the RIT ASL and Deaf Studies Community Center (RADSCC) to present a workshop to the RIT Sports Medicine Office to help athletic trainers develop communication skills to effectively work with deaf and hard-of-hearing student-athletes in the trainers' room. The program also has hosted workshops for coaches and captains on how to improve team dynamics with a deaf athlete involved.

Given the increasing importance of athletics to universities around the United States—and the increasing focus on developing good physical health as a society—athlete development is an important factor in long-term planning for an institution's future. In fact, it may be the single most important factor in long-term planning for a student's future. The support that student-athletes receive from the program, from NTID, and from RIT Athletics will stand them in good stead long after graduation. Though NTID's Athlete Development Program is still in its infancy, its future looks bright.

Sean "Skip" Flanagan is the current NTID Athlete Development Program Coordinator.

Notes

1. " 'Big splash' Created by NTID Athletes," *FOCUS Magazine* (May–June 1971): 16.

2. "U.S. Scores Final Second Victory, 6–5," *FOCUS Magazine* (January–February 1974): 9.

3. Jean Ingham, "Gaining the Competitive Edge: From Workout to Workday," *FOCUS Magazine* (Summer 1988): 8–11.

4. "Students React to Present, Hope for Future." *FOCUS Magazine* (January–February 1974): 11.

5. Ann Kanter, "Telling It Like It Is," *FOCUS Magazine* (Summer 1986): 10–13.

6. Kanter, "Telling It Like It Is," 11.

7. Kanter, "Telling It Like It Is," 12.

8. Ibid.

9. Rochester Institute of Technology Athletics Department, "Ronald Rice," http://www.ritathletics.com/hof_rit. aspx?hof=134.

10. "Athletics: John Reid," *FOCUS Magazine* (Summer/Fall 1977): 9.

11. Rochester Institute of Technology Athletics Department, "John Reid." http://www.ritathletics.com/hof_rit. aspx?hof=109.

12. "Athletics: John Reid."

13. Rochester Institute of Technology Athletics Department, "Marie (McKee) Benson," http://www.ritathletics.com/hof_rit. aspx?hof=172.

14. Kathleen S. Smith, "Going the Distance." *FOCUS Magazine* (Summer 1994): 8.

15. Smith, "Going the Distance."

16. Frank A. Kruppenbacher, "'Go Tech!': RIT's Deaf Athletes." *FOCUS Magazine* (Fall/Winter 2001): 7–10.

17. Rochester Institute of Technology Athletics Department, "Kristine Gray." http://www.ritathletics.com/hof_rit. aspx?hof=114.

18. Rochester Institute of Technology Athletics Department, "Matt Hamill." http://www.ritathletics.com/hof_rit. aspx?hof=162.

19. "Hollywood Comes to Campus." *FOCUS Magazine* (Fall/Winter 2009): 17.

20. "Profiles in College: Tony Wallace." *FOCUS Magazine* (Spring/Summer 2002): 15.

21. Rochester Institute of Technology Athletics Department, "Tony Wallace," http://www.ritathletics.com/hof_rit. aspx?hof=175.

22. Lisa Demer, "Standoff Follows Shooting Deaths of Two Hoonah Officers," *Alaska Dispatch News*, August 29, 2010.

23. Frank A. Kruppenbacher, "NTID/RIT Rookies of the Year." *FOCUS Magazine* (Spring/Summer 2003): 21.

24. Rochester Institute of Technology Athletics Department, "Mike Lawson." http://www.ritathletics.com/hof_rit. aspx?hof=200.

25. Kruppenbacher, "NTID/RIT Rookies of the Year."

26. J. Roger Dykes and Frank A. Kruppenbacher, "RIT Sports Hall of Fame Inductees." *FOCUS Magazine* (Fall/Winter 2005): 13.

27. Rochester Institute of Technology Athletics Department, "Meredith Ray." http://www.ritathletics.com/hof_rit. aspx?hof=140.

28. Rochester Institute of Technology Athletics Department, "Meredith Ray."

29. Dykes and Kruppenbacher, "RIT Sports Hall of Fame Inductees."

Section 2

The Place

Leading the Way

Dr. Gerard Walter

Introduction

In 1930, a deaf teacher from the Minnesota School for the Deaf wrote, "A national technical institute for the deaf...located in a large manufacturing city, is what deaf young Americans need more than anything else...Such an institution should include several buildings filled with modern machines, appliances, tools, materials, dormitories...a gymnasium, library, tennis courts, trees, shrubs, flowers, a director, a staff of competent instructors, and 500 students...A dream, yes, and a possibility."[1]

In 1965, the National Technical Institute for the Deaf Act (Public Law 89-36) was signed into law by President Lyndon B. Johnson. This bill provided for the establishment of a postsecondary institute for technical education for people who are deaf or hard-of-hearing. Ultimately, more than 20 colleges and universities around the country applied to host this National Technical Institute for the Deaf (NTID) on their campuses. Rochester Institute of Technology (RIT) in Rochester, New York, was one of the institutions that applied. Rochester had a large deaf community, and was very receptive to the idea of hosting NTID. In 1966, RIT was officially selected as the host institution for the new NTID.[2]

Since its founding, NTID has had six leaders: D. Robert Frisina (1967–1976), William E. Castle (1977–1994), James DeCaro (1995, 2010), Robert Davila (1996–2003), T. Alan Hurwitz (2004–2009), and, as of this publication, Gerard Buckley (2011–present). What is interesting about these six individuals is that they are all still alive, have all known each other

professionally and personally, have communicated with each other about their experiences as leader, and thus have had the luxury of learning from each other. These relationships have resulted in an unusually high level of mission continuity that is seldom achieved when organizations change leadership. Along with this continuity, each of these leaders has also brought a personal perspective and focus to the growth and development of NTID during his tenure. This chapter does not attempt to be a compendium of the activities of each leader but, instead, focuses on the unique contributions each individual has made to NTID.

D. Robert Frisina set the stage as NTID's first director. As a young leader, he eloquently articulated what the college was to become, as well as what the role he filled should be. James DeCaro, who twice served as an interim leader of NTID, has described Frisina's role in setting the stage for those who would follow him.

It began with the indomitable Dr. Robert Frisina, NTID's first director, who hired me in 1971 to teach civil technology. I often have said of Bob, 'He was never my mentor, but always my mentor.' While he didn't formally instruct me on how to be a good teacher, and later, an administrator, I only had to watch him in action to see excellence defined.[3]

Frisina constantly emphasized not doing business as it had been done in the past, but bringing to bear all the creativity and technical competence possible to help deaf and hard-of-hearing persons succeed. Throughout this chapter you will see this creativity by the emphasis placed on the use of technology and innovation in the design and delivery of NTID's curriculum, in its broad range of support services for students, and by the promotion of a vibrant artistic and cultural environment. As one who has worked closely with each of these individuals during more than 40 years at NTID, I can tell you that while each had his own views, they all had, as their primary focus, the personal and professional growth of the deaf and hard-of-hearing students who enrolled at RIT.

D. Robert Frisina (1967 – 1976)

On January 13, 1967, D. Robert Frisina, was appointed RIT Vice President for NTID. Frisina was a young, energetic, and innovative educator of individuals who were deaf or hard-of-hearing. A World War II veteran, he graduated from Westminster College in 1949 and taught at the Missouri School for the Deaf. Later he joined the faculty of the Kendall School, an elementary and secondary school located on the Gallaudet campus. Frisina then pursued graduate studies at Northwestern University and, in 1955, was awarded a PhD in audiology. Eventually he returned to Gallaudet and became the director of the Hearing and Speech Center.[4]

In 1964, Frisina was appointed dean of the Gallaudet College Graduate School. With his experience in teaching deaf and hard-of-hearing children, audiology, and higher education administration, he brought to NTID a resume that uniquely fit the leadership needs of this new institution. In addition, Frisina had the knack of encapsulating in a few words the goals that would motivate his staff and those individuals supporting this "new idea" in Congress. He said that the college had to be "innovative" if it was to succeed in graduating deaf and hard-of-hearing students who were "technically competent" and could compete with their hearing peers in the workplace.

Frisina lost no time in establishing NTID as one of the colleges of RIT and in hastening the enrollment of its first class. Less than two years after his appointment, in fall 1968, 70 deaf and hard-of-hearing students enrolled at the college. One year later, NTID's first technical programs were offered. Included in these

D. Robert Frisina

programs were architectural drafting, mechanical drafting, machine tool operation, and office practice and bookkeeping. A student interpreter training program was also established; this was the first school in history to offer such a program. In addition, he worked tirelessly to educate staffers in the U.S Department of Education and subcommittees of Congress about the role NTID would play in improving the socio-economic status of its graduates. Frisina knew that understanding this was critical for those who controlled the NTID purse strings. Thus he established a foundation for the positive relationships NTID would have with government officials needed by each of the NTID leaders who were to follow.

He also worked selflessly for the welfare of deaf and hard-of-hearing students. He was a true innovator in every sense of the word, and to hear him tell the story of "life in the trenches" as he worked to get NTID up and running is nothing short of inspirational. Thousands of deaf and hard-of-hearing graduates, and current students, owe much to Frisina and his innovative vision for what he called The Grand Experiment. As RIT Trustee Arthur L. Stern stated, "Few leaders anywhere in the nation could have matched Dr. Frisina's dynamic leadership in charting the course for the National Technical Institute for the Deaf."[5]

Frisina Quotes

In essence, what is at stake here is the socio-economic status of present and future generations of people who are born with or who sustain deafness in very early life.[6]

During these first few years of its existence, NTID has grown steadily as a proving ground for inventing approaches to teaching and learning, for developing new employment opportunities, for probing new dimensions in the communication and in the psycho-social aspects of deafness, and for applying and measuring the effectiveness of new technology in education.[7]

In 1976, Frisina accepted increased responsibilities at Rochester Institute of Technology and became Senior Vice President for Institutional Advancement for all of RIT. He left NTID in the capable hands of William E. Castle, whom he had hired in 1968 to be Director of Instructional Affairs.

William E. Castle (1977 – 1994)

Prior to his coming to NTID, William Castle had served as the Associate Secretary of Research and Scientific Affairs for the American Speech and Hearing Association. In 1967, he worked on the *Final Report on the Seminar on Skills and Knowledge Needed by Audiologists and Educators of the Deaf*, published by the American Speech and Hearing Association. While Frisina firmly established NTID at RIT in the minds of the U.S. Congress, Castle moved NTID onto the international stage, and followed Frisina's creative lead by expanding NTID's role in supporting and promoting the arts for

William E. Castle

and by deaf and hard-of-hearing persons.

Castle led NTID and served as Vice President of RIT for Government Relations from 1977 through 1994. By 1977, most of NTID's curricular programs were well established. Therefore, he emphasized significant outreach programs, including congressional relations, international relations, a Special Speakers Series, and a Deaf Artists series. Following the lead of his predecessor, he spent an enormous amount of time in Washington, DC, developing strong, lasting relationships with members of Congress. This was done primarily to maintain appropriate federal funding for NTID. He managed, in the process, to obtain honorary degrees from RIT for some members of Congress, and to obtain special grants for new programs in other colleges of RIT that

---

deaf and hard-of-hearing students could pursue.

He had a way of making deaf and hard-of-hearing students feel special, and he always welcomed them into his office. Castle helped originate the NTID Student Government, when, in 1971, he had a group of students write a constitution. In addition, he strongly supported the arts as a critical part of NTID. This support followed Frisina's belief in the role of the arts at a technical institution. When the NTID buildings were being designed, Frisina was asked why a theater was included in those plans. His response was that we must provide students with a well-rounded education, including personal and social development, and communication skills. He felt that the cultural arts and technology are not mutually exclusive—that they are critical elements of a postsecondary curriculum, each fostering creativity in the other.

As a result, Castle provided a budget to support a Special Speaker Series that brought many celebrities, both deaf and hearing, to NTID to provide deaf and hard-of-hearing students with role models and insights into the greater world. During his administration, he used the Mary Switzer Art Gallery as a venue to invite deaf and hard-of-hearing artists from the United States and other countries to exhibit their works. From these exhibits, he often purchased works of art to create a permanent collection for continuing exposure of deaf and hard-of-hearing students to this part of their culture. To extend these endeavors campus-wide, in 1980, the President of RIT provided a special budget to Castle to initiate the Creative Arts Program in Complementary Education for all of RIT. Among other things, this program encouraged deaf and hard-of-hearing and hearing students to form musical groups, and to promote the production of Broadway musicals at NTID's Robert Panara Theatre. It also lent support to the already-existing Sunshine Too! group of performers, who signed as they sang.

Because other countries showed a strong interest in NTID as a model program, he frequently traveled abroad. These visits fostered relationships with the already-established Tsukuba Technical Institute for the Deaf in Japan, a consultation arrangement with the Princess of Thailand regarding creating the Ratchasuda College for the Handicapped, and the creation of a sister institution with the N.C. Bauman Institute of Moscow's State Technical University. His visits also led to grants

of millions of dollars from the Nippon Foundation and helped convince Congress to allow NTID to admit international students who were deaf or hard-of-hearing.

Other programs created during this time included the National Center for Employment of the Deaf, the Joint Educational Specialist Program between RIT and the University of Rochester, the Educational Interpreting associate degree program, and the International Center for Hearing and Speech Research.

Castle Quotes

I foresee such a program [RIT Complementary Education] giving us ways to enhance the communications comfort and therefore interaction, and yes, integration among deaf and hearing students, among other student groups, and among staff and students. I also foresee such a program giving a new, enriched quality to the total campus life of RIT.[8]

I have seen the Institute mature from infancy to its current position as a world-renowned leader in the education of people who are deaf. I am intensely proud of that position, and a bit nostalgic as well, as I recall NTID's beginnings more than a quarter century ago. I have been privileged to be at or near the helm since NTID moved from congressional legislation to reality.[9]

NTID has always been in a class of its own: a college that meets the unique needs of deaf students in a way that no other institution in the world has done as well.[10]

In 1994, William Castle retired from NTID after more than 25 years in key leadership roles. He left the college temporarily in the hands of James DeCaro, the Academic Dean of NTID, who served as Acting President of NTID for just over one year while RIT conducted a national search for a new leader.

James DeCaro (1995, 2010)

Hired at NTID in 1971, James DeCaro was the first faculty member in NTID's Civil Engineering Technology Program. He holds bachelor's and master's degrees in civil engineering, and a PhD in instructional technology from Syracuse University. He has served NTID as a Staff Chairperson, Instructional Developer, Department Chair, and Division Director. From 1985 to 1998, he was Dean of NTID, and served as NTID's Interim President and RIT Vice President in 1995 when William E. Castle retired, and again in 2010 following the departure of T. Alan Hurwitz in December 2009.

He is the past director of NTID's Postsecondary Education Network-International, a multinational collaborative network of colleges and universities serving deaf and hard-of-hearing students that was funded by more than $11 million in grants from the Nippon Foundation of Japan. DeCaro also is Immediate Past Director of the NTID Center on Access Technology, which focuses on the application of innovative technologies to facilitate access to educational settings for deaf and hard-of-hearing people. He was awarded an Honorary Doctorate in 2003 by Bauman Moscow State Technical University (Russia) for his contributions to the postsecondary education of people who are deaf and hard-of-hearing. He has been a Rotary International Scholar at University of Newcastle upon Tyne (England), and a Fulbright Senior Scholar at Orebro University (Sweden). He holds an honorary professorship at Tianjin University of Technology (China). In 2008, he received the FESCO Award (Foundation for Encouragement of Social Contribution) from Japan for his service to humanity. He has been inducted into RIT's Innovation Hall of Fame in recognition of his many achievements and his positive effect in our global society.

During his second stint as interim leader of NTID in 2010, DeCaro initiated NTID's Strategic Decisions 2020. Implementing any strategic plan requires much collaboration and at least a small dose of risk-taking, qualities of any good leader. This plan continues NTID's legacy and belief in the role of thoughtful strategic planning, as DeCaro describes:

> This scenario is most agreeable with me, as I always have enjoyed a good challenge. I accepted one when

James DeCaro

I came to NTID nearly 40 years ago. I had no experience with either deafness or teaching, but when Bob Frisina shared during my interview his vision of what NTID could be, I began to believe in what this college could accomplish. Four decades later, I am still a believer. We have managed to change with the times and continue to grow in ways that no one would have dreamed possible. The technological preparation our students receive today is second to none, and the barriers that have been broken in terms of accessibility and career options for them are mind-boggling. In the forefront of everything we do, day in and day out, is the belief that our job no longer is to advocate for these students, but instead to give them the skills they need so that, upon entering the competitive job market, they cannot be denied. We must be singular in our focus in this regard, and we do not strive to emulate others. We must aspire, every day, to be "NTID at RIT."[11]

Robert Davila (1996 – 2003)

After a national search, Robert Davila was appointed as NTID's first deaf leader. Davila became deaf at eight years of age, the result of a severe case of spinal meningitis. Learning about a special school for deaf children and determined that her young son should have a fair shot at life, Davila's mother sent him to the California School for the Deaf (CSD). After graduating with honors from CSD, he entered Gallaudet University, where he obtained a bachelor's degree in 1953, followed by a master's degree from Hunter College and a doctorate in education from Syracuse University.

Prior to being appointed to the top post at NTID, Davila served as Assistant Secretary for the Office of Special Education and Rehabilitative Services in the U.S. Department of Education from 1989 to 1993, during the administration of George H.W. Bush. In addition, he had experience teaching high school mathematics, being an assistant principal, and serving as a K-12 superintendent. During the 1970s and 1980s, he worked at Gallaudet College as a professor, administrator, and vice president. Before his appointment at NTID, he served as Headmaster of the New York School for the Deaf at White Plains from 1993 to 1996.

At NTID, Davila focused his energies on the role of technology in enhancing the learning of deaf and hard-of-hearing persons, and providing outreach to the broader population of postsecondary learners nationwide. During his term, NTID was selected as the site for the Northeast Technical Assistance Center to provide outreach and training for deaf and hard-of-hearing students pursuing postsecondary education in colleges and universities other than NTID or Gallaudet. And, in 2001, the Postsecondary Education Network-International was created with support from the Nippon Foundation to set up and develop programs to support students who were deaf or hard-of-hearing in higher education institutions in 10 countries, including NTID's sister institutions in Russia and Japan.

In 1999, NTID implemented its first online course, Internet Technologies I, and in 2001, NTID hosted its first National Symposium of Instructional Technology and Education of the Deaf, which attracted national and international attendees. An annual conference that continued for many years, it emphasized

Robert Davila

Davila's belief as to the critical role of technology:

Why is this emphasis on using technology to educate deaf and hard-of-hearing students so important? We believe that it helps "level the playing field" for these students as they prepare to enter the mainstream work force. It not only provides them with specific tools, but also offers them the opportunity to develop essential skills that enable them to adapt to the demands of the workplace by successfully applying basic knowledge and job-related skills.[12]

Davila also continued the emphasis on the arts begun by previous NTID leaders. He promoted a fundraising activity for development of the Joseph F. and

Helen C. Dyer Arts Center. Groundbreaking occurred in 2000, culminating a two-year campaign to raise several million dollars from largely deaf and hard-of-hearing donors. The Dyer Arts Center was completed in 2001, and Joseph and Helen Dyer committed additional funds for maintenance of the center.

NTID established a Bachelor of Science degree in ASL/English Interpretation as part of its strategic goal to be a leader in interpreter training. The Master of Science program in Secondary Education (MSSE) was also expanded to accommodate 50–60 enrolled students.

Davila Quotes

Nothing has given me more pleasure and pride than interacting with our students. Every initiative I have undertaken has been motivated by a desire to provide our students with opportunities to achieve their fullest potential.[13]

NTID is also implementing a new Bachelor of Science degree in American Sign Language and English Interpretation—the college's first ever. The program offers advanced specialized training to develop greater interpreting skills, as well as practical experience and coursework in interpreting in elementary, middle/secondary, and postsecondary settings. It also provides training and experience in working with oral deaf, hard-of-hearing, and deaf-blind people. The New York State Education Department recently informed the university provost of its approval to initiate the program.[14]

NTID cultivates and nurtures today's students to become tomorrow's leaders. We do this through our cutting-edge academic programs that prepare our graduates to "hit the ground running" and land jobs in fields that didn't even exist a decade or two earlier. We do this through the dazzling array of opportunities we set before them to help them become leaders, to grow and challenge themselves far beyond what they thought they were capable of when they arrived at RIT.[15]

Davila announced his retirement from RIT/NTID in 2003 and was appointed by President George W. Bush to serve on the National Council on Disability, a 15-member group that advises the President and Congress on matters affecting the education, rehabilitation, employment, and independent status of the country's 52 million persons with disabilities.

On December 10, 2006, Davila was named the ninth President of Gallaudet University, the first of two NTID leaders to hold that position.

T. Alan Hurwitz (2003 – 2009)

After a national search, T. Alan Hurwitz was the fourth to be appointed to lead NTID, beginning on December 1, 2003. Hurwitz was initially hired by NTID in 1970 as an Educational Specialist in RIT's College of Engineering after working for McDonnell Douglas Corporation for five years. He holds a BS in Electrical Engineering from Washington University in St. Louis, an MS in Electrical Engineering from St. Louis University, and an EdD in Curriculum and Teaching from the University of Rochester. He subsequently held a number of progressively responsible positions at NTID, including Chair of the Engineering and Computer Science Support Department, Director for NTID Support Services, Associate Dean for Educational Support Services, Associate Vice President for Outreach and External Affairs, and Associate Dean for Student Affairs.

Hurwitz had been active in a variety of professional and deafness-related organizations, and served on a number of boards of organizations for persons who are deaf or hard-of-hearing, including the Rochester School for the Deaf and the National Captioning Institute. He is a former president of the National Association of the Deaf, and has traveled and lectured extensively both nationally and internationally.

Hurwitz's main focus was on curriculum reform and access to RIT/NTID's curricula and careers for all deaf and hard-of-hearing students. One of his first actions as leader was to create a "2010 Strategic Vision" group to assess where NTID should be headed for the following five to ten years. Four major initiatives resulted from the deliberations of this group.

First, he realigned and combined academic departments between traditional technical education and baccalaureate programs to allow faculty and staff with similar discipline backgrounds and training to provide seamless guidance and support to students who aspire to advance from associate degree programs to baccalaureate programs (e.g., NTID Engineering Technology faculty with the RIT College of Engineering and the RIT College of Applied Science and Technology support faculties, and NTID Business Technology faculty with the RIT College of Business support faculty). As a result, NTID's curricula were restructured around three distinct areas of study: career-focused sub-baccalaureate degrees, transfer degrees leading to baccalaureate studies, and baccalaureate/master's degrees.

Second, the continued growth of enrollments in the other colleges of RIT by deaf and hard-of-hearing students with diverse communication preferences resulted in demands for expansion of the amount and variety of support services being offered. As a result, he realigned existing resources and acquired additional funding to expand NTID's sign language interpreting, speech-to-text captioning program, and general support services for students enrolled in the other colleges of RIT.

Third, he promoted the development of formal preparatory programs with selected community colleges for students who wanted to come to NTID, but were not academically ready. Through the efforts of the Northeast Technical Assistance Center and the Postsecondary Education Program Network, NTID worked closely with community colleges to develop readiness programs that emphasized reading and writing, mathematics, career awareness, and interpersonal growth. In addition, Hurwitz established a formal educational outreach consortium to share NTID's expertise with others and to improve education and career development opportunities for deaf and hard-of-hearing people. Outreach programs for deaf and hard-of-hearing youth in grades 7-11 were also created. Examples of these programs include MathCounts, National Science Fair, National Essay Contest, National Digital and Animation Arts Contest, TechGirlz, ACT prep class, and career exploration for AALANA middle school students, in addition to NTID's traditional Explore Your Future program.

Finally, he successfully acquired $2 million from Communication Services for the Deaf to construct a new Student Development Center at NTID. This grant

T. Alan Hurwitz

enabled NTID to build a $4.5 million, two-story, 30,000-square-foot building to extend students' learning experiences by fostering their potential for leadership and community service, and to provide opportunities to explore other interests through a variety of nontraditional educational and recreational activities.

Hurwitz Quotes

One of my goals in the next few years is to create Centers of Excellence at NTID, where educators of deaf and hard-of-hearing people can access the latest research in technology and pedagogy. Teamwork, group projects and discussions, and creative learning environments will be hallmarks of these centers.[16]

It's hard to know what the NTID of tomorrow will look like for future students, and what programs those students will be interested in studying. Many probably haven't even been invented yet. But one thing is certain... NTID will still be here, helping prepare students for the world—and perhaps the universe—in which they will live.[17]

During his term at the helm of NTID, applications for admission continued to increase, and enrollment was the highest in NTID's history. In addition, students continued to find good jobs upon graduation, despite tough economic times.

On October 18, 2009, Dr. Hurwitz was selected as the 10th president of Gallaudet University. He took office on January 1, 2010, becoming the second NTID leader to have been named president of Gallaudet University.

Gerard Buckley (2011 – present)

A graduate of NTID, Gerard Buckley was selected as its sixth, and as of this publication, current president. He assumed that role on January 1, 2011.

A native of St. Louis, Missouri, Buckley received a BS degree in Social Work from RIT in 1978, an MSW from University of Missouri, and an EdD in Special Education from the University of Kansas. He has more than 30 years of experience in higher education, including more than 20 years serving in a variety of capacities at NTID. From 1990 to 1993, Buckley served as Chairperson and Assistant Professor in the Department of Educational Outreach, followed by five years as Director of NTID's Center for Outreach and Assistant Professor on the RIT/NTID Social Work Support Team. He has twice received the NTID Student Congress Faculty/Staff Humanitarian Award and was named Distinguished Alumnus by NTID in 1985 and by RIT's College of Liberal Arts in 1996. From 1998 to 2003, he served as NTID Associate Dean for Student Services, and he held the position of NTID Assistant Vice President for College Advancement with responsibility for the admissions, placement, marketing, and outreach operations from 2004 until becoming President.

Outside of NTID, he has served as President of the Board of the American Deafness and Rehabilitation

Gerard Buckley

Association and as President of the Lexington School for the Deaf's Board of Trustees in New York City. He has also served on the National Advisory Board of the National Institute of Health's Institute on Deafness.

Buckley represents the fulfillment of what D. Robert Frisina called the Grand Experiment that created NTID. He noted that the fruits of this experiment would be realized when its graduates entered the workplace and competed on par with their peers who hear. That has happened now for many of NTID's graduates. "With the appointment of Gerry, another historic milestone has been achieved—a graduate of the college, who has had a successful and distinguished career in the national workplace, and at NTID, is taking the helm. I am ecstatic that the baton has been passed to the next generation, and I'm glad that I was here to witness it and be part of it," said Dr. James DeCaro.

Buckley played a critical role in the development of Strategic Decisions 2020, the college's blueprint for the next decade.

My top priority is to continue to strengthen our relationship with Congress and the Department of Education regarding budget and operations. I'm also working closely with students, faculty and staff to implement Strategic Decisions 2020, a plan that will guide our work for the next decade. We continue to further NTID's integration with RIT, and to foster new and productive relationships with our colleagues throughout the university.[18]

Buckley was also actively involved in raising funds to build Rosica Hall, a facility on the RIT campus that is the focal point of NTID's research and innovation efforts for students, faculty, and staff. He is focusing his efforts on developing partnerships with business and industry consistent with NTID's mission, and directing NTID to take a more active role in sustainability. He has established an NTID committee for sustainable practices to engage the NTID community fully in this RIT-wide priority.

As I look to the future, I envision that our portfolio of career-focused associate degree programs will be enhanced with programs in areas such as healthcare and sustainability, that our highly successful associate and bachelor's degree programs will continue to grow, and that new bachelor's degree programs will result from collaboration between NTID and RIT's other colleges. I also see a new generation of outstanding students, faculty, and staff thriving, and driving innovation further as they work together in [Rosica] Hall to produce groundbreaking research that improves the educational and employment success of deaf and hard-of-hearing people nationally and internationally. And I see our alumni network engaged and proud to be an integral part of the RIT/NTID family, helping with recruitment, placement and fundraising work.[19]

Conclusion

This chapter has reviewed the unique contributions made by the six leaders who have guided NTID during its first half-century. However, during this time, there have been a variety of continuing challenges that have resulted in changes that the drafters of the initial legislation could not have anticipated. One such change is in the nature of the host institution, RIT. When selected, RIT was a regional technical college that offered many associate degrees in career areas required by prominent industries in the greater Rochester area (Kodak, Xerox, Bausch & Lomb, Taylor Instruments, Stromberg-Carlson, and General Dynamics, among others.) Many readers today may not even recognize some of these companies as major employers in Rochester. Yet it was RIT's relationships with these companies that supported its selection as the career-oriented institution to host NTID. The fact that RIT was not a traditional university system and had only begun granting baccalaureate degrees less than a decade before the establishment of NTID also contributed to RIT's selection as the host institution. Anyone looking at RIT today would hardly recognize it as the same institution. During NTID's first 50 years, RIT has grown to be ranked as one of *U.S. News and World Report*'s National Universities, and is currently the tenth largest private university for undergraduates in the United States. These changes have certainly required flexible and adept leadership at NTID. How does one continue to adhere to the original intent of the NTID legislation and still remain an integral part of the greater and ever-changing Rochester Institute of Technology? Certainly, a challenge for any leader.

As the NTID legislation was making its way through Congress in the mid-1960s, a rubella epidemic was raging across the United States. During these years, the number of children born deaf or hard-of-hearing increased by another third. As a result, in the mid-1980s, NTID was faced with an increase of a third more students applying for admission. Up until this time, NTID had a target population of 750 students, but enrollment grew to more than 1,100 by the late 1980s. The leadership had to seek additional funding to support the staff and infrastructure needed to accommodate the increased number of students seeking admission beyond the 750 for which the original buildings and staffing were designed. Even beyond this "Rubella Bulge," enrollments continued to rise and currently stand at more than 1,200 deaf and hard-of-hearing students—nearly double the original projections made in the mid-1960s.

Another major challenge for the leadership of NTID has been a sea change in the way that deaf and hard-of-hearing students are educated in the United States. Public Law (PL) 94-142 was enacted by the United States Congress in 1975. This act required all public schools accepting federal funds to provide equal access to education, and one free meal a day, for children with physical and mental disabilities. Before enactment of this law, about 85% of deaf and hard-of-hearing children were educated in a relatively small number of residential schools created specifically for individuals who were deaf or hard-of-hearing. Over the next quarter of a century, the statistics reversed, so that today more than 80% are being educated in their local public school systems.[20] This change has not only affected NTID's approach to recruiting students for admission, but also has had a profound impact on the communication preferences of entering students and their expectations for support services provided by the university as a whole.

Another change not foreseen by those who sought the establishment of NTID was in the structure of the U.S. economy—the movement from a manufacturing economy to an information-based economy. NTID was established to provide deaf and hard-of-hearing persons access to a manufacturing economy, and as previously stated, RIT was a natural fit for this. However, with the growth of the service sector in our economy, and the availability of jobs in this sector, NTID, as well as RIT, was required to provide curricula in these areas. The information economy and its emphasis on quality communication skills has traditionally created barriers for persons who are deaf or hard-of-hearing. Thus, NTID's leadership has been challenged to make NTID a leader in using advanced technology to support improved communication between persons who are deaf and hard-of-hearing and persons who are hearing.

NTID has been blessed with leaders who have skillfully managed the complexities of a federally-funded organization within the broad context of an evolving private university system, while adapting to the changing cultural, educational, and economic

makeup of its target population. The continued success of this Great Experiment has its roots in the clarity of mission that was initially articulated by Robert Frisina, and has been reaffirmed by each of his successors. The fact that NTID has been able to continue to grow while adapting its curricula to accommodate these changes testifies to the quality of leadership at the Rochester Institute of Technology who, ultimately, were responsible for appointing each of the six individuals profiled in this chapter. These sentiments are best summed up by James DeCaro:

> From the first time I set foot on this campus as a new member of the faculty in 1971, it was clear to me that I was expected to take risks, and develop and implement new ways of teaching people who are deaf...but to do so in a calculated and systematic fashion. That is, develop new approaches to reaching out to people who are deaf...finding innovative ways to meet their educational needs. The educational history of people who are deaf was one of underachievement and low expectations. For almost 40 years now, I have been given the freedom to pursue these ends...and not only at the college of NTID, but across the university. RIT is an institution that has thrived on innovation and change and has been nimble and flexible in providing its people with the opportunity to innovate. For this, I am most appreciative and thrilled.[21]

Dr. Gerard Walter, retired, is the former Director of Institutional Research at NTID.

Notes

1. Peter W. Peterson, "A Dream and a Possibility." *The Vocational Teacher*, no. 1 (1930): 8.

2. Edward L. Scouten, *Turning Points in the Education of Deaf People*. (Danville, IL: Interstate Printers and Publishers, Inc., 1984).

3. James DeCaro, "Defining Excellence." *FOCUS Magazine* (Spring/Summer 2010): 2.

4. Scouten, *Turning Points*.

5. Rochester Institute of Technology, "2011 Innovation Hall of Fame." YouTube video. 6:47. Posted June 2011. https://youtu.be/llbaSlEl24g.

6. D. Robert Frisina, "We Have Made a Beginning." *FOCUS Magazine* (February/March 1975): 2, 22.

7. Frisina, "We Have Made a Beginning," 22.

8. William E. Castle, "An Overview." *FOCUS Magazine* (Spring 1980): 1.

9. William E. Castle, "From the Director's Desk." *FOCUS Magazine* (Winter 1995): 2.

10. Castle, "From the Director's Desk," 2.

11. DeCaro, "Defining Excellence," 2.

12. Robert Davila, "Adapting with Technology." *FOCUS Magazine* (Fall 2000): 2.

13. Robert Davila, "State of the Institute" (lecture, National Technical Institute for the Deaf, Rochester, N.Y., 2003).

14. Robert Davila, "Pausing to Celebrate and Reflect." *FOCUS Magazine* (Fall/Winter 2001): 2.

15. Robert Davila, "Preparing the Next Generation of Leaders." *FOCUS Magazine* (Spring/Summer 2003): 2.

16. T. Alan Hurwitz, "Strategic Visioning 2010: Realizing the Dream." *FOCUS Magazine* (Fall 2004/Winter 2005): 3.

17. T. Alan Hurwitz, "Charting the Course." *FOCUS Magazine* (Spring/Summer 2004): 3.

18. Pamela L. Carmichael, "NTID's New President: An interview with Gerard J. Buckley." *FOCUS Magazine* (Fall/Winter 2010): 3.

19. Carmichael, "NTID's New President," 5.

20. United States Department of Education, "IDEA Part B Child Count and Educational Environments Collection." (2015-16). https://www2.ed.gov/programs/osepide-a/618-data/static-tables/index.html#part-b

21. Greg Livadas, "James DeCaro Inducted into RIT's Innovation Hall of Fame." *NTID News* (2010). http://www.ntid.rit.edu/news/james-decaro-inducted-rits-innovation-hall-fame

A Commitment to Equality
Diversity at NTID

Dr. Charlotte LV Thoms and Dr. Ila Parasnis

NTID has promoted inclusion of deaf and hard-of-hearing students in society since it was established in 1968 and has addressed issues related to diversity among deaf and hard-of-hearing students, and among NTID faculty and staff for several decades. In this chapter, we discuss affirmative action efforts and professional activities that have addressed diversity issues. We also list a few courses related to diversity developed by faculty, as well as presenting profiles of several diverse faculty and staff members. Our sources include NTID's annual report to the Department of Education, *FOCUS Magazine,* personal interviews, and our personal knowledge.

Our account is not exhaustive, and we may have missed some significant events or the recognition of some significant people. Any omissions are not intentional. We value the contributions of everyone who promotes diversity and inclusion at NTID. We also note that, given time and chapter length constraints, discussion of diversity related to hearing status, gender, and nationality is not addressed in this chapter, although these are also important aspects of diversity at NTID.

Affirmative Action Efforts

Details regarding the racial/ethnic demographics of students and faculty/staff for the early years of NTID are not available, but records and annual reports to the Department of Education (starting in 1979) that do include information about diversity are available. The records from 1979 show that the percentage of accepted students who were racial/ethnic minority was

7.8%, while the percentage of racial/ethnic minority faculty and staff members working at NTID was 2.8%. By 2016, the numbers had changed dramatically for students, with 39.6% identifying themselves as racial/ethnic minority students or "other." The increase in the number of diverse faculty and staff is smaller, compared to the increase in the number of diverse students, but by 2016, 12.6% of NTID employees were members of racial/ethnic minorities, showing that the workforce is also changing in its composition.

Table 1 shows the total number of accepted students in 1979—the number of registered students is not available—and registered students in 1989, 1999, 2009, and 2016, along with numbers and corresponding percentages for each racial/ethnic group, all derived from the NTID annual report for each year. Table 2 shows the total number of faculty and staff at NTID for the same years. The tables provide snapshots of racial/ethnic diversity at NTID and highlight the success of affirmative action efforts over time.

In 1979, NTID established a minority advisory group, and plans were formulated for participation in the National Scholarship Service and Fund for Negro Students workshops in Louisiana.[1] At that time, NTID spent 33% of its available advertising resources for advertisements in *Communicade, Deaf American, Annals of the Deaf, Ebony,* and *Afro-American Opportunities,* and in major urban newspapers such as *The New York Times, Washington Post* and *Chicago Tribune* in an effort to reach those in protected classes. However, these attempts

Table 1. Race/Ethnicity of Students at NTID

This table shows the number of accepted students in 1979 and registered students for the rest of the years. The students are categorized as white, Asian, Black/African American, Hispanic/Latino, Native Americans, and Other which includes those who self-identified as mixed races. The table shows numbers as well as percentages for each category.

Year	White	Asian	Black/African American	Hispanic/ Latino	Native American	Other/Two mixed races	Total Students
1979	319 (92.2%)	4 (1.2%)	14 (4.0%)	7 (2.0%)	2 (0.6%)	NA	346 (100%)
1989	988 (90.1%)	25 (2.3%)	36 (3.3%)	41 (3.7%)	6 (0.6%)	NA	1,096 (100%)
1999	758 (76.2%)	75 (7.5%)	86 (8.6%)	73 (7.4%)	3 (0.3%)	NA	995 (100%)
2009	773 (68.0%)	91 (8.0%)	117 (10.3%)	112 (9.9%)	8 (0.7%)	35 (3.1%)	1,136 (100%)
2016	637 (60.4%)	115 (11.0%)	120 (11.4%)	151 (14.3%)	unknown	31 (2.9%)	1,054 (100%)

Table 2. Race/Ethnicity of NTID Employees

This table indicates the total number of employees categorized as White; Asian, Native Americans, and Other as one group; Black; and Hispanic. The table shows numbers as well as percentages for each category.

Year	White	Asian/Native Americans/ Other	Black	Hispanic	Total Employees
1979	467 (97.1%)	4 (.8%)	7 (1.5%)	3 (.6%)	481 (100%)
1989	538 (92.8%)	18 (3.1%)	24 (4.1%)	unknown	580 (100%)
1999	483 (91.7%)	11 (2.1%)	23 (4.4%)	10 (1.8%)	527 (100%)
2009	542 (91.2%)	11 (1.9%)	32 (5.4%)	9 (1.5%)	594 (100%)
2016	498 (88.5%)	21 (3.7%)	29 (5.1%)	15 (2.7%)	563 (100%)

did not yield any response.[2] In June 1980, a 12-hour, cross-cultural orientation at NTID was piloted for staff. Its goal was to increase the quality of communication between deaf and hard-of-hearing and hearing staff, and to help staff identify what it meant to take responsibility for communicating. The program was intended to address the needs identified by the Communication Task Force, according to the *NTID 1980 Annual Report*. These early reports suggest that NTID was taking steps to serve the number of racial/ethnic minority students and to retain them.

Affirmative action efforts at NTID starting in 1986 were influenced by the following two events. That year, the summer edition of *FOCUS* reported a letter received in November 1985 from alumna Ronnie Mae Tyson, a 1984 graduate, inquiring about the lack of publicity about Black graduates who were successful. She provided William E. Castle, the director of NTID, with a list of examples of alumni with noteworthy careers. Her letter arrived six months after Louis Stokes, a Black member of the U.S. House of Representatives from Ohio, visited NTID around May of 1985 and expressed his concerns.

In a 1986 *FOCUS* article, "Telling It Like It Is," Kanter stated, "Dr. Castle had learned of a concern on the part of Representative...Stokes...about the number of minority students, faculty, and staff at NTID."[3] James (Jim) DeCaro, Professor and Dean Emeritus, said in March 2017, "The NTID efforts to bring AALANA [African American, Latino, Asian, and Native American] students and faculty to our college took on increased urgency with a visit of Democratic Congressman Louis Stokes to NTID....During his visit he asked specific questions about our student and faculty numbers. We were 'encouraged' to improve our outcomes..."[4]

This article reported that in January 1986, Castle strongly reiterated the need for an Affirmative Action/Equal Employment Opportunities program for faculty and staff. As Table 2 shows, the percentage of NTID minority faculty and staff increased from 2.9% in 1979 to 7.2% in 1989. It is reported that Congressman Stokes said, "NTID is an example of the progress that can be made when people are committed to change and equality of opportunity."[5] In 1999, the number of racial/ethnic minority faculty and staff rose to 8.3%, and by 2009, the number was 8.8%. As of 2016, this number is 11.5%, the highest it has ever been.

In the '80s, annual reports focused on Affirmative Action and referred to minorities, underrepresented minorities, or members of protected classes, reflecting the terms used in the general field in those times. There was a shift in the narrative in 1991 to refer to diversity and inclusion commitments, which mirrored the general narrative in the field of diversity. This narrative is still used to reflect NTID's diversity and inclusion philosophy. The *NTID 1991 Annual Report* states,

NTID's commitment to recognize, celebrate, and value cultural diversity and individual differences is grounded in the nation's continuing effort to forge a pluralistic society. It does not arise merely from political pressures nor rest solely on public law. It is based in NTID's fundamental mission, the nature of the changing student body, and the changing nature of the world. Diversity is an asset upon which NTID can educationally capitalize, not a hurdle or governmental edict, which must be complied with. Simply put, it is a pedagogical opportunity for faculty and staff and a learning opportunity for students. Therefore, it is incumbent upon the NTID community to vigorously pursue a course of action that capitalizes on its diversity and continues to promote and nurture pluralism as a central theme.[6]

NTID Departmental Activities Related to Diversity

Training and Development Department

This department offered 14 workshops and 6 focus groups in the 1990 Multicultural Awareness Program for 218 participants.[7] In 1993, this department offered a multicultural education program in which 33 events were offered to 492 participants.[8] The department continued to offer various diversity-related workshops and Black History Month celebrations, along with the Affirmative Action Advisory Committee through 1994.

NTID Professional Development Program

Since the late '90s, the NTID Professional Development Program has offered hundreds of workshops, presentations, and panel discussions to NTID faculty and staff that have included specific events related to diversity and inclusion. Hope Williams, Program Manager since 2012, notes that she has organized more than 400 professional development and training programs aimed to increase faculty's knowledge and skills, and ultimately to enhance their teaching performance and the educational experiences of their students.[9]

NTID Student Life Team

The Student Life Team (SLT), under NTID Student & Academic Services, has been involved in organizing and supporting various campus events and activities that increase awareness of diversity and inclusion. One notable SLT event is the Cultural Celebration Weeks that they sponsor and organize, in which each culture is celebrated and presented from the deaf and hard-of-hearing perspective. According to Yvette Chirenje, Senior Staff Assistant, NTID Student Life Team, the following cultural weeks are currently celebrated at NTID: ALLY Week, Asian Deaf Week, Black Deaf Week, Deaf International Awareness Week, Deaf Womxn Week, Jewish Deaf Week, Latin American Deaf Week, and Native American Deaf Week.

Chirenje notes that the SLT also provides support to the diverse student clubs under RIT Student Government. (These are covered in another chapter in this book.) She also notes that the SLT supports a paraprofessional group, "Step Up," 5–6 ethnic student paraprofessionals who mentor first-year minority students under the Career Exploration Studies (CES) program.[10]

Johnnie Brown

Professional Activities and Initiatives Related to Diversity
The Annual Potluck Luncheon

The Annual Potluck, Black History Luncheon, or Black History Month Pot Luck Lunch Celebration, as it has been referred to over the years, is a celebration of diversity that started at the grassroots level in the '90s. The event was encouraged by Johnnie Brown (also known as "JB" or the "Mayor of NTID") from Facilities Management Services (FMS) when a few employees from FMS and a handful of NTID faculty members talked informally about good food and cultural traditions.

In their reminiscence about this event, Williams and Vincent Daniele (retired NTID faculty) said, "These conversations resulted in sharing, learning, and often good-naturedly teasing each other about how one person might know more than the other about food, cooking, and eating well. From time to time, a group of seven to ten faculty members and FMS staff ended up going to lunch together at some of Rochester's soul-food restaurants."[11]

As the event grew, Brown enlisted the help of Williams and others, and received support from the Dean's Office from then-Interim Dean DeCaro in the mid-1990s. Although potluck dishes were a hallmark of the luncheons, space and funding were also provided by the Dean's Office. An early version of the expanded luncheon was a warm-weather outdoor cookout in the LBJ courtyard—the area that is now the Dyer Arts Center—where NTID faculty and FMS staff prepared and grilled food. When the courtyard was enclosed, the event moved indoors and became an annual event during the month of February. The name changed to the Black History Luncheon, and Brown added guest speakers to the event. Presenters have included local artists, entrepreneurs, and educators.

The latest event was held on February 22, 2017 and had more than 100 faculty and staff participants. The luncheon has been one of the most consistent efforts to model diversity and pluralism. Brown and so many others have been able to demonstrate how easy it is to learn from each other and enjoy our diversity with a plate, a platform, and people.

Deaf Identity: Diverse Perspectives Conference

Ila Parasnis received funding from the NTID Division of Communication Programs to organize a one-day conference on April 23, 1993, called *Deaf Identity: Diverse Perspectives,* in which 14 experts considered issues regarding racial/ethnic minority Deaf people and Deaf women within the context of Deaf identity. The presenters from NTID were Simon Carmel, Karen Christie, Susan Foster, Vicki Hurwitz, Waithera Kinuthia, Carl Moore, Michael Stinson, J. Matt Searls, Teena Wax, and Dorothy Wilkins. Presenters external to NTID and well known in the field of deaf education were Gilbert L. Delgado, Joseph Fischgrund, Katherine Jankowski, and Linda Lytle. This conference drew more than 100 people and was well received by the NTID and Rochester-area Deaf community. It helped bring fresh insights into the experiences of diverse Deaf people, as they live in both Deaf and hearing worlds.

Scholarship Related to Diversity

NTID faculty members have published scholarly work related to racial/ethnic diversity, such as book chapters or journal articles. Dianne K. Brooks published a book chapter, "In Search of Self: Experiences of Postlingually Deaf African Americans," in *Cultural and Language Diversity and the Deaf Experience,* edited by Ila Parasnis.[12] In 2003, Susan Foster and Waithera Kinuthia published a research study in the *Journal of Deaf Studies and Deaf Education*, which explored the ways in which deaf and hard-of-hearing college students with Asian American, African American, and Latino American backgrounds think about and describe their identities.[13] As members of a research strand on diversity and minority issues, Parasnis (facilitator), Susan D. Fischer, and Vincent S. Samar conducted two research projects related to diversity from 1998 to 2003, and published their findings in *The American Annals of the Deaf* in 2005. One was about the perceptions of diverse educators regarding racial/ethnic minority deaf and hard-of-hearing college students, role models, and diversity; and the other was about deaf and hard-of-hearing students' attitudes toward racial/ethnic diversity, campus climate, and role models.[14, 15]

NTID Diversity Group

Alex Jones, Thomastine Sarchet, Sarah Bauman-Sarchet, and Alvin C. Merritt Boyd III served on the NTID Diversity Group established by the Office of the President in 2012. Jones served as the chair from 2012–2014, and Pamela McClain Christopher has been the chair since 2014. The goals of this committee are to provide a professional support community for faculty and staff members of color at NTID; to improve the work climate experience for AALANA faculty, staff, and students; to ensure that AALANA faculty, staff, and students form partnerships and collaborations; and to serve as a resource for the college, from interviewing candidates for administrative roles to mentoring faculty, staff, and students.

Workshops Organized by the AALANA Faculty Advisory Council

On March 18, 2016, Charlotte LV Thoms, then-Chairperson of the AALANA Faculty Advisory Council (AFAC, a group of tenured RIT/NTID AALANA faculty members who leverage their wealth of experience and wisdom to advocate for and to mentor pre-tenure AALANA faculty members) coordinated two half-day workshops. These workshops (additionally sponsored by the Office of the Provost, NTID's Office of the President, and the Division for Diversity and Inclusion) were presented to both the RIT and NTID faculty. Both workshops detailed the goals of AFAC in ensuring success for diverse faculty in mentoring and productivity.

Joy Gaston Gayles, a workshop facilitator from the National Center for Faculty Development and Diversity, presented *Solo Success: How to Thrive in the Academy when You're the Only ___ in Your Department* and *Re-thinking Mentoring: How To Build Communities of Inclusion, Support & Accountability*. She not only discussed the pressures of underrepresented faculty and the struggles in classroom dynamics related to race, class and gender, but also addressed strategies for increasing productivity, teaching efficiently, and building strong and healthy professional relationships.

NTID Courses Related to Diversity

There have been several academic courses related to diversity taught at NTID over the years. Some examples of classes on diversity that were taught in 2016–2017 include:

- *The Black Experience*: Developed and taught by Shirley Allen (early 1990s), and Catherine Clark and Kathy Davis (1997–2011)
- *Deaf People and the Holocaust*: Developed and taught by Patti Durr (2004–2006) and by J. Matt Searls (2009–2012)
- *Deaf Women's Studies*: Developed by Vicki Hurwitz (featured in the *FOCUS Magazine* Winter 1995).[16] Taught by Hurwitz (1995–2002) and Karen Christie (2003–2013)[17]
- *Diversity in the Deaf Community*: Developed and taught by J. Matt Searls (2013–)
- *Educational and Cultural Diversity*: Developed and taught by Patricia DeCaro and J. Matt Searls (1998–2004). Taught by Searls (2005–2011) and Ila Parasnis (2005–)
- *Individual and Social Identity*: Developed and taught by Thomas Warfield (2010–)

Profiles of Diverse Faculty and Staff

Diverse faculty members have contributed significantly to the mission of NTID. In this section, we profile a small selection of faculty who show the diversity of expertise and experience at NTID. This highlights significant contributions made by such individuals to promote diversity at NTID. Brief profiles of the two authors are listed at the beginning of this chapter, and additional profiles follow.

Charlotte LV Thoms

was recognized by the state of Massachusetts and the U.S. House of Representatives for her advocacy role on behalf of people with disabilities and issues related to women.

In 2015, Thoms, along with Sharon Burton from Florida Institute of Technology, published a book chapter on the impact of inclusion in disability-studies education.[18] In 2016, Thoms and Burton published on the impact of inclusion in disability-studies education, as well as in a recent journal article on the transcultural diversity and inclusion model.[19,20] Thoms states:

> As senior faculty, I often have ALANA and non-AL-ANA faculty and staff come to me when life in academe is challenging to say the least. Helping people see their value, their worth is critical to enjoying life. When I see someone I have talked with in the hallway, and the look on the person's face indicates it's not a day of joy or accomplishment, I sign "Never." That sign means "*Never let what others think of you become what you think of yourself.*" We have to remember we are agents of change: changing the world one student at a time, one diversity-related chat at a time, and one caring glance that we both know means "*Never.*"[21]

Charlotte LV Thoms

Charlotte LV Thoms, Associate Professor in NTID's Business Studies Department, was the first Black faculty member hired in that department. Thoms joined the department in 1991. She earned a master's degree from the University of Rochester and Rochester Institute of Technology in the Joint Educational Specialist Program (JESP), the predecessor of the MSSE Program. She later earned an EdD in 2011 from the University of Rochester in higher education administration. Thoms has served on various NTID and RIT committees and in local Rochester community organizations. She has served on the NTID Faculty Congress for more than ten years, and has chaired (or co-chaired) the Congress (2015–2017). She also served on the Institute Retention Committee for the Diversity Task Force in 2002.

Recently, Dr. Gerard Buckley appointed Thoms as NTID Director of Diversity Recruitment and Retention for African, Latino, Asian, and Native American (ALANA) faculty and staff positions. In 2012, Thoms

Ila Parasnis

Ila Parasnis joined NTID in 1979 as an Assistant Professor in the Communication Research Department and is presently Professor in the MSSE program. Parasnis earned a PhD in psychology from the University of Rochester. She has published extensively in peer-reviewed journals and has given more than 100 presentations at local, national, and international conferences about her research in deaf education. She edited a book, *Cultural and Language Diversity and the Deaf Experience* (1996, Cambridge University Press) and was the invited guest editor of the 150th year reference issue of the *American Annals of the Deaf* in 1997 on cultural identity and diversity in deaf education. She has also published *Attention Deficit Scales for Adults: Sign Language Version (ADSA-SLV)*, which is the first sign language-based computerized ADHD screening test for deaf adults.[22] The test addresses the issue of language diversity within the deaf community by providing the test items in ASL, in English-based sign with voice, or in print.

Ila Parasnis

Alvin C. Merritt Boyd III

In the 1991–1992 academic year, Parasnis, along with NTID faculty member Dominique Lepoutre, received the NTID New Faculty Initiatives Grant to organize a colloquium series entitled, "Cultural and Language Diversity in Education." Parasnis and Lepoutre invited four internationally-known researchers (Drs. Kenji Hakuta, François Grosjean, Josiane Hamers, and Carol Padden) and 12 NTID faculty and staff members to discuss the topics of bilingualism and bilingual education, diverse perspectives of deaf people, and their relevance to deafness and deaf education. At the time, the sociocultural model of deafness was just beginning to gain acceptance by educators and other professionals working with deaf and hard-of-hearing students, so this series was well received, with nearly 100 in attendance.

Parasnis has been active on numerous NTID and RIT committees, including the NTID Faculty Council (1983 to 1990) and the RIT Commission for Promoting Pluralism (2002–2006). She co-organized Expressions of Diversity Annual Conferences (2004–2006), and

organized Campus Week of Dialogue events focusing on deaf, hard-of-hearing and hearing students (2003), on international students (2004), and on women (2005). She served on the Board of Directors of both the United Nations Association of Rochester (2000–2002) and the Rochester International Council (2004–2006), and on the Board of Trustees of the India Community Center (1999–2000); in addition, she organized several community events related to diversity for each of these organizations. Parasnis remains active in the field of diversity and deaf education. In her writings and in her presentations, she explains the importance of understanding the multidimensionality of identity and intersectionality, and of recognizing individual differences among students, in order to create an optimal teaching-learning environment.

Alvin C. Merritt Boyd III
In 2004, Alvin C. Merritt Boyd III joined NTID as an American Sign Language and Interpreting Education

---

(ASLIE) student and completed a degree in the MSSE program in 2005. He began working at NTID in 2007 and is currently a lecturer in the Business Studies department and also Special Assistant for Diversity and Inclusion to President Buckley since September 2011. Boyd earned an EdD from St. John Fisher College and received an award for his dissertation, "Experience and Perceptions of Full-Time, Non-Tenure-Track Faculty at a Four-Year University." His dissertation also earned the Leo and Margaret Goodman-Malamuth Dissertation Award for 2017 from the American Association of University Administrators.

Boyd is co-chair, along with Thomastine Sarchet, of the NTID Diversity, Equity, and Inclusion Committee, which fosters active dialogue among community stakeholders and promotes engagement in ongoing diversity and inclusion initiatives at RIT. As co-chair, along with Jessica Cuculick, of the NTID Fellows Program for Academe, their mission is to work towards diversifying the faculty by increasing the number of postsecondary science, technology, engineering, and math (STEM) instructors and professors from historically underrepresented groups who are qualified to teach deaf, deaf-blind, and hard-of-hearing college students. Boyd has contributed significantly to NTID efforts to recruit and to retain racial/ethnic minority faculty, staff, and students.

Catherine Clark

Catherine Clark

Catherine Clark is an audiologist and Associate Professor who has worked in the Communication Studies and Services Department since 1986. While at NTID, Clark earned a professional doctorate in Audiology (2009) and established cochlear-implant services. She is viewed as a cochlear-implant expert in the Rochester community and has presented her research at national conferences. She notes one of her proudest accomplishments has been teaching a course titled "The Black Experience." Clark credits Shirley Allen and Kathy Davis, fellow faculty members who also taught this course, as great mentors.

Clark has been active in local community service organizations such as the Big Brother/Big Sister program and Rochester Black Deaf Advocates (RBDA) to support deaf and hard-of-hearing colleagues and to provide role models for her "little sister," an African American deaf student named LaToya, whom she

mentored for 12 years. LaToya has in turn become active in RBDA. Since 2014, Clark has been involved in efforts to empower deaf and hard-of-hearing people in Ethiopia and is contributing to the Model Deafness Center in Bahir Dar, Ethiopia, where she has provided audiological services to more than 100 individuals.

Clark has received local and national recognition for her work and is the recipient of the Isaac L. Jordan, Sr. Faculty/Staff Pluralism Award from RIT in 2011 and the Oticon FOCUS on People Award in the Practitioner category in 2016. Clark says, "I truly enjoy my work with students and colleagues. It's much more than a job; it has been an empowering career. NTID has provided tremendous professional growth!"[23]

Ellen Renee Johnson

Since 2011, Ellen Renee Johnson has been the Senior Staff Assistant in the Business Studies Department. She earned an MS in Accounting from Kaplan University and an MS in Management/Strategic Leadership from

Ellen Renee Johnson

Hope Williams

Roberts Wesleyan College. She is currently studying for CPA certification.

Johnson is a board member and coordinator for the NTID Diversity Group (2012–). She was a member of the committees for Signing in Public Spaces (2012–2015) and Improving Services for Underprepared Students (2012). She is a mentor in the Business Studies department for Administrative Support Technology (AST) students (2012–) and serves on the AST Mentoring Committee (2012–).

Johnson self-published a book, *Our Daughters: Let's Teach Them.*[24] She started Innercity Upkeep, Inc., a non-profit organization that plans to hire youth and young adults to work 20 hours/week keeping their neighborhoods clean. When asked what she brings to deaf and hard-of-hearing students, Johnson replied:

I'm an overcomer. I overcame the obstacles of poverty and surpassed everyone's expectations. From being a high school dropout to earning a robust

college education, a career, and homeownership, I now ignite the passion in others to achieve greatness in the midst of humble beginnings. When I talk to students, I empathize with them. They know I understand when people think you can't achieve because of something outside of yourself.[25]

Hope Williams

Hope Williams started in 1992 as an Office Systems Specialist at NTID. She became an Instructional Technology Specialist in 2003 and has been the Manager of Professional Development since 2012. Williams earned an MS in Instructional Technology from RIT. She has provided strategic vision and leadership to multidisciplinary teams of faculty and staff, and is particularly proud of her service to the university as a liaison among diverse groups of individuals. Williams wants to be remembered as someone who was always willing to help others and contribute to the university in a thoughtful and meaningful way. Her advice to new incoming NTID staff is:

T. Jane Doctor

John T. Reid

Keep an open mind, be compassionate and take advantage of the opportunities and benefits available at RIT. Be a lifelong learner and strive to be a T-shaped professional by honing your interpersonal, technical and disciplinary skills. Respect others and be civil—even if you disagree with them![26]

T. Jane Doctor

T. Jane Doctor is a member of the Seneca Wolf Clan from the Tonawanda Reservation, one of the nations of the Haudenosaunees, or the Iroquois Confederacy. Her tribe is located near Akron, New York. Doctor graduated from Empire State College with a BS in Cultural Studies. She joined NTID in 1993 and is a Senior Mechanical Technician who manages the Engineering Studies Lab.

Doctor has been active in raising awareness about Native American cultures at RIT, as well as in the Rochester community. She has served the RIT community on the RIT President's Native American Advisory Council since 2014. In 2016, she became the Assistant Director of the Office of NTID Tribal Education, under RIT's Future Stewards Program, an outreach program for Native American students; she travels throughout the country sharing the NTID story with students. She served as president of the 1993–94 Board of Directors of the Native American Cultural Center of Rochester and has been an active member of Ganondagan Historic Site in Victor, New York, since 1991. Doctor believes her greatest contribution to NTID is what she calls "raising students." She teaches them about life and her culture, and many call her "Dr. Mom."

John T. Reid

John T. Reid, known as "JT," is currently senior admissions counselor for NTID Admissions. He earned a MEd from the University of Arizona, focusing on counseling and guidance. Reid came to NTID as a student in 1973 to pursue his degree in social work and to continue his wrestling career. Reid competed in the Deaflympics in Sweden in 1973, in West Germany in 1981, and in

New Zealand in 1989.

In the early years, Reid remembers that the majority of the student body was white. He was one of only 10 Black deaf or hard-of-hearing students; there were even fewer Asian, Latinx, and Native American deaf or hard-of-hearing students. Rapport and socialization were centered on his choice of communication; therefore, ASL was more important to him than race. There were no deaf or hard-of-hearing student organizations related to diversity, and the NTID Student Congress (NSC) was probably the only organization on campus centered on deaf and hard-of-hearing students. In the late 1970s and early 1980s, the number of diverse deaf and hard-of-hearing students gradually began to increase.

When Reid was at NTID as a student, he did not consider professors who were not Black as role models, because they did not reflect his race or ethnicity. He took a class taught by a Black professor, Dr. Kijana Crawford, and did not believe there was a difference until she showed concern regarding a homework assignment. That concern, he recalls, was the turning point of his perception, as he realized the importance of having a role model who reflected his race or ethnicity. Although he never took a course with Dr. Shirley Allen, who was probably the only Black Deaf faculty member at NTID in the early and mid-1970s, he spent a lot of time visiting her in her office to chat, seek counsel, or even cry on her shoulder. He thought of her as his role model, or second mom, who understood him and his background.

From 1980 to 1983, Reid was the Assistant Educational Specialist for the Division of Human Development. He left NTID to attend graduate school at the University of Arizona where he earned an MEd in Counseling and Guidance. In 1993, JT returned to NTID as an admissions counselor for the Office of NTID Admissions. He later became the Coordinator of Multicultural Student Programs for the NTID Student Life Team, and then resumed his duties as an admissions counselor.

When Reid visits schools across the country, he shares with deaf and hard-of-hearing students the diversity of RIT/NTID, because he wants incoming students to feel comfortable when they decide to enroll here. He also tells them the story of his turning point.

Joseph C. Hill

Reid believes that NTID needs to hire more diverse faculty, staff, and administrators to correspond to the proportion of diverse students. He thinks they would serve as good role models to the students. "Perhaps," he says, "every NTID department, which has contact with students regularly, can establish a goal to maintain a certain percentage of diverse faculty within the department. If the goal is met and maintained, NTID would actually serve deaf and hard-of-hearing students of color very successfully."[27]

Reid has served on many RIT committees, such as NTID Diversity Group, RIT's Commission for Promoting Pluralism, the National Black Deaf Advocates, and Partners in Deaf Health, as well as other local organizations.

Joseph C. Hill

Joseph C. Hill became an assistant professor in the NTID Department of American Sign Language and Interpreting Education in 2015. He has a PhD in linguistics from Gallaudet University, and he is the first Black Deaf faculty member with a doctoral degree in this department. Hill is a co-author of *The Hidden Treasure of Black ASL: Its History and Structure*, which discusses the history and language of the African American Deaf Community from scholarly and linguistic perspectives.[28] Hill also published a book in 2012, entitled *Language Attitudes in the American Deaf Community*.[29] He has served on the board of Discovering Deaf Worlds since 2015, as well as on the editorial boards of *Sign Language Studies* and *The Journal of ASL and Literature* since 2013 and 2015, respectively.

Hill notes that he carries with him a unique view on education, language, and social justice that he always infuses into his teaching and research. He says that he feels very fortunate to work at NTID where he can be around students of color, and show them that it is possible to achieve more than they have been taught to believe. He says:

> Growing up, I didn't see deaf people who were in a professional role, and it was even rarer to see Black Deaf people like me in that role. I truly thought I was a rare kind who aspired to be a college educated professional. I was proven wrong when I went to my first National Black Deaf Advocates conference in Indianapolis in 1998 and saw a good number of Black Deaf professionals. It was inspiring to see them in real life, and, at the same time, disappointing that it had taken so long for me to see them. So I want to change that for deaf and hard-of-hearing students of color at NTID.[30]

Kathy L. Davis

Kathy L. Davis' career at NTID spans a period from 1976 until her retirement in 2013, having worked as an assistant professor in the Counseling and Advising Services Department. She has a master's degree in higher education and counseling from the College at Brockport, SUNY. While employed, Kathy earned a business certificate in administrative leadership from RIT, a certification as a nationally certified counselor from the National Board of Certified Counselors (NBCC), and later licensure in mental health counseling from New York State.

Kathy L. Davis

Davis remembers working for several years as the only Black counselor/faculty member of her department. With Allen, Davis co-developed and taught the first Black-history social-science course offered at NTID, entitled "The Black Experience," (previously discussed). Davis worked with Clark for 14 years to co-develop and teach the course.

Davis served as an early advisor of the NTID Ebony Club, was a member of the RIT Gospel Ensemble (30 years) and an active member of NTID's Affirmative Action/Equal Employment Opportunities Program. The efforts of this program led to an increase in the number of registered racial/ethnic minority students and faculty. Along with other NTID faculty and administrators, Davis traveled to various high schools across the country to provide career-development seminars for parents, administrators, and deaf and hard-of-hearing high-school students in preparation for postsecondary education.

She remains most proud about having provided personal, mental health, and career counseling to

Shirley J. Allen

later, was promoted to Associate Professor. Before retiring in 2001, she was a mentor to faculty, staff, and students, and developed the "Black Experience" course to increase awareness related to Black history. During her time at NTID, Allen earned an EdD from the University of Rochester in 1992. She conducted—what was probably the first music program for faculty, staff and students—singing for enjoyment. She also volunteered as a faculty advisor to several NTID and RIT student organizations. "I thoroughly enjoyed my time teaching and counseling at NTID/RIT," she says, "and will always carry fond memories."[31]

Thomas Warfield

Thomas Warfield has been teaching dance at NTID since 1998. He has an MFA from the University of Utah. He is a Senior Lecturer and Director of Dance in the NTID Performing Arts Department. He teaches four dance courses that include jazz and hip-hop, and a course titled "Individual and Social Identity." Warfield has performed, from stage to television to film, in more than 100 cities around the world as a singer, dancer, actor, model, composer, choreographer, director, producer, educator, activist, and poet. He is active within RIT, as well as in the local Rochester community.

Warfield has received numerous awards for his creative work, as well as for community service. For example, he was named a 2015 Community Champion Honoree by the Empire State Pride Agenda for his commitment to advancing LGBT equality and justice in Western New York. He also received the Isaac L. Jordan, Sr. Faculty/Staff Pluralism award from RIT in 2009, for making a significant contribution to diversity efforts on campus and within the Rochester community.

Warfield chaired the board of ARTWalk, which transformed the Neighborhood of the Arts with the ARTWalk Alive Festival (2004–2008). Two of the many highlights of his NTID career have been winning the 2004 OOBR (Off Off Broadway) Award for Choreography, for the NTID production of *Emperor Jones* that was presented in New York City, and an original project, *AstroDance*, combining dance and astrophysics through a collaboration between NTID and the RIT College of Science that was funded by the National Science Foundation. This dance performance premiered

hundreds of NTID students, who, once they graduated, increased their footprint in the workplace. After attending and presenting at national and international conferences on counseling and advising diverse student populations, Davis and her fellow counselors then integrated those cutting-edge methodologies in their work and services at NTID.

Shirley J. Allen

A native of Tyler, Texas, Shirley Jeanne Allen aspired to become a musician, most likely in rock-and-roll. However, she became ill during her third year in college and lost her hearing from the medication used. After returning to school, she continued her music and presented her senior piano recital, even after losing her hearing. She subsequently transferred from her hearing college to Gallaudet and graduated with a degree in English/Education.

Allen joined NTID in 1973 as an assistant professor in the Department of General Education, and

Thomas Warfield

Thomastine A. Sarchet

at the Rochester Fringe Festival and gave eight RIT/NTID students an opportunity to tour the east coast of the United States in 2012–2013. Warfield is also the founder/artistic director of PeaceArt International, a local/global outreach non-profit organization utilizing the arts and the creative process to foster world peace.

Warfield feels that his proudest achievements have been how he has made an impact on his students' lives. He feels grateful that he has been able to pass his knowledge and wisdom on to his students. He says, "working at NTID has allowed me to grow artistically in ways that I would have never imagined. It allowed me to maintain the integrity of artistic expression and expand that experience to non-professional dance performers."[32]

Thomastine A. Sarchet

Thomastine A. Sarchet joined NTID in 2006 as a Research Assistant in the Center for Educational Research Partnerships (CERP). From 2011 to 2016, she worked as Senior Project Associate, and later as

the Associate Director, for the Pre-College Education Network, a grant-funded project supported by the Nippon Foundation of Japan. In 2016, President Buckley established the Center for International Educational Outreach and appointed Sarchet as its director. She is also a member of NTID's Administrative Council and a Research Associate Professor in the MSSE Program. Sarchet has an MS in Secondary Education and is currently finishing her doctorate at the University of Rochester in teaching and curriculum, with a focus on international education partnerships.

As a part of her duties, Sarchet, along with Bakar Ali, Senior Project Associate, work in other countries to help local communities develop and implement programs and training in education for deaf and hard-of-hearing individuals. Along with Jonathan Holmes, International Enrollment Specialist, Sarchet is also heavily involved in recruiting and retaining international students at RIT/NTID. She notes that currently 45 deaf and hearing international students from

22 different countries are attending RIT/NTID. She has been part of RIT's Partnerships in Pluralism and RIT's Strategic Planning Task Force for Diversity and Inclusion, and served as a mentor for Women of Color, Honor and Ambition (WOCHA). She was on the board of the NTID Diversity Group (2012) and is a co-chair of a newly formed NTID Diversity, Equity and Inclusion committee. Sarchet is a recipient of the Isaac L. Jordan, Sr. Faculty/Staff Pluralism award from RIT in 2011. Sarchet states:

> When it comes to diversity, we cannot let ourselves get comfortable. We use the term often, but it has multiple meanings and multiple realities in our community. If we hit a milestone, we should celebrate; but at the same time, we should be looking ahead to the next one. Those milestones are dynamic and fluid. We must continually re-visit and self-reflect on what it means and what our responsibilities are to foster a diverse, inclusive community. Inclusive excellence is a process of becoming, striving, which is never done. Thus...ever onward.[33]

Conclusion

The goal of this chapter was to recognize the diversity of NTID, especially through the contributions of particular individuals. From the employee who empties the trash cans, to those who fill students' minds with dreams, knowledge, and ideas, people of color have contributed to the success of NTID and to the deaf and hard-of-hearing students who have attended NTID and have made an impact on the world. NTID celebrates diversity because, together, we are making a difference through setting policy, doing research, teaching in the classroom, offering access services, providing counseling, and, yes, keeping the building clean.

In the past 50 years, NTID has made significant strides in providing educational opportunities by maintaining cutting-edge expertise in a variety of disciplines through the work of a talented and dedicated faculty and staff. It has also been committed to a philosophy of diversity and inclusion. Recent dialogues among NTID Student Congress, Ebony Club, and the NTID administration have underscored how implementing this philosophy into action is an ongoing effort that takes time,

collaboration, and critical analysis.

We believe that in the future, NTID faculty and staff can become agents of change by incorporating diversity into all educational efforts. Providing professional development related to diversity and creating an inclusive campus climate are important efforts, but a concerted effort to address diversity in curricular and educational practices will benefit the multicultural community of deaf and hard-of-hearing learners.

Dr. Charlotte LV Thoms is a faculty member in NTID's Business Studies department, as well as the current Director of Diversity Recruitment and Retention at NTID. Dr. Ila Parasnis is a research faculty member in the Master of Science in Secondary Education (MSSE) program.

Notes

1. National Technical Institute for the Deaf, *FY1979 Annual Report* (Rochester, N.Y.: Rochester Institute of Technology, 1980): 6.

2. NTID, *FY1979 Annual Report*, 19.

3. Ann Kanter, "Telling It Like It Is," *FOCUS Magazine* (Summer 1986): 10.

4. James DeCaro, personal communication, 2017.

5. Harry G. Lang and Karen K. Conner, *From Dream to Reality: The National Technical Institute for the Deaf* (Rochester, N.Y.: Rochester Institute of Technology, 2001): 103.

6. National Technical Institute for the Deaf, *FY1991 Annual Report* (Rochester, N.Y.: Rochester Institute of Technology, 1992): 61.

7. National Technical Institute for the Deaf, *FY1990 Annual Report* (Rochester, N.Y.: Rochester Institute of Technology, 1991): 46.

8. National Technical Institute for the Deaf, *FY1993 Annual Report* (Rochester, N.Y.: Rochester Institute of Technology, 1994): 48.

9. Hope Williams, personal communication, 2017.

10. Yvette Chirenje, personal communication, 2017.

11. Vincent Daniele, personal communication, 2017.

12. Dianne K. Brooks, "In Search of Self: Experiences of Postlingually Deaf African Americans," in *Cultural and Language Diversity and the Deaf Experience*, ed. Ila Parasnis (Cambridge, UK: Cambridge University Press, 1996): 246–257.

13. Susan Foster and Waithera Kinuthia, "Deaf Persons of Asian American, Hispanic American, and African American Backgrounds: A Study of Intraindividual Diversity and Identity," *Journal of Deaf Studies and Deaf Education* 8, no. 3 (2003): 271–290.

14. Ila Parasnis and Susan D. Fischer, "Perceptions of Diverse Educators Regarding Ethnic-Minority Deaf College Students, Role Models, and Diversity," *American Annals of the Deaf* 150, no. 4 (2005): 343–349.

15. Ila Parasnis, Vincent J. Samar, and Susan D. Fischer, "Deaf College Students' Attitudes Toward Racial/Ethnic Diversity, Campus Climate, And Role Models," *American Annals of the Deaf* 150, no. 1 (2005): 47–58.

16. Deborah Waltzer, "Making Herstory," *FOCUS Magazine* (Winter 1995): 14–16.

17. Karen Christie, personal communication, 2017.

18. Charlotte L. Thoms and Sharon L. Burton, "Understanding the Impact of Inclusion in Disability Studies Education," In *Impact of Diversity on Organization and Career Development,* ed. C. Hughes (Hershey, PA: IGI Global Publishing, 2015): 186–213.

19. Charlotte L. Thoms and Sharon L. Burton, "Learning, Development and Training: The Influence of Synergies through Educational Evolution," *International Journal of Adult Vocational Education and Technology* 7, no. 4 (2016): 85–104.

20. Charlotte L. Thoms and Sharon L. Burton, "Transcultural Diversity and Inclusion Model: A New Framework for an Enlightened Society," *Advances In Developing Human Resources* (in-press).

21. Charlotte Thoms, personal communication, 2017.

22. Ila Parasnis, Gerald P. Berent, Vincent J. Samar, Santo J. Triolo, and Kevin R. Murphy, *Attention Deficit Scales for Adults: Sign Language Version* (Rochester, N.Y.: Rochester Institute of Technology, 2008).

23. Catherine Clark, personal communication, 2017.

24. Ellen Renee Johnson, *Our Daughters: Let's Teach Them* (Charleston, S.C.: CreateSpace Independent Publishing Platform, 2016).

25. Ellen Renee Johnson, personal communication, 2017.

26. Hope Williams, personal communication, 2017.

27. John T. Reid, personal communication, 2017.

28. Carolyn McCaskill, Ceil Lucas, Robert Bayley, and Joseph C. Hill, *The Hidden Treasure of Black ASL: Its History and Structure* (Washington, D.C.: Gallaudet University Press, 2011).

29. Joseph C. Hill, *Language attitudes in the American Deaf Community* (Washington, D.C.: Gallaudet University Press, 2012).

30. Joseph C. Hill, personal communication, 2017.

31. Shirley J. Allen, personal communication, 2017.

32. Thomas Warfield, personal communication, 2017.

33. Thomastine A. Sarchet, personal communication, 2017.

Buildings of the National Technical Institute for the Deaf

Erwin Smith

Soon after the National Advisory Board officially announced RIT as the location for the National Technical Institute for the Deaf on November 14, 1966, Dr. Frisina engaged the architectural firm of Hugh Stubbins and Associates to design the new campus.[1] The groundbreaking was held in 1971. Construction took three years to complete, and the dedication of the $27.5 million NTID facilities took place on October 5, 1974.[2] Lady Bird Johnson, the keynote speaker and widow of former President Lyndon B. Johnson, began "Lyndon would have enjoyed today." The former First Lady also planted a tree in memory of the late president during the ceremony.[3]

The original concept for NTID consisted of five buildings: an administrative/academic building, three dormitories, and a dining hall. While the buildings opened in 1974, the official naming ceremony didn't occur until 1979.[4] NTID's buildings were officially named the Lyndon Baines Johnson Building; Alexander Graham Bell, Mark Ellingson, and Peter N. Peterson Halls; and the Hettie L. Shumway Dining Commons.

Lyndon Baines Johnson Hall

Lyndon Baines Johnson Hall was named after the 36th U.S. president who, on the morning of June 8, 1965, signed Public Law 89–36 that would revolutionize technical education for the deaf community by creating the National Technical Institute for the Deaf.[5] LBJ Hall continues to be the main academic building at NTID. In addition to the classrooms, laboratories, administrative, and faculty offices, LBJ Hall is home to the Robert

F. Panara Theatre, dedicated in 1988, and the Joseph F. and Helen C. Dyer Arts Center, dedicated in 2001.[6, 7]

Robert Panara served on the National Advisory Board for the establishment of NTID. He began his career at NTID in 1967 and became its first deaf professor. He established the English Department at NTID, founded the NTID Drama Club, and was a founding member of the National Theatre of the Deaf.[8]

Joseph and Helen Dyer were deaf college graduates who were long-time supporters of NTID.[9] Helen was also an accomplished oil painter.[10] In 1997, they funded the Joseph F. and Helen C. Dyer Endowed Scholarship Fund to benefit RIT/NTID students in good standing, and in 2000, they provided $2.5 million to fund the construction and on-going support of the Joseph F. and Helen C. Dyer Arts Center at NTID.[11]

Mark Ellingson Hall

At 12 stories high, Ellingson Hall (referred to as Tower A) is the tallest building on the RIT campus. It was dedicated in honor of Mark Ellingson, the President of RIT from 1936 through 1969.[12] A former teacher, Ellingson guided the merger between the Empire School of Printing and the Mechanics Institute in 1937. Then, in 1944, the Athenaeum and Mechanics Institute was renamed "Rochester Institute of Technology."[13] Planning for the move to Henrietta began in 1961, in the last decade of his term, and NTID opened its doors in 1968.[14] Ellingson Hall continues to be the primary dormitory for NTID students.

Above: A group of NTID administrators overlook what will later become the Frisina Quad from LBJ Hall.
Below: LBJ and Ellingson Halls under construction during the winter.

Above: The front of LBJ Hall, including the iconic "Split Cube" sculpture by Carl Zollo.
Below: Ellingson Hall is visible from the third floor of LBJ Hall as both are being constructed.

Peter N. Peterson Hall

Peterson Hall (referred to as Residence Hall B) was dedicated in honor of Peter N. Peterson. Peterson was a deaf vocational education teacher of deaf students who conceived the idea of a national technical institute for the deaf in the 1930s.[15] He believed that young deaf persons, if properly educated in technical and professional fields, would be able to compete with their hearing peers in the labor force. Peterson Hall is still used as a dormitory. It also contains several apartments used for visitors to NTID.

Residence Hall D

Residence Hall D was originally dedicated as Bell Hall in honor of Alexander Graham Bell, the inventor of the telephone. Bell is a controversial figure in the history of deaf education, even though both his mother and wife were deaf.

Bell was convinced that learning to speak and lip-read was the only way for deaf people to succeed in society.[16] He also supported a law, which was never passed,

that would have prevented deaf people from marrying one another, in hopes of preventing future cases of congenital deafness.[17] Because of these beliefs, and after the Alexander Graham Bell Association criticized a Coca-Cola Super Bowl advertisement that featured the use of American Sign Language, NTID students successfully petitioned to have his name removed from the building.[18]

Today Residence Hall D is home to visitor apartments, the NTID Center for Access Technology, and Margaret's House (RIT's day care center).

Hettie L. Shumway Dining Commons

The Shumway Dining Commons was dedicated in honor of Hettie L. Shumway. Shumway, the wife of RIT benefactor F. Ritter Shumway, was the strongest supporter of having the National Technical Institute for the Deaf brought to RIT during the 1960s.[19] When Shumway discovered the search for a host institution for NTID, she told RIT President Mark Ellingson, "I just heard about a wonderful thing I think we should have at RIT. We are a technical institute. We ought to be in this field."[20]

She met with and convinced civic leaders, educators and Board of Trustees members about the benefits that might come of hosting NTID.[21] If not for Hettie Shumway, NTID might not be on the RIT campus.

Top: A group of NTID administrators stand in the unfinished Shumway Dining Commons and observe Ellingson and Peterson Halls during the construction process. Above: The exterior of the Shumway Dining Commons soon after construction.
Below left: The dining room of the Shumway Commons before the construction of Rosica Hall.
Below right: Hugh L. Carey Hall.

An aerial photograph reveals the SDC as it is being constructed.

Hugh L. Carey Hall

The next building erected by NTID was Carey Hall in 1984.[22] Carey Hall was dedicated in honor of Hugh L. Carey on October 14, 1984 during NTID's 15th Anniversary Celebration and Homecoming Weekend.[23]

Hugh Carey was once Governor of New York State and a member of the House of Representatives from 1960 to 1974.[24] In 1965, he proposed the NTID bill in the U.S. House of Representatives, and he was a member of NTID's first National Advisory Group, established to guide the development of the college and to enforce regulatory compliance.[25]

In 1991, an addition was built to the south side of Carey Hall, nearly doubling the size of the building to accommodate the expanding number of interpreters and captionists needed to serve the growing number of deaf students pursuing degrees in the other RIT colleges. The Department of Access Services, as well as NTID Research and the Information Computing Studies program, called Carey Hall home.

CSD Student Development Center

NTID's landscape remained mostly unchanged until the Student Development Center was built, connecting Lyndon Baines Johnson Hall with the Shumway Dining Commons. The home of the popular dining location, The Commons, was originally called the Hettie Shumway Building.

Beginning in 2005, it was expanded to a new facility based on the concept of promoting students' experience and opportunities through leadership, community service, and recreational activities. In 2007, the SDC was named as the Communication Service for the Deaf (CSD) Student Development Center. Communication Service for the Deaf, Inc. (CSD) is a non-profit organization for the deaf and hard-of-hearing community.

The NTID Student Congress, various multicultural organizations for deaf and hard-of-hearing students, and the NTID Student Life Team continue to call the SDC home.

NTID President Dr. Gerard Buckley speaks to a crowd assembled to celebrate the 10th Anniversary of the SDC.

The Frisina Quad.

D. Robert Frisina Quad

Also on April 27, 2007, the quadrangle surrounded by LBJ, Ellingson, and Peterson Halls, and the CSD Student Development Center was dedicated in honor of D. Robert Frisina, the Founding Director of the National Institute for the Deaf at RIT. The Frisina Quad is the venue for many events throughout the year, including the annual Apple Festival, welcoming students back to school every fall. It is now home to the Jan Strine Memorial Labyrinth. Ms. Strine, an Assistant Professor at NTID for 30 years, was a mentor to many deaf students over the course of her career.

The Jan Strine Memorial Labyrinth.

Sebastian and Lenore Rosica Hall

The newest NTID building on the RIT campus, Sebastian and Lenore Rosica Hall, is devoted to innovation and research for students, faculty, and staff of the National Technical Institute for the Deaf and RIT. The groundbreaking for the $8 million, two-story 23,000-square-foot building occurred on October 14, 2011, and the building officially opened on October 11, 2013.[26] Rosica Hall was made possible through a $1.75 million grant from the William G. McGowan Charitable Fund, along with numerous private donations.[27]

The Rosicas were long-time advocates for deaf and hard-of-hearing people. Lenore was William McGowan's sister and worked as a speech pathologist. Sebastian worked as an audiologist at the St. Mary's School for the Deaf in Buffalo, New York, for forty years, and was a trustee of the McGowan Charitable Fund.[28]

Sebastian and Lenore Rosica Hall is a unique facility intended to help bring deaf and hard-of-hearing students and their hearing peers, along with faculty and corporate partners, together in the innovation process.

The ribbon-cutting ceremony for Rosica Hall.

A student presents a poster to Sarah Gordon ('07) in the light-filled corridors of Rosica Hall.

Erwin Smith *is the Assistant Vice President for Information Technology & College Operations.*

Notes

1. Hugh Stubbins, *Architecture: The Design Experience* (New York: John Wiley and Sons, 1976): 148–151.
2. Rochester Institute of Technology Archives, "Dedication Ceremony." https://library.rit.edu/depts/archives/dedication-ceremony-0.
3. Ibid.
4. National Technical Institute of the Deaf, "History." http://www.ntid.rit.edu/history.
5. Ibid.
6. Ibid.
7. Joseph F. and Helen C. Dyer Arts Center, "About the Gallery." https://www.rit.edu/ntid/dyerarts/content/about-gallery.
8. NTID Performing Arts, "Our History." https://www.ntid.rit.edu/theatre/our-history.
9. Dyer Arts Center, "History." https://www.rit.edu/ntid/dyerarts/content/history.
10. Ibid.
11. Ibid.
12. Rochester Institute of Technology, "History of RIT: Presidents." https://www.rit.edu/overview/history-rit-presidents.
13. Ibid.
14. Ibid.
15. Jack R. Gannon, *Deaf Heritage: A Narrative History of Deaf America* (Washington, DC: Gallaudet University Press, 2011): 51.
16. Casey Dehlinger, "The Renaming of Bell Hall." *Reporter Online* (March 21, 2008).
17. Ibid.
18. Ibid.
19. Kathleen S. Smith, "NTID Experiment Proved Truly Grand." *University Magazine* (Spring 2003).
20. Ibid.
21. Ibid.
22. Ibid.
23. Rochester Institute of Technology, "Hugh L. Carey Hall." http://www.rit.edu/fa/facilities/maps.
24. Ibid.
25. Ibid.
26. Greg Livadas, "NTID's Rosica Hall Officially Opens on Campus." *University News* (October 10, 2013).
27. National Technical Institute of the Deaf, "Sebastian and Lenore Rosica Hall." http://www.ntid.rit.edu/rosica-hall.
28. Ibid.

The Changing Face of the NTID Research Enterprise: 1968–2017

Dr. Ronald R. Kelly

NTID's research enterprise has undergone numerous transformations during the college's first 50 years. Seven primary factors have guided the direction of NTID research and influenced subsequent changes:

1. Early advocacy, governance and original mission statement
2. Updated mission statement
3. Organizational restructuring, 1968–2017
4. Evolving expectations about research focus
5. Evolving roles of research and instructional faculty
6. Expanded funding options to support research
7. Scholarly productivity and dissemination

The ever-changing face of the NTID research enterprise will be discussed within the context of these seven factors.

Early Advocacy, Governance and Original Mission Statement

Research has been integral to the National Technical Institute of the Deaf (NTID) since the college was founded. Advocate S. Richard Silverman, Director of the Central Institute for the Deaf in St. Louis, Missouri, speaking at the initial House Committee on Education and Labor's House Resolution 7031 on April 27, 1965, emphasized that the proposed NTID would offer technical training, expose deaf students to an environment of diverse economic opportunities, fulfill a strong need for research, train professionals and reduce communication barriers for deaf people.[1] Dr. D. Robert Frisina, first director and Vice President of NTID for RIT, developed the original mission statement, which consisted of eight objectives inspired by his extensive review of the records of the National Advisory Board.[2] Three of the eight co-equal original mission objectives referred to research:

- To conduct research in the occupational and the employment-related aspects of deafness
- To develop and evaluate new imaginative instructional technology for application in the education of deaf students
- To disseminate information regarding…research findings…

Throughout the early years, Dr. Frisina consistently likened NTID to "a grand experiment," emphasizing the need for scientific data to document successful outcomes. He articulated the goal of the grand experiment, which was "…to determine whether deaf students, when provided appropriate education, could earn parity in the economic mainstream."[3] That is, would NTID's curriculum be able to "…produce young men and women who will be competitive in the open marketplace?"[4]

Frisina's perspective influenced early hiring at NTID. Among the first staff brought on board were E. Ross Stuckless, who was appointed Director of Research and Training at NTID in September 1967, and William E. Castle, hired in April 1968, not only for his experience with government and higher education, but particularly because of his research, clinical, and teaching background in communication.[5]

Updated Mission Statement

Two decades after NTID's founding, there had grown the perception among instructional faculty and administrators that researchers were pursuing scholarly studies that were not always consistent with the goals of the college and with student improvement. Furthermore, during that same period, promotion requirements surrounding scholarly publication had resulted in a disproportionate number of researchers at the senior faculty rank of Professor. As a result, a strategic-planning effort between 1990 and 1992 updated the original mission statement to comprise two distinct parts: a primary mission focused on instruction, and a secondary mission that included research, among other secondary missions.

The Strategic Planning Committee further stated that researchers were to henceforth conduct primarily applied research that focused on improving teaching and learning, rather than conducting basic and theoretical research. Additionally, they stressed the need to expand the concept of scholarship to include the creation of artistic productivity that would henceforth count toward promotion. The revised and updated 1992 NTID Mission Statement with clarifying statements pertinent to research and scholarship reads:

The *primary mission* of the National Technical Institute of the Deaf is to provide deaf students with outstanding state-of-the-art technical and professional education programs, complemented by a strong arts and sciences curriculum, that prepare them to live and work in the mainstream of a rapidly changing global community and enhance their lifelong learning. *Secondarily*, NTID prepares professionals to work in fields related to deafness; undertakes a program of *applied* research designed to enhance the social, economic and educational accommodation of deaf people; and shares its knowledge and expertise through outreach and other information dissemination programs [emphasis added.][6,7]

Specific to the secondary mission, in its role as a national (and international) institution, NTID's revised mission listed additional specific points, two of which were relative to research and scholarship:

- Conducting applied research that improves the teaching and learning processes; advances the study, technology, and application of communication strategies; and assesses the occupational and community experiences of deaf people
- Promoting scholarship that enhances professional practice and supports the creation of artistic works[8]

In response to the updated NTID Mission Statement in 1992, throughout the last decade of the 20th century, researchers were assigned to research strands that reflected the new emphasis on a program of applied research that included teaching and learning, communication, access and instructional technology, and occupational/employment experiences. However, with the advent of the 21st century and with further re-organization, the research strand approach was gradually abandoned as increased emphasis and focus were given to obtaining external funding to support research.

Organizational Restructuring 1968–2017

During the first 50 years of operation, NTID re-organized multiple times to create environments that produced research and data essential to the functioning of a large and complex college. The re-organization of research operations was influenced by a variety of factors, including:

- attempts to re-focus and guide research in new directions
- consolidation of research resources to eliminate duplication
- budgetary constraints
- increasing the number and monetary amount of externally funded research projects
- influence from the university leadership to evolve RIT into a comprehensive and PhD-granting research institution

Between 1967 (the planning year) and 2012 (the year which saw the elimination of the last remaining pure research department), there were 10 different operational departments at NTID with research responsibilities (see Table 1, column 1). Some departments operated for only 2–6 years, while the longest operating research department existed for 20 years before being re-organized. While most of the departments had names that identified their research focus, the last standing department was generically named the Department of Research (2010–2012) because it was staffed by faculty from educational, communication, and cognition/language research areas.

In 2012, NTID moved to a fully center-based research model that consisted of two extant research centers and two newly created research centers (see Table 1, column 2). These centers were:

- Center for Educational Research Partnerships (CERP), established in 2004, Marc Marschark, Director

Table 1.
The Ever-Evolving Research Landscape, including planning year 1967 and 1968–2012

NTID Departments with Research Responsibilities	Research Centers	Institutional Research
Research & Training 1967–1973		Institutional Research 1968–present
Office of Program Analysis 1973–1984		
English Department 1974–1978		
Educational Research & Development 1975–1995		
Communication Research 1978–1994		
Postsecondary Career & Institutional Research 1985–1994		
Applied Language & Cognition Research 1994–1998		
Educational Research 1995–1998		Institutional Research 1995–September 2016
Department of Research & Teacher Education 2005–2010	CERP 2004–present CAT 2006–present	
Department of Research 2010–2012		
	Teaching & Learning Jan 2012–present REACH Jan 2012–present	
	Cognition & Learning Aug 2016–present	Institutional Research, Assessment, & Strategy October 2016–present

Rosica Hall.

- Center for Access Technology (CAT), established in 2006, James J. DeCaro, Director
- Teaching & Learning Research Center, established January 2012, Susan B. Foster, Sara Schley, and Christopher Kurz, Co-Directors
- *REACH* Center — Research on Employment and Adapting to Change: Center for Studies on Career Success, established January 2012, Ronald R. Kelly, Director, and Gerald P. Berent, Associate Director

Four years later, on August 1, 2016, the Center for Cognition and Language Learning was established with Peter C. Hauser as Director.

The first NTID research center was established by Professor Marc Marschark in 2004. He proposed a research agenda that involved international relationships and focused on pre-college deaf and hard-of-hearing populations, both of which precluded the use of NTID research funds. As a result, he created the self-supporting Center for Educational Research Partnerships (CERP), whose research activities are completely funded through external grants.

Completion of Rosica Hall in summer 2013 advanced the research center model. Rosica Hall was designed for the purpose of conducting research specific to deaf and hard-of-hearing people. James J. DeCaro, Interim President of NTID from 2009 to 2010, provided the leadership and impetus for building a dedicated facility for NTID research; he facilitated the transition of NTID away from the research department model that had predominated since 1968 and toward a research center model. With Rosica Hall dedicated solely to research activities, NTID has made a highly visible and long-term commitment to the future of research, as well as to the related national and international leadership the college will provide to the field of deaf education.

NTID institutional research has functioned continuously in one form or another since 1968 (see Table 1, column 3). Dr. Gerard Walter, the college's first

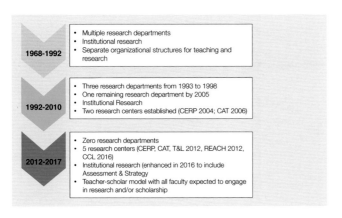

1968-1992	• Multiple research departments • Institutional research • Separate organizational structures for teaching and research
1992-2010	• Three research departments from 1993 to 1998 • One remaining research department by 2005 • Institutional Research • Two research centers established (CERP 2004; CAT 2006)
2012-2017	• Zero research departments • 5 research centers (CERP, CAT, T&L 2012, REACH 2012, CCL 2016) • Institutional research (enhanced in 2016 to include Assessment & Strategy) • Teacher-scholar model with all faculty expected to engage in research and/or scholarship

Figure 1. Organizational Changes Affected Both Teaching and Research Faculty Roles.

Primary focus: 1968-1990s
Continuing focus: 1968-2017

| Research focus on improving education of DHH students through:

1. Teaching & learning
2. Communication
3. Instructional technologies
4. Employment experiences

…and Institutional Research | 2002

Todd Pagano hired:

• Raised visibility of discipline-based research

• Facilitated undergraduate students' participation in scientific research as investigators | 2010-present (7 years)

Official emphasis on discipline-based research (*Strategic Plan 2020;* 2010) |

Figure 2. Evolving Research Focus 1968 – 2017

institutional researcher, served in that capacity for 37 years (1967 and 1968–2004). Dr. Sara Schley served as the second Director of Institutional Research from 2004 to 2009. Richard C. Dirmyer, Director since 2009, saw an expansion of his title and role to Assistant Vice President for Institutional Research, Assessment, and Strategy in October 2016. The overall purpose of institutional research and assessment activity at NTID has been to support institutional program planning, evaluation, and decision-making. Specific historical responsibilities have included examining demography, conducting predictive analytics and data analysis/interpretation, as well as developing reporting recommendations. More recently, the responsibilities of institutional research have expanded to philosophies, consulting on statistics, and assessing the structured administrative unit.

In summary, organizational restructuring affected the expectations and roles of both teaching and research faculty (see Figure 1). From 1968–2012, NTID established and modified multiple research departments that separated research functions from teaching functions. In 2012, the last remaining research department was eliminated, and the teaching and research functions were fully integrated, with all faculty expected to engage in research and/or scholarship relevant to their fields as "teacher-scholars."

Evolving Expectations About Research Focus

During the first two and a half decades of NTID, research focused primarily on improving the teaching

and learning of NTID students, as well as on the employment and career outcomes of graduates. The research goals included improving teaching, learning, communication skills (signing, speaking, listening, reading and writing), instructional technologies, and employment experiences/outcomes (see Figure 2). In 1992, the college's research focus was broadened to include populations outside NTID. In fact, 1992 marked two important changes in the focus of NTID research. First, the focus of research was expanded beyond just NTID students and graduates, pulling in pre-college deaf and hard-of-hearing populations. This occurred due, in part, to the growing recognition that understanding deaf and hard-of-hearing students' learning experiences and cognitive development prior to college was essential to improving their college experience. Second, the focus of research broadened even further once external funding was allowed, since federal funding agencies require impact beyond just one institution. This expansion of focus also laid the groundwork for an increased effort to contribute to the study and practice of deaf education on a national level.

Further changes in NTID's research focus occurred in 2002 with the hiring of Todd Pagano. First, Pagano raised the visibility of discipline-based research, which, up to that point, had not been emphasized or supported by NTID. Second, within the context of discipline-based research, Pagano encouraged the participation of undergraduate deaf and hard-of-hearing students as investigators in the scientific research process, which also included presenting and publishing their scholarly findings (see Figure 2). This brought the broader disciplinary principles taught in the classroom into students' hands. With discipline-based research, Pagano's work with students enabled those students to develop stronger skills, better understanding of the research process, and greater clarity regarding future career options.

Because of Pagano's success with involving undergraduate students in discipline-based research, in 2010, NTID officially emphasized and supported discipline-based research in the new *Strategic Plan 2020*.[9] Of course, the research emphasis on improving educational outcomes of deaf and hard-of-hearing students has been continuous throughout NTID's 50-year history. With Pagano's arrival, and due to the changes wrought by the *1992 Strategic Plan*, the focus has shifted to more direct and immediate effects on the educational outcomes of NTID students, as well as to increasing the published output in order to contribute to the field of deaf education in general, continuing the trend begun by the *1992 Strategic Plan*.

Evolving Roles of Research and Instructional Faculty
In terms of the expectations and roles of faculty, the organizational structure and hiring practices of NTID during its first 24 years fostered the separation of teaching and research. From 1968 to 1992, instructional faculty were expected only to teach and not to contribute to scholarly research. Conversely, faculty assigned to research departments were expected only to conduct research and not to teach. Of course, there were exceptions to this imposed division of labor, as some instructional faculty did conduct scholarly research, and some researchers did occasionally teach classes on a limited basis (relative to interests). But the prevailing organizational structure and hiring practices during NTID's first 24 years created two very different professional cultures—one for teachers and one for researchers.

The 1992 strategic planning effort began to bridge these two cultures by broadening the concept of "scholarly activities" and applying it equally to all faculty, not just researchers. This effort continued from 1992 to 2010 (see Figure 3). Beginning in 2010, NTID implemented the teacher-scholar model for all NTID faculty, consistent with the other RIT colleges.

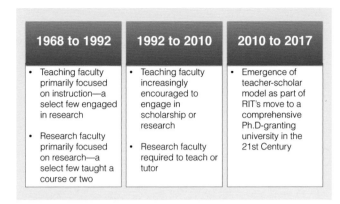

Figure 3. Changing Expectations of Both Research and Instructional Faculty

Expanded Funding Options to Support Research
From 1968 until the *1992 NTID Strategic Plan*, NTID research was supported entirely by an annual funding allocation from Congress and disbursed through NTID's annual internal budgetary process (see Table 2). Prior to 1992, the NTID administration did not allow faculty to develop research proposals for external funding from federal agencies. The administrative perception, accurate or not, was that any additional funding received from the federal government for research would potentially have a negative impact on NTID's annual federal budget allocation.

The *1992 Strategic Plan*, however, placed greater emphasis on external funding to support research.[10] From that point forward, research faculty were increasingly encouraged to seek external funding for research projects. Since federal funding agencies are concerned with broad impact, and generally will not fund research limited to a single organization, this change in funding source helps explain the expansion of research populations beyond NTID. As noted elsewhere in this chapter, prior to 1992, the NTID research focus was restricted to NTID students and NTID graduates. This represents a sea change from the pre-1992 status quo.

Since the mid-1990s, NTID research has been supported through a combination of funding that includes:

1. Internal NTID budgetary sources for
   • Salaries for tenured and tenure-track faculty

Table 2.

1992 Strategic Plan Changed the Funding of NTID Research.

First 25 Years (1968 to 1992/1993)	Second 25 Years (1992/1993 to 2017)	
Research funded only from NTID budget	**1992–2012**	**2012–2017**
No additional federal funding for research pursued	*Strategic Plan 1992* (p. 37) called for greater emphasis on external funding to support research	All research centers require minimum external funding of $500,000 to maintain center status
	Faculty increasingly encouraged to seek external funding	

Table 3.

Summary of External Funding 2001–2016.

Years	# Grants	Total $M	# < $100K	# 100K–500K	# $500K–$1M	# $1–4M+
2001–2005	32	$20.35M	7	9	7	8
2006–2010	58	$27.06M	25	13	7	11
2011–2015	65	$22.75M	41	11	7	5
2016–present	8	$1.95M	4	3	1	0
Total	163	$72.11M	77	36	22	24

Table 4.

NTID Faculty Recognized by RIT Sponsored Research Million Dollar PI Club 2001–2016.

Research Grants = 6		Non-Research/Training or Service Grants = 7	
1. D. Robert Frisina	2002	1. Laurie C. Brewer	2002
2. Michael S. Stinson	2005	2. James J. DeCaro	2003
3. Marc Marschark	2006	3. Dianne Brooks	2003
4. Peter C. Hauser	2011	4. Gerald C. Bateman	2004
5. Lisa B. Elliot	2014	5. Susan B. Foster	2006
6. Ronald R. Kelly	2014	6. Jeffrey Rubin	2006
		7. Donna A. Lange	2008

- Allocations for major programs and initiatives
- Seed funding for research ideas
2. External funding sources from
  - Federal grants
  - State grants
  - Foundation grants

Table 3 presents a summary of the external funding received from 2001 to the present. During this 15-year period, NTID faculty received 163 grants totaling $72.11 million dollars. Equally impressive, since 2001, when RIT Sponsored Research Programs established a "Million-Dollar P.I. [primary investigator] Club," 13 NTID faculty have been recognized for receiving external funding exceeding one million dollars (see Table 4).

Scholarly Productivity and Dissemination

Since NTID's founding, scholarly contributions to the field of education of deaf and hard-of-hearing students,

Table 5.

Scholarly Productivity and Dissemination 1968–2016.

Years	Publications	Presentations/papers at national/international conferences
1968–1984[11]	700+ research articles in 35 journals	500
1985–1999[12,13]	364 research articles	423
2000–2012[14]	374 research articles and book chapters, 31 books	573
2013–2015[15]	96 research articles, 34 book chapters	345
Total	1599 publications	1841

as well as to one's discipline area, have been required for promotion and tenure, consistent with RIT requirements. As noted previously, however, these requirements were not always applied equally to instructional faculty and research faculty until 2010–2012, when NTID officially adopted the teacher-scholar model for all faculty, and organizational restructuring eliminated the only remaining research department, placing all faculty instead in academic home departments.

Regardless of the organizational changes and evolving expectations for instructional and research faculty roles, published scholarly contributions occurred from the earliest years of NTID. Table 5 presents a summary of scholarly productivity and dissemination by NTID faculty over the initial 50 years.

Summary

As documented herein, research has been an integral part of NTID's 50-year history from the beginning, starting with the planning discussions in Congress. While the importance of research at NTID has always been recognized, there have been different perspectives on how research should be organized and what should be its focus. The NTID research enterprise experienced a number of transformations from 1968–2017 due to changes in the mission statement, organizational restructuring, evolving expectations for the focus of research and the roles of faculty, and expanded funding options. Regardless, throughout the various changes, researchers and teaching faculty have continuously made scholarly contributions, as reflected by their extensive publications and presentations.

While a number of factors have been identified herein as having influenced the NTID research enterprise throughout its 50-year history, only a few significantly influenced the historical trajectory of how research was organized and funded. The factors that have had the greatest impact on the NTID research enterprise are:

- *1992 Strategic Plan*, which encouraged researchers to seek federal grants, both expanding the funding options for research and broadening the research populations beyond NTID college students and graduates
- The 2004 creation of the Center for Educational Research Partnerships (CERP), the first self-supporting research center, which provided the basis of funding support for implementing all future NTID research centers
- *Strategic Plan 2020* (finalized in 2010), which adopted the teacher-scholar model for all NTID faculty, consistent with other RIT colleges, and articulated an official emphasis on pursuing discipline-based research, leading to the 2012 elimination of the one remaining research department and full implementation of the research center model with a dedicated research building in Rosica Hall.

Based on the transformations of the NTID research enterprise during the first 50 years, it is reasonable to predict that in the next 50 years, NTID research will continue to adapt and transform to meet the future challenges facing NTID, its students and its graduates.

_____

Dr. Ronald R. Kelly *is a research faculty member in the Master of Science in Secondary Education (MSSE) program, and Director, REACH Center for the Study of Career Success.*

Notes

1. Harry G. Lang and Karen K. Conner, *From Dream to Reality: The National Technical Institute for the Deaf.* (Rochester, N.Y.: Rochester Institute of Technology, 2001).

2. Lang and Conner, *From Dream to Reality,* 35–36.

3. Lang and Conner, *From Dream to Reality,* 38.

4. Lang and Conner, *From Dream to Reality,* 45.

5. Lang and Conner, *From Dream to Reality*, 39.

6. NTID Strategic Planning Committee, *Strategic Plan: An agenda for Action.* (Rochester, N.Y.: National Technical Institute for the Deaf, 1992): 9.

7. National Technical Institute for the Deaf, *FY92 Annual Report.* (Rochester, N.Y.: National Technical Institute for the Deaf, 1992).

8. NTID Strategic Planning Committee, *Strategic Plan,* 10.

9. NTID Strategic Vision Planning Committee, *Strategic Decisions: 2020.* (Rochester, N.Y.: National Technical Institute for the Deaf, 2010).

10. NTID Strategic Vision Planning Committee, *Strategic Decisions,* 37.

11. Lang and Conner, *From Dream to Reality, 83.*

12. National Technical Institute for the Deaf, FY85–89 Annual Reports. (Rochester, N.Y.: National Technical Institute for the Deaf, 1985–1989).

13. National Technical Institute for the Deaf, FY99 Annual Report. (Rochester, N.Y.: National Technical Institute for the Deaf, 1999).

14. National Technical Institute for the Deaf, NTID Annual Research Reports, 2000–2012. (Rochester, N.Y.: National Technical Institute for the Deaf, 2000–2012).

15. National Technical Institute for the Deaf, NTID Annual Research Reports, 2013–2015. (Rochester, N.Y.: National Technical Institute for the Deaf, 2013–2015).

The Evolution of Access Services

Stephen Nelson

Introduction and Roots

The birth and development of access services coincides closely with NTID's history. In 1965 when federal legislation was passed to establish NTID, the Registry of Interpreters for the Deaf (RID) was also being formed. The deaf leaders who joined in the development and celebration of NTID's founding lived lives and pursued educations without the benefit of legally recognized rights to access services. An enormous shift in opportunity was beginning. The coincident birth of the interpreting field and NTID foreshadowed the coming disability-rights movements that won legal protections afforded by Section 504 and Individuals with Disabilities Education Act (IDEA) legislation in the 1970s, and the 1990 passage of the Americans with Disabilities Act (ADA).

Despite stories to the contrary, interpreters were, in fact, employed at NTID from the start. However, they were few in number and were not nearly the resource they became at RIT and in the world at large. Notetaking was yet to be established as an access service, and no technology existed for creating text captions in real-time. Before sign language interpreting grew as a profession, interpreting was mainly provided by hearing children born in deaf families or hearing educators, i.e., skilled signers who helped friends and family members, usually as volunteers.

When NTID began, faculty member James Stangarone, later a national RID president, was charged with finding qualified interpreters, and he turned to

Alice Beardsley for assistance. Beardsley, an alumna of Rochester School for the Deaf who had subsequently regained her hearing through surgery, served as NTID's first interpreter. With the arrival of NTID's charter class in 1968, Beardsley helped find adult children of Deaf adults (CODAs) to fill the need for interpreting services. They worked as NTID's first interpreters. Department of Access Services (DAS) members have since established, funded and championed a scholarship awarded to interpreting students at NTID in Beardsley's name.

As much as NTID opened new opportunities for technological education, it also revolutionized postsecondary education for deaf and hard-of-hearing people by providing rich access to mainstream college and professional environments. Interpreting was a "disruptive technology," and newcomers to the field were inspired as contributors to a large, noble, empowerment effort. As training programs arose to catch up with unrelenting increases in demand, American Sign Language (ASL) was gaining wider recognition and respect. Idealists and others were drawn to the inherent worth of interpreting, the endless intellectual challenges of the task, and the immediate gratification of providing effective communication and growing opportunities for deaf and hard-of-hearing people. As much as we loved the work, few of us in those early years could imagine the multi-decade careers we ultimately enjoyed as interpreters.

A strong partnership between deaf leaders and pioneer interpreters set aspirations high. The 1970s saw intensive training begin with the Basic Interpreter

Training Program (BITP), hand-selecting students for a 10-week summer program designed to move them from novice signers to beginning interpreters. The limited timeframe and methodology of that era left much to be learned through daily interaction with deaf signers and experienced interpreters. The bootstrapping of this new educational technology called interpreting was fiercely pragmatic. Best practices were developed and shared within a guild not well understood by, or well integrated with, traditional deaf education. Interpreters sought RID certification to demonstrate competence, as other credentials were unavailable. RID evaluations in those early decades were conducted by live panels of deaf and hearing experts, predating the associate, baccalaureate, and master's degree programs, or the ubiquitous video assessments that followed. The interpreting experiment grew in a shared community of deaf and hearing people from its start.

Growth and Establishment of the Department of Interpreting Services

A culture of "can-do" and "must-cover" drove both interpreters' skill development and the rapid expansion of interpreting services. With leadership from future NTID President T. Alan Hurwitz and Anna Witter-Merithew, interpreters worked as hours were available—without set shifts—organized by content areas associated with the various RIT colleges. Empowering young adult students lifted NTID above the oral/manual controversies of educating deaf and hard-of-hearing children. Interpreters sought to meet the diverse needs that older students brought to us, regardless of their backgrounds. A value of communication eclecticism celebrated all needs as important and valid. Many students from oral backgrounds learned sign language to help them gain greater access both to a deaf community they discovered at NTID, and to technical course content taught at a breakneck pace in RIT programs.

Interpreter training and the provision of service were completely intertwined in these early years, led in the late 1970s by Witter-Merithew, a widely-honored builder of the interpreting field. She is currently serving as the Interim Executive Director of the RID after a long career in a wide range of leadership roles.

Office space was limited in those days, and inter-preters could be seen hanging out in the College Union (now the Student Alumni Union) cafeteria between assignments, often with deaf students engaged in mutually supportive conversation. Administrative space was scattered across a small set of offices in the basement of the Union, NTID's Lyndon Baines Johnson Building (now LBJ Hall), and some in the NTID support departments housed in various colleges.

In those early days, necessity drove innovation. The growth and establishment of systems and practices that made NTID uniquely accessible among the world's universities began to take place during the 1980s. For example, oral-interpreting training was provided, and NTID leadership helped establish RID certifications to serve non-signing deaf students who could benefit from interpreters skilled in presenting a more easily speech read source than from an unfamiliar speaker. Teams of oral interpreters from NTID served several conferences of the Alexander Graham Bell Association for the Deaf and Hard of Hearing before the development of real-time captioning.

Over the course of the 1980s, the Department of Interpreting Services (DIS) joined the wider community in the push for professional recognition of sign-language interpreting. Kathy Gillies took over leadership as chairperson of DIS in the early 1980s, and served for most of this dynamic, foundational decade. ASL was being "discovered" and popularized. Interpreting was a cool, challenging, and gratifying job, seeking professional recognition. Many DIS members volunteered for RID, serving on boards, undertaking projects, becoming raters for certification tests, and even hosting state and regional RID conferences at NTID.

Creativity and entrepreneurial energy also abounded in a corner of NTID far from its LBJ headquarters. Homegrown systems employing newly available technology allowed DIS to keep pace with continuous increases in demand. Macintosh computers helped us handle the explosive growth. MacPlus and Mac SE computers with nine-inch black-and-white screens were networked to impact printers capable of printing request forms using print merges from Excel spreadsheets into Microsoft Word forms.

Moving and Growing

Because of the ongoing growth in demand, DIS moved constantly, starting the 1980s in the basement of the College of Science (then called Building 08) and now in Gosnell Hall, with a Scheduling Office dispatching and redeploying interpreters as they became available. Students' requests began on paper. Copies were distributed to assigned interpreters with originals held in binders in the Scheduling Office, a still-critical central dispatch that addresses unfilled needs and last-minute changes. The "Board Log" developed, named for the blackboard on which it was created each day, tracking last-minute needs and assignments. Jo Carol Vedock was the first of a small list of cherished schedulers whose office backstopped all sorts of last-minute needs. Vedock was followed by DIS's beloved Barb Weir, who expanded the office with student staffing to help with evening needs and ceaseless volume growth. This process is still essential, continuing even with today's 21st-century data systems.

Gosnell Hall also held a small, single, repurposed classroom serving as a drop zone, break, preparation, and holding area for staff interpreters. DIS moved from there to a small group of offices in Booth Hall, which had been converted from three classrooms: one for DIS and two for the neighboring NTID interpreter training program. Soon after that, DIS moved to a newly constructed "Link Building," a hallway-shaped addition connecting Ross and Carey Halls. Finally, DIS was relocated to a large addition constructed on the south side of Carey Hall, which is still occupied by DAS. Interpreters noted with some amusement that each relocation moved DIS further way from the core of campus and into the wetlands.

The need for access extended to co-curricular and residence-hall settings. Interpreters were superimposed in "video bubbles" in the corner of TV screens to interpret news and popular TV shows before closed-captioning was invented. In Ellingson Hall (known as Tower A), InterCom provided interpreting for phone calls to home or sweethearts, or to order pizza or book flights, in an era before teletype (TTY) or video relay services (VRS) existed. Weekly movies shown on film by the College Activities Board were interpreted live before video and captioning made captioned movies routine. The need

arose for emergency medical and Public Safety calls on a 24-hour basis, so a crisis-interpreting system was built and staffed.

Initially, services for non-academic areas were coordinated and actually promoted to a campus unfamiliar with interpreting by "liaison interpreters," who worked closely with the specific campus life areas that they served. Each liaison had assigned areas to coordinate, educate about interpreting, and serve as an expert interpreter and potential mentor to interpreters new to the area. Meredith Ray worked first as a liaison for TV and InterCom before moving to serve Physical Education and Athletics. Aaron Gorelick stayed busy helping student clubs realize that they could make themselves accessible to deaf participants with our services. These roles and titles changed to Coordinators as demand for non-academic services grew. Through most of the '80s, Mike Rizzolo led a Campus Life Core Team created to better manage this growing demand and improve services in yet another unique content area.

Everything we now see as common practice needed to be invented, tried, and refined by practitioners. As new jargon was encountered, English words could be fingerspelled. But how often should one spell a term? What signs would best represent new terms? Answers to countless questions were hammered out in the early years of NTID. To best serve academic needs and to support development of content expertise, interpreters were gathered in core teams focusing on specific content areas. Core teams served Social Work, Liberal Arts, Business and Computers, Science/Engineering, and other areas of focus, while all resources were shared across teams to optimize coverage. Lead Interpreters supervised each team, coaching interpreters with developing skills and functioning as experts on interpreting and content for a rapidly growing staff.

As the 1980s drew to a close, lead interpreters and core teams shrank to five, and then four, teams with four managers. Previously, lead interpreters had been housed with, and reported to, academic-support department chairs. By decade's end they, as managers, and the staff interpreters they supervised were centralized to form NTID's largest department, DIS. During the '80s, the hours of interpreting provided increased by nearly 25,000 hours annually (from 35,544 hours provided in academic year 1980–81 to 60,372 hours in academic year 1988–89).

Working conditions and pay improved with full-time salaried professional staff contracts starting for all staff interpreters during the academic year of 1979–1980. This was adjusted to 10-month full-time contracts several years later. NTID began a three-level career ladder in 1986 to encourage the continued development and retention of staff. Advancement up that ladder depended on skills demonstrated through RID certification.

The severe shortages of interpreters and the growing numbers of students cross-registering into bachelor's degree programs pushed demand higher, and forced creative strategies for the provision of services. As NTID bulged in response to increased numbers of deaf students from the maternal rubella epidemic of the 1960s, resources for interpreting were increasingly strained. Dedicated and motivated interpreters worked heavy loads, and many overloaded hours beyond their shifts to help meet needs. Fiercely denying that interpreting was a "helping" profession, interpreters avoided any study or professional discussion of the need to set boundaries with their clients or to limit the hours worked by each interpreter.

Fortunately, some programs became especially popular with deaf and hard-of-hearing students and attracted large numbers to shared services, like the highly integrated deaf and hearing BS Social Work program that helped prepare many deaf leaders, including prominent alumnus NTID President Gerard Buckley.

Changing Practices
As the 1980s closed, Liza Marshall began her long leadership as Director of DIS in 1988, and a full-blown crisis erupted at DIS: an epidemic of cumulative trauma disorder (CTD), or "overuse syndrome". At the worst, fully half of the staff interpreters were working reduced hours due to injury; several people left their careers due to injury. Anger and fear troubled the entire community. Initially, denial of a problem ruled the responses of colleagues and administrators. Medical providers were often uninformed about the nature of the work, and diagnoses were inconsistent. The community, deaf students, and interpreters alike, raised the strongest

concerns. Shock and fear was gripping the interpreting community. A "black armband" rally, showing solidarity among interpreters and concerned deaf students, loudly communicated the alarm as the 1990s approached.

In response to these concerns, our then-dean, Dr. James DeCaro contracted with experts from the University of Rochester Medical Center's Center for Occupational Rehabilitation (COR), who closely studied NTID interpreters. COR discovered that the epidemic's cause was overuse syndrome, or cumulative trauma disorder. Based on deliberations and their findings, COR provided intensive training on safer biomechanics, focusing on reducing excessive wrist deviations, improved posture, eliminating ballistic or tense signing, and learning to utilize short rests while interpreting by positioning arms and wrists in restful neutral positions—all markers of non-symptomatic interpreters discovered in studies of DIS interpreters and consistent with COR's expert knowledge.

Workloads were adjusted downward, and a permanent shift in thinking—making concern for health and safety a priority—changed DIS forever. COR offered a holistic framework for understanding the many factors contributing to injury. Comprehensive understanding and intervention resulted in a complete reversal of the crisis—albeit, sadly, after a significant number of staff suffered career-ending injuries. Training on biomechanics and work safety continues to this day.

Injuries depleting an already-short supply of qualified interpreters, and reduced workloads to protect those still working, significantly constrained provision of services in the academic years 1989–90 and 1990–91. Nearly 5000 hours of needs were left unfilled in those years—a roughly 9% drop in service. The crucial need to retain and to develop the skills of interpreters was evident.

One strategy adopted was the establishment of a four-level career ladder for interpreters. Unlike previous promotion systems, demonstration and assessment of readiness was satisfied by managers' observation on the job and an in-house skill assessment, rather than on RID certification. The ability to advance as a working interpreter helped retain experienced people, who now saw a path to advance in their career. Added pay levels recognized, and added incentive to develop, advanced skills. NTID continued to be a strong supporter of RID after this change, but multiple delays with RID certification test availability that negatively impacted staff, and uncertainty about the match between RID assessment criteria and NTID needs, made the move inevitable.

By the end of the 1990s, interpreting service levels provided by DIS grew from an overuse-injury-induced low of 51,767 hours in 1990–91 to a record-high 84,590 hours in 1998–99, an increase of over 32,000 hours (63%). The trend line of increase begun in the 1980s and continuing in the 1990s would not shift downward, as more NTID students matriculated into baccalaureate and graduate programs at RIT, and as the RIT community enjoyed growing levels of interaction between deaf and hearing members.

The unrelenting growth of interpreting continued in the 2000s, accompanied by a number of big changes at DIS, including the establishment of a new Department of Access Services (DAS). DIS became DAS by incorporating notetaking and a newly established real-time captioning service. A tumultuous and productive decade saw big impacts from technology applications and some unanticipated challenges.

During this decade, the demand for sign language interpreters grew tremendously and somewhat unexpectedly. With the advent of video relay services quickly replacing older TTY-based services, competition for qualified interpreters drove salaries skyward. As VRS exploded in the mid-2000s, DAS saw numerous relatively new staff members drawn away by salaries nearly double their NTID earnings. We no longer called DAS the largest interpreting service in the world, as enormous telecoms hired hundreds and hundreds of video interpreters for well-funded call centers.

Due to the lack of peer institutions for comparison, NTID had always struggled to benchmark the pay of access providers. RIT's regular benchmarking of higher-education positions did not cover the unique services of DAS. A couple of focused salary surveys had previously found NTID interpreter pay rates lagging, and modest adjustments were made. In 2008, DAS's most recent salary survey was conducted by an outside firm. A resulting pay increase of nearly 30% for all staff interpreters was phased in over the following two fiscal years.

Those generous pay increases came at a helpful time, following another challenge to the morale of interpreters. Interpreters had fought for recognition, pay, working conditions, and professional respect from the start of the field. NTID was a leader, training and employing the best postsecondary interpreters in the world. When RIT settled a lawsuit regarding the misclassification of some employees as exempt from the federal Fair Labor Standards Act (FLSA), many others at RIT were caught up in the case. The largest number of those impacted were interpreters. Although long recognized at NTID and many other places as professionals, a prior U.S. Department of Labor ruling had opined that "...staff interpreters would not qualify as professional employees."

After years of private contention with strong support from NTID, it became clear that defending the exempt classification was untenable. In spring 2007, all interpreters and coordinators were moved to non-exempt classifications, with guarantees to keep their benefits whole, grandfathering in vacation and sick leave, among benefits. Numerous changes were required and implemented to ensure compliance with FLSA, including establishing overload pay and revised methods to spread pay across 12 months for those contracted for 10 months. Although the move to hourly pay was a blow to those who had worked for years to gain recognition of interpreting as a profession, the persistent support by NTID executives was unprecedented, and reflected the value of interpreting to the college.

The highly experienced interpreters at NTID continue to provide a tremendous resource for the coaching and mentoring of newly graduated interpreters, as they begin working in a richly educational and supportive environment.

Notetaking at RIT/NTID

According to Jimmie Wilson, an early coordinator, trainer and champion of notetaking, in 1968, when the first 70 deaf and hard-of-hearing students were registered into RIT classes with sign language interpreters, no other access services were envisioned. Although these NTID students were all cream-of-the-crop high-school graduates with high hopes for success in mainstream RIT classes, when the first grades were posted, most had failed. Wilson reported that the students said they could not remember what had happened in the class, and they could not look down to take notes for themselves.

Dr. Ross Stuckless and Marilyn Enders established that NTID needed to support students' notetaking needs, and to develop a system to meet those needs, starting with volunteers in classes, writing on carbonless (NCR, or no carbon required) copy paper. Soon, the program and student numbers grew. Paper photocopies of notes taken initially by volunteer students were distributed to deaf and hard-of-hearing students. Some paid professionals with subject-matter knowledge were enlisted as tutor/notetakers to better provide accurate notes and to tutor outside of class. Wilson, who was an interpreter/tutor in the early 1970s, was one of those professional notetakers. Research and refinement of the notetaking service led to the training of upperclassmen with good grades already earned in the courses they were hired to support.

At that time, it was expected that these notetakers could also act as tutors, and the program was called the Tutor/Notetaker Training Program (T/NTP). The two-day training program included information about deafness, NTID, and the need for the notes, with extensive feedback on several practice notetaking sessions. From the beginning, employing hearing students as tutors did not work as well as expected, so by the late 1970s, the program was soon changed to a one-day training session for notetaking alone, while NTID support faculty undertook the tutoring responsibilities. Notetakers were almost always hired from among students currently enrolled in the classes for which they took notes. Throughout a series of re-organizations, notetaking coordination remained with NTID faculty support teams until it was moved into the newly formed Access Services near the start of the new millennium.

Like other access services at NTID, notetaking grew and demonstrated its value to the success of deaf and hard-of-hearing students in mainstream classrooms. Practices were established, and acceptance became widespread in the initial decades of NTID. The adoption of notetaking as an access need became the norm nationally, and even internationally, while students with an array of disabilities also found benefits from the service. Technology advances enhanced the provision of notetaking services, moving from NCR paper, to copy machines, to images of paper notes scanned and securely distributed via the Internet to authorized recipients.

Now in the 21st Century, DAS is increasingly providing text transcripts of professional real-time captioning or student-produced Microsoft Word files in formats that can be downloaded, searched, highlighted, or edited by deaf and hard-of-hearing students.

A Missing Piece for Access: Real-Time Captioning Develops

The possibility of real-time captioning (RTC) in RIT classes was investigated at NTID by Dr. Ross Stuckless and others starting in the early 1980s. Closed captioning (CC) had been demonstrated in the 1970s, and with set-top decoders, CC was beginning to grow on network TV. The computer-aided stenographic technology used to create closed captions in real-time proved difficult and expensive to adopt for classroom use. Early efforts focused on preparing open and closed captions to be added to media shown in classrooms.

An alternative was found in an NTID-developed shorthand typing system called C-Print™. Dr. Michael Stinson, a deaf researcher at NTID, was the visionary and inventor of C-Print. During his tenure as a college student, Stinson's inability to benefit from sign-language interpreters led him to envision a system that produced text in a live setting. Based on Stinson's own educational access needs, his ideas and desire for a text-providing system led to the development of the C-Print speech-to-text system.

C-Print is software that uses a set of rules that allows a trained captionist to type fewer keystrokes by using phonetic shortcuts. The captionist types the sounds that they hear, thus the meaning of "C-Print," which stands for "SEE print". Over the years, many individuals contributed to the success and development of C-Print. Stinson writes,

In 1989, a team of developers and researchers— myself included—sought to provide better access to communication for deaf and hard-of-hearing (D/HH) students. Our team began working on a new form of technology and support service called C-Print, and, soon after, that never-tried-before technology changed the face of communication access. I am very proud to have led our team in a journey that has been travelled along with hundreds of dedicated C-Print service providers, students, educators, and administrators. Our commitment to providing the best possible educational experience for students who are D/HH has never wavered.[1]

Research and development of C-Print continued for many years. The Real-Time Captioning Department was established in April 1997. At that time, NTID had one trained captionist, then called an operator, to provide captioning support for cross-registered NTID students enrolled in RIT classes. In April 1997, four additional captionists were hired. The captionists at that time used C-Print™ software in order to keep up with the rapid speech rates encountered in RIT classes.

From 1997 to 1999, the C-Print captionists were housed in Peterson Hall, on the east side of the RIT campus, under the direction of Pamela Francis, who coordinated C-Print for NTID. Research was conducted to see if this system could be a successful stand-alone support service for cross-registered deaf and hard-of-hearing RIT students. Due to limited staffing, only select students were allowed access to captioning as a live support service. The provision of captioning was limited to classes that were in session Monday through Friday, between the hours of 9 a.m. and 5 p.m. Demand for captioning support kept growing.

The development of this new real-time captioning service paralleled and borrowed from earlier access services, yet differed in many ways. The young field struggled with terminology and even with developing an accurate description of their product. Disputes about the accuracy of terms (such as Communication Access Realtime Translation or CART, computer assisted notetaking, verbatim vs. paraphrase, and so on) veiled competition among approaches. Should it be called "speech-to-text"? While accurate, that was a differently connoted term than "real-time captioning" (not that anything like a picture or video was actually captioned). Real-time captioning prevailed because the term resonated better as referring to English text, in an era when closed captions had recently been adopted. The dedicated focus of NTID captionists using C-Print software

forged the ideal tool to meet the needs of the students they served, ultimately quieting initial concerns. Like other access services, over time the best practices and terminology took shape. It wasn't until the mid-1990s that widespread provision of real-time captioning as a part of Access Services began in earnest.

As tough as it seemed for interpreters and their struggle to gain widespread recognition as a profession, our colleagues in real-time captioning had it rougher. They were just beginning a journey, like the one interpreting professionals had been through, to establish recognition, working conditions, pay rates, a career ladder, and best practices. Their positions were always classified as non-exempt hourly and clerical, probably because initially women with long office careers and good typing skills were hired and trained as captionists.

When Liza Marshall retired after more than 15 years at DIS in 2003, her values and consensus-building style were well imprinted on DIS. Leadership for the later part of the decade was passed to DAS Director Stephen Nelson, a longtime member of Marshall's management team. He sought to build an Access Services identity that welcomed the quickly expanding team of captionists, then called Special Access Services and led by manager Ann Marie Kuntz, a long-time member of the C-Print team.

As interpreters had once been, captionists were new. They didn't fit an existing position, and their work was not well-understood. They also shared a fierce concern about meeting students' needs as a top priority. Positions were added, up to 15 per year, with each new hire trained on the job using C-Print software. Between 2004 and 2016, over 100 individuals were hired and trained in-house as captionists as the service grew. Struggles with technology diminished as networking and software improved.

While C-Print was initially the only captioning software used at RIT, in July 2012, several RIT captionists trained on the TypeWell transcribing system. TypeWell, a program like C-Print that uses an abbreviated spelling system, rather than C-Print's phonetically-based method, provides online training supported by a live-instructor component. Captionists at RIT now use a mix of C-Print and TypeWell software.

There are currently 55 captionists on staff, and

On Giants' Shoulders
A Tradition of Excellence in Teaching

Dr. Todd Pagano

Prologue

When I was first asked to write a chapter on teaching excellence for NTID's history book, I was flush with feelings of both flattery and trepidation. I have been humbled and honored to receive teaching recognitions and accolades (which was likely an impetus for being asked to write this chapter), but also skeptical that I could do justice to the many years of dedicated teaching excellence that NTID has witnessed. In order to convince myself to take on this assignment, I had to first take a step back and think as to whether I actually *could* write such a chapter.

In doing so, I was reminded of one of my favorite books, *On the Shoulders of Giants* by Stephen Hawking.[1] (Yes, I am a scientist!) In the book, Hawking compiled the seminal reports of some of the great scientists of the past, including Nicolaus Copernicus, Isaac Newton, Galileo Galilei, and Johannes Kepler. With each report, Hawking discussed how the works of science are built on the efforts of their predecessors. In fact, the title of the book is derived from a quote by Isaac Newton, in which he stated, "If I have seen further, it is by standing on the shoulders of giants." The metaphor loosely means that one can discover new things based on the prior discoveries of others and on the foundations laid by those discoveries. When I reflect on my teaching career at NTID, I cannot help but think of Hawking's book and message. Perhaps I could write this chapter not because of what I have accomplished, but rather because I have discovered my teaching successes by "standing on the shoulders of giants."

Though he retired before my career began, I did have the good fortune of meeting Prof. Robert Panara. It did not take me long to recognize that he was a giant in Deaf education and of NTID's history—and the career that I had ahead of me was already (at least partially) paved by his efforts. Likewise, my career did not overlap much with NTID's founding director, Dr. D. Robert Frisina, but I have come to know him within the past few years. Dr. Frisina recently told me that "the birth and evolution of NTID required scholarship, adaptability, creativity, and collaboration..." and that he personally sees me as a "superb teacher, creative mentor, and innovator of community partnerships", the likes of which are necessary for the "continued advancement of NTID."[2] The words of this "giant" in NTID's history, and my revelation that I am enjoying my own teaching success because it has been built upon the hard work of my predecessors, ultimately led me to agree to write this chapter.

It should be noted that much of what is written here is based on my personal observations of NTID's commitment to student learning and success, as well as the characteristics that I believe constitute teaching excellence. In particular, I am a strong proponent of student-centered teaching and maximizing student success, which are two topics that are intentionally woven throughout this chapter. Like any other trade or profession, teaching excellence requires commitment and practice. NTID has a history of professional development focused on supporting faculty in their attainment of teaching skills and strategies, and to this end, I invited Dr. L.K. Quinsland (long time NTID faculty member and professional development specialist) to share some of NTID's past efforts in this area. It is my hope that readers will reflect on some of the great teachers they have had–at NTID or elsewhere–and find a renewed appreciation for the contributions of outstanding educators in their lives.

Introduction

NTID has a long history of sincere dedication to teaching excellence and a focus on optimizing student success. Prof. Robert F. Panara and the first cohort of NTID faculty clearly had a devotion to student learning that still resonates today with even the newest of NTID faculty members. It has been well-known among NTID faculty that a good teacher can have a profound impact on students in the classroom, in their careers, and in their lives. NTID faculty have been known to allow their passion for teaching and student learning drive their teaching– and research, for that matter–and many truly love what they do.

The quest for excellence in teaching requires a dedication to professional development. Although the development of teaching skills is a never-ending journey, many of those who have devoted effort to improving their teaching have been recognized with awards and honors, as well as receiving ever-important accolades from their students and peers.

How teaching excellence is measured can take a variety of forms and is often dependent on the situation and environment. In its early years, due to the uniqueness of students and faculty, NTID was an incubator of teaching methodology, often measured in quantity, productivity, and success of individual students. Faculty spent considerable time reflecting on teaching effectiveness and self-awareness on an individual basis. Expertise in one's discipline did not guarantee a successful teaching experience, nor did competency in sign language in itself guarantee competent teaching.

Though some faculty were effective teachers in hearing environments, they often realized, after arriving at NTID, that without knowledge of sign language and/or deaf and hard-of-hearing education or strengths in specific disciplines, they were not adequately prepared to maintain their teaching competencies. Likewise, some faculty with experience in the instruction of deaf and hard-of-hearing students sometimes had to enhance and/or update their knowledge in the discipline if they were teaching in technical fields. So, throughout the phases of NTID's evolution, faculty worked very hard and took their pursuit of teaching excellence very seriously. The summer months were deemed times to work to develop new curricula and hone teaching skills in anticipation of the next school year. For the first decade or so of NTID's existence, faculty were working according to a 12-month contract.

Formal awards for teaching excellence were not common in the earlier years of NTID. Accolades were mostly directed from within NTID, coming from one's peers, and great pride was taken in the uniqueness of NTID's mission. A faculty member's success was often measured by the nod from a student's head and an index finger moving up and down next to their temple, signing that they understood a particular concept. It is important to note that, although awards can be flattering, it is most often the gratitude expressed by a student, or a congratulatory comment from a colleague, that are most desired and appreciated by teachers. Despite the lack of available awards to be had in the earlier years of NTID, there was tremendous satisfaction and celebration of accomplishment as a result of students applying skills and knowledge learned at NTID after graduating and gaining employment.

NTID is a unique institution of higher learning, where deaf and hard-of-hearing students learn the roots of their trades, applied knowledge, self-advocacy, and lifelong learning skills—and do so side-by-side with their hearing peers on campus. Many NTID students benefit from applied curricula structured to allow individuals to gain employment and contribute immediately to their host organizations. Inasmuch as it is anticipated that graduates might face workplace communication, cultural, and attitudinal barriers, it is imperative to give students a competitive advantage by ensuring that they are well-trained in the skills of their discipline and in the soft skills needed for workplace success.

When an instructor is able to get a concept through to students, it can change their lives. It can be life-changing if it means they get a job because of that nugget of gained information. With the emphasis on developing career-focused skillsets and lifelong learning, a significant level of curriculum development and the use of innovative pedagogical strategies and technologies are required of the teaching faculty.

Students supported by NTID are enrolled in degree-granting programs at NTID, as well as in the other colleges of RIT. Students in NTID programs benefit from direct instruction from the professor and smaller class sizes that allow for lecture, active learning activities, collaborative learning, and hands-on experiences. Faculty in these programs are versed in best practices for the education of deaf and hard-of-hearing students, and the curriculum is optimized for student success in career attainment or continuing education at the next level.

NTID students enrolled in the other colleges of RIT are additionally supported by faculty tutors, advisors, sign language interpreters, and captionists. It is important to note that tutoring is inherently a form of teaching, and the term "teaching" encompasses tutoring activities. Throughout this chapter, faculty whose responsibilities predominantly involve tutoring are celebrated alongside those whose primary role is classroom teaching. In fact, many NTID faculty members perform both classroom teaching and tutoring. Regardless of the form of the teaching, the emphasis on teaching excellence at NTID is shared by the administration, academic counselors/advisors, programs/departments, support service providers, staff, and faculty alike.

Traits of Effective Teachers

Sometimes it seems as though a professor is a naturally talented instructor. While there is certainly an innate talent component to teaching, NTID faculty approach their pursuit of teaching excellence with purpose and self-reflection. Some of the traits of an effective teacher at NTID can be found in the non-exhaustive list below.

Student-Centered Teaching and Sharing the Mission of Student Success

When teachers actually convince (not just try to convince) their students that they care about their academic progress and success (in the current coursework, in their careers, and in their lives), students are more likely to meet them halfway in the classroom. This is part of the essence of the shared mission of learning. The learning process is only partially the responsibility of the instructor because it is shared with the students. Students put effort into their coursework and can (and should) take some of the ownership of their learning process.

The shift in teaching focus, away from passive learning and toward active learning (where students are active participants in the learning activities), is another component of student-centered teaching and learning. Although "student-centered teaching" is a term that has more recently made its way into the mainstream vocabulary, NTID may have been well ahead of its time because there are many stories over its history of conscious and active participation of students in the learning process. This co-dependence of teaching and

Active learning is critical to empowering students for lifelong learning. Students learn better by doing, and by placing the students in the right environment with the right project/assignment and giving them appropriate feedback, learning will predictably occur. It is crucial that students take ownership of their work, including learning from their mistakes. If this happens, then there will be knowledge/experience transfer to the job later, and they will become stronger, lifelong learners.

-Jim Mallory, Faculty Member and Eisenhart Award Recipient

learning, with instructors and students working collaboratively, is seen today in the most vibrant and successful classes at NTID.

The acts of conducting successful student-centered teaching and sharing the mission of student success place quite a bit of responsibility on the professor. The best instructors are continually asking themselves: How does this classroom or tutoring activity that I am planning directly relate to student success? A good, student-centered instructor typically has a passion for showing students how the information that they are learning in class directly relates to their lives, the real world, and to success in their future careers (which often helps to enculturate students into their selected disciplines). Effort is also required for the instructors to get to know their students. It is important to know the students as individuals, as their backgrounds, personalities, and identities can give clues to ways of tailoring course material and activities to optimize student success. Students get to know instructors and can often begin to see their teachers as good role models.

The instructor-student relationship can be demonstrated by the reciprocal nature of teaching and learning, where the instructor must also learn. And in the context of the shared mission of student success by the teacher and the student, instructors should be willing to learn, not only by keeping current in their fields, but also by learning from their students. Acquiring, modifying, and improving teaching skills are dynamic processes that can be continually developed through feedback from students and peers, as well as through comprehensive self-reflection.[3]

Adaptability and Understanding of Various Learning Styles

While keeping in mind the ever-changing student population that enters the classroom, effective teachers must continually adapt modes of teaching in order to reach students with a range of learning styles. Educational theories and best practices in teaching and tutoring have changed over the years. Lectures are now often interspersed with active and collaborative learning, online components, and ever-advancing classroom technologies. In fact, more and more, NTID faculty are adopting "flipped classroom" or "blended" approaches to teaching, in which students view pre-recorded lectures outside of the assigned class time and work on problem-solving and non-passive modes of learning during regular class time.

Although NTID has traditionally used direct instruction in the classroom, our classroom is now evolving. To keep up with the current trends in education, NTID has started to offer a flipped classroom experience where students basically watch a pre-recorded (accessible) lecture and come to class to do homework, and even more recently has started to offer some completely online courses (with possibly a future goal of completely online programs).

-Stacey Davis, Faculty Member and NTID Teaching Award Recipient

Attention to Lifelong Learning

Effective teachers understand that students need to acquire lifelong learning skills. Whereas learning the content and skills of their disciplines is paramount, so too is guiding students to become productive learners unto themselves. Today at NTID, faculty are increasingly adding metacognitive material to course instruction and tutoring initiatives. When a student can better understand how they best think and learn (the definition of metacognition), new avenues are opened to improve their overall knowledge acquisition and learning processes.

Self-Reflection

The task of self-reflection is extremely important to good teachers. An effective teacher will never repeat an unsuccessful lesson in the same way if they have taken a step back and reflected on what might have gone wrong with the lesson. It is important to strive continually to improve what is done in the classroom. Self-reflective teachers often ask themselves: How can I improve on what I just taught in order to maximize student success the next time I teach this topic? An important aspect of the reflective process is to seek peer and student feedback related to the efficacy of how certain topics were taught and to use that information to adapt and improve. Polling the students in a course or tutoring group to gauge how learning is progressing is a trait of an effective teacher. NTID has long been an institute-wide leader in collecting feedback from students and peers about teaching effectiveness.

Communication

Communication between teachers and their students—and among students in the classroom or workgroup, for that matter—is ubiquitously important in any type of learning environment. In an academic setting, effective communication is paramount for relaying course expectations and requirements, disclosing assignment/exam/project evaluations, or in the actual act of delivering the course material and content. Especially as it relates to the latter, classroom communication is unique at NTID.

Here, classroom communication is as critical as anything else in the classroom, in tutoring sessions,

during extramural activities, or anyplace where incidental learning can occur. All NTID faculty members are expected to devote time and effort annually to work continuously toward improving communication skills, and support is provided to assist faculty in their communication development efforts. Especially in technical programs, instructors need to not only effectively communicate content discourse for students' employment or continuing education success, but also model communication traits necessary along their paths of lifelong learning. The whole of the NTID community is encouraged to keep communication access at the forefront of their minds in all of their interactions.

Adherence to Standards

Effective teachers do not lower their learning expectations for students. Instead, they bring all students up to those standards. At NTID, deaf and hard-of-hearing students are held to the same learning expectations as their hearing peers. In the applied programs at NTID, instructors strive to prepare students for eventual success in the workforce, and students often succeed in exceeding the expectations and industry standards they will face in their careers. In the same vein, faculty at NTID want to make sure that their students become self-advocates, upstanding citizens, and lifelong learners.

Teaching Beyond the Classroom

NTID professors have also been known to share in the activities and successes of students outside the classroom. Many faculty members will get involved in students' co-ops or job searches, host classes on field trips, or work with students in research, creative, or independent learning environments. Faculty members are also sometimes able to support students extramurally, through working together in student clubs and organizations or by attending students' theatrical plays, athletic events, or other student-sponsored activities.

Discipline Expertise

The credentials of NTID faculty have come in many forms over the years. Many professors have had significant industrial experience, are experts in Deaf education, or have terminal degrees in their discipline. All of these credentials bring a wealth of knowledge and experience to the instruction of NTID students. In order to ensure the course content that is being conveyed is high-quality, current, and relevant to the field, it is important that faculty possess these competencies.

Teacher-Scholars

Related to disciplinary expertise, many good professors at NTID are also good researchers, and there is a natural link between teaching and scholarship. The greater faculty members' disciplinary knowledge (which often comes from one's research/scholarship agenda), the more flexibility they have to relay the course material from different and creative angles. Currency in one's field is critical, and it is often the case that one's research efforts inform their teaching, and vice versa.

NTID professors conduct research within their disciplines (science, engineering, psychology business, etc.) and/or related to investigating strategies to improve student learning. Scholarship of Teaching and Learning (SOTL) and Discipline-Based Education Research (DBER) are two current types of research methodology that investigate new and effective ways of teaching that enhance learning, whether in general or in specific disciplines. NTID faculty members have been conducting research in these two areas that clearly demonstrate the marriage between teaching and scholarship.

Highlights of Faculty Teaching Development at NTID

The spirit and history of innovation at NTID has brought it recognition as the leader in technical education for deaf and hard-of-hearing students. Quality learning requires exceptional teaching, and the skills of an effective teacher require continual practice and development. NTID has a notable history in support of faculty development. Dr. Larry K. Quinsland, faculty member from 1974 to 2015, has contributed this history of Faculty Teaching Development at NTID.

In the early years, NTID experienced rapid growth in teaching faculty and staff, requiring the development of a quality orientation process for new instructors. Initially, orientation sessions were conducted by Drs. D. Robert Frisina and William Castle, along with support staff, with much of the development time allocated to the acquisition of sign language skills. Most new teaching faculty could have been characterized as experts in

their respective disciplines with little to no prior teaching experience. Very few had prior teaching experience, even fewer had experience interacting with deaf and hard-of-hearing students, and a limited number had degrees in Curriculum/Instruction, Education, or Special Education. It was soon recognized that in addition to sign language skill acquisition and development, teaching support was needed for faculty to become competent in the classroom and teaching laboratory.

In the late 1970s, the Office of Teaching Effectiveness (OTE) was created by Richard Curwin, who was hired with faculty development experience. He took the lead in designing support for both new and veteran teaching faculty. Larry Quinsland and Mary Lou Basile, both with prior teaching experience in the field of deaf and hard-of-hearing education, became facilitators of classroom-skill and knowledge development in OTE, while concurrently teaching their own NTID classes. This context allowed them to share their own current student teaching/learning interactions with the faculty who were simultaneously sharing their experiences when involved in OTE activities. At the time, faculty were on 12-month contracts, which allowed them to focus intensively on teaching improvement activities during the summer. Basile utilized her experiences training new NTID faculty and staff in sign communication development to assist faculty in developing early communication proficiency in the classroom. Quinsland focused on teaching skills that helped to make new content and concepts visual in the classroom and teaching laboratory. Members from NTID technology support areas were included to demonstrate new classroom technologies as they became available.

In the early 1980s, it was recognized that, while the faculty who availed themselves of OTE teaching improvement activities became skilled teachers, some of the faculty who did not participate were opting to leave. In fact, for many newly hired teaching faculty, the prior sense of professional competence could not be quickly re-established in the classroom without assistance. Consequently, the Office of Faculty Development (OFD), chaired by Dr. Harry Lang, was established with the goal of providing all new teaching faculty with support during their first year. In addition, the OFD provides support for veteran faculty who either volunteered to work with OFD teaching consultants, or were referred to OFD for the confidential teaching improvement skill and knowledge development that was offered.

The OFD First Year Experience included a continuation of NTID-wide orientation sessions and a First Year Teaching Faculty Seminar Series led by OFD program coordinators and members of the NTID community. The primary focus of the First Year Experience was on developing teaching knowledge and skills through the Faculty Consultations Program. All new faculty, regardless of prior experience, were required to participate as part of their first-year expectations.

The kick-off event was the summer Microteaching Program taught by Peter Haggerty, Larry Quinsland, and Keith Mousley. Faculty were immediately exposed for several weeks to a "class" of students and were asked to prepare lessons in their content area(s). Students were trained by the teaching consultants to assume various student characteristics and to offer critique of lessons with the goal of improving teaching presentation and interaction skills in preparation for the fall quarter. Participants quickly developed confidence and basic teaching planning skills that were applied to their course preparation.

At the completion of Microteaching, all new faculty were matched with a faculty consultant each quarter for the first year. Teaching faculty consultants were senior faculty members who were trained by OFD to facilitate the development of teaching skills on a one-to-one, confidential basis. New faculty were videotaped at least once each week using a split-screen two-camera video process that was developed in conjunction with the NTID Technical Support Department. This allowed the new instructor and the faculty consultant to discuss teaching and communication on a regular basis, for the purpose of encouraging the new instructor to revise and experiment with new teaching strategies that would be revisited and discussed at the next consultation session. Faculty from the Sign Communication Department were also invited to consult with the new instructor during faculty consultant sessions, using the same teaching materials, videotapes, and confidentiality guidelines.

The Faculty Consultations Program was successful in that it significantly improved retention of new teaching faculty, as well as initiated an expectation on the part of faculty to continually offer critique and experiment with the ultimate goal of improving one's teaching skills and knowledge throughout their teaching career. An interesting outgrowth of this process was that department chairpersons began to incorporate ongoing faculty development into the annual expectations of teaching faculty, with the focus being primarily on faculty members to define their own areas of effort and to describe their outcomes to themselves and to their colleagues within their departments.

RIT Consultations

NTID became involved in providing support for RIT campus-wide professional development and support for other colleges and universities serving deaf and hard-of-hearing students, as well as professional organizations nationally. In the 1970s and 1980s, RIT had an office sponsored by the RIT Faculty Council providing faculty support. Members of OTE and OFD served on this committee, sharing faculty-development techniques and conducting campus-wide presentations and workshops for RIT faculty several times a year. Individual consultations were provided to RIT colleagues in other colleges who had deaf and hard-of-hearing students in their classrooms and laboratories.

External Professional Consultations

Faculty-development presentations and workshops were designed and presented on the campuses of Gallaudet University and regional programs, as well as on several other campuses. These interactions were planned and facilitated primarily by Larry Quinsland and involved other NTID faculty. Additional presentations and workshops were presented on the campuses of state residential schools and day programs for deaf and hard-of-hearing students.

In addition, OFD faculty became members and sometimes leaders of several important professional organizations that focus on deaf and hard-of-hearing educational issues. Chief among these was the Convention of American Instructors of the Deaf (CAID), which is believed to be the oldest teaching organization in the United States. Several NTID faculty assumed responsibility for keeping CAID alive and coordinated several national conferences for teachers to share successful teaching and learning strategies.

OFD teaching consultants became members of the Professional and Organizational Development (POD) Network in Higher Education. POD serves as the primary organization for professional faculty developers in the United States. NTID faculty introduced POD members to special education issues on college campuses and stimulated members to consider students with alternative needs. Several additional presentations and workshops were conducted at the American Educational Research Association (AERA) and the National Science Teachers Association (NSTA).

During NTID's years of growth and development, new teaching faculty received intensive orientation and training in the field of teaching and learning with deaf and hard-of-hearing students. Many current senior faculty still comment on the importance of that introduction and how it benefited them throughout their career. Due to the establishment of a trained core of skilled teaching faculty, centralized teacher training for new faculty and support for veteran faculty was discontinued. The Office of Faculty Development was dismantled in the 1990s. However, NTID has continued to offer various professional development activities for its faculty and staff with the support of NTID's administration. Hope Williams has long organized many of these activities. In 2016, the new position of Professional Development Coordinator for Teaching Excellence was established and quickly occupied by Stacey Davis. The NTID community is currently discussing further mechanisms for bolstering their professional development offerings.

Recognition of Teaching Excellence

Students and colleagues often inform faculty when they notice that good teaching is occurring, either formally through evaluations and observations or informally through comments about how their teaching is having an impact. Outcomes related to graduation and retention rates or co-op and employment success are other indicators of teaching success (even if the teaching in support of those metrics is less visible). As stated previously, formal awards are just one way in which a professor can be recognized for teaching excellence. Although they can publicly overshadow other forms of

recognition, they are dwarfed by the massive number of instances in which a student has informed their teacher about their teaching impact. Today there is a host of avenues through which instructors can be formally recognized for their teaching excellence. These honors and awards can be at the institute or university level, but can also come from external local, national, or international organizations.

NTID Institute-Level Honors

NTID understands the importance of teaching excellence and established a formal awards process for recognizing great teaching and tutoring in 2013. Teaching awards are given annually in up to three categories of tenured faculty, pre-tenured faculty, and lecturer faculty. NTID faculty members who have been honored with these awards are listed below.

NTID Teaching/Tutoring Award for Tenured Faculty
Keith Mousley, 2016
Mark Pfuntner, 2015
Brian Trager, 2014

NTID Teaching/Tutoring Award for Pre-Tenure Faculty
Austin Gehret, 2016
Gary Behm, 2015
Scot Atkins, 2014
Annemarie Ross, 2013

NTID Teaching/Tutoring Award for Lecturers
Eric Kunsman, 2016
Stacey Davis, 2014
Carla Deibel, 2013

RIT University-Level Honors

RIT has a longer tradition of awards dedicated to teaching excellence. Many NTID faculty have received these honors over the years. NTID faculty members who have been honored with these awards are listed as follows:

The Eisenhart Award for Outstanding Teaching
The Eisenhart Award for Teaching Excellence is perhaps the most well-recognized of RIT's teaching awards. It has been given, in one form or another, since 1965. Tenured faculty who have at least seven years of teaching

experience are eligible for this award, and two to four awards are generally given annually.

Christopher Kurz, 2014–2015
Linda Fleishman Gottermeier, 2012–2013
Paula Grcevic, 2005–2006
Patricia Durr, 2003–2004
Sidney L. McQuay, 2000–2001
Sidney Barefoot, 1999–2000
James Mallory, 1998–1999
Mary Louise Basile, 1997–1998
Donald Beil, 1996–1997
Lynette Finton, 1995–1996
Joan Carr, 1994–1995
Marilyn Mitchell, 1993–1994
Lorna Mittelman, 1992–1993
Paula Grcevic, 1991–1992
Robert Keiffer, 1989–1990
Paul Peterson, 1988–1989
Maria Shustorovich, 1986–1987
Peter Haggerty, 1985–1986
Roxanna B. Nielsen, 1984–1985
Donna Gustina Pocobello, 1983–1984
Harry G. Lang, 1982–1983
Jack Slutzky, 1981–1982
Beverly J. Price, 1980–1981
Julie J. Cammeron, 1978–1979
Edward L. Scouten, 1977–1978
Loy Golladay, 1975–1976
Robert F. Panara, 1974–1975
Lawrence Mothersell, 1970–1971

The Richard and Virginia Eisenhart Provost's Award for Excellence in Teaching

The Richard and Virginia Eisenhart Provost's Award for Excellence in Teaching is similar to the Eisenhart Award for Outstanding Teaching. However, the Provost's Award was established in 1989 to recognize newer faculty (those who have taught three years or less) for teaching excellence. The competitive honor is given to only one (and occasionally two) professors annually.

Peter C. Hauser, 2004–2005
Todd Pagano, 2004–2005
Reed Gershwind, 1991–1992

Outstanding Teaching Award for Non-Tenure-Track Faculty

Tenured and tenure-track instructors have long been eligible for the RIT-wide recognitions described above, but to honor the valuable contributions of non-tenure-track faculty, the Outstanding Teaching Award for Non-Tenure-Track Faculty was established in 2011. One award is given annually.

Heather Smith, 2016–2017

Provost's Award for Excellence in Mentoring

As discussed in this chapter, professional development is essential for faculty to hone their skills in teaching. The Provost's Award for Excellence in Mentoring was established in 2011 to recognize the efforts of mentors in helping others to become effective faculty members. One to five awards are given annually.

Todd Pagano, 2012–2013

Provost's Award for Excellence in Advising

The academic advising of students is another critical aspect of student success. The Provost's Award for Excellence in Advising was established in 2015 to recognize primary academic advisors for exceptional work in support of students. Two awards are given annually.

Veronika Talbot (Experienced Advisor), 2015–2016

Excellence in Student Learning Outcomes Award

Improving student learning can occur at the department level. Academic departments at NTID are continually assessing their programs' curricula and related learning outcomes to optimize student success. The Excellence in Student Learning Outcomes Award was established in 2014 to recognize one department annually that excels at assessing and continually improving student learning.

Administrative Support Technology Program (Mary Lou Basile, Adriana Kulakowski, Tracy Magin, Mary Beth Parker, and Kathleen Szczepanek), 2015–16

External Honors

Over the years, several NTID faculty members have been honored for teaching excellence by external organizations. Inasmuch as there is not a compiled list of faculty who have been recognized by external organizations, the list below is by no means exhaustive. Some of the honors are given for multiple reasons, but are always, at least in part, in recognition of teaching excellence or support for teaching excellence.

Stanley C. Israel Award (American Chemical Society)
Annemarie Ross, 2012
Todd Pagano, 2008

Daniel T. Cloud Award (National Center on Deafness)
James DeCaro, 1996

Excellence in Teaching Award (Science Teachers Association of New York State)
Todd Pagano, 2016

Thomas Francis Fox Award (Empire State Association of the Deaf)
T. Alan Hurwitz, 1980

Outstanding Undergraduate Science Teacher Award (Society for College Science Teachers)
Todd Pagano, 2016

Outstanding Young Man of America (Jaycees)
Sid McQuay, 1980

United States Professor of the Year (Council for the Advancement and Support of Education & Carnegie Foundation for the Advancement of Education)
Todd Pagano, 2012

Conclusion

Indeed, NTID has a rich and remarkable history of teaching excellence—one that is only balanced by its bright future. The physical act of teaching has changed somewhat since NTID admitted its first class of students. What has not changed, however, is the accepted understanding at NTID that a great teacher can have a profound impact on a student. Technology in the classroom has transformed over the years and will continue to do so—virtual reality being one such tool that could greatly benefit the teaching toolkit. Courses are now frequently offered online, either entirely or in part, with little to no time spent in a traditional classroom space. Active and collaborative learning (including learning

communities) are increasingly becoming the norm throughout the nation in academia. The needs of the job market are ever-changing, and at an applied institute of higher learning (like NTID), programs are constantly being assessed and new programs are being developed to meet the needs of the job market. Employers of NTID students are increasingly demanding that graduates have critical-thinking and problem-solving skills, the ability to work as a valued member of a team, and global and social awareness. Surely, NTID will continue to evolve to meet these changing expectations and will continue to flourish, due in no small part to its commitment to teaching excellence.

Epilogue

In the prologue, I mentioned Stephen Hawking's "giants" metaphor. Another giant of NTID whom I met early in my career was Dr. Harry Lang, whose name has surfaced a couple of times in this chapter related to teaching excellence. As a promoter of physics, he, no doubt, appreciates my references to the "giants" of physics and to Stephen Hawking. I have enjoyed reading Dr. Lang's book, *Silence of the Spheres*.[4] In fact, he opens the book with a quote also from Johannes Kepler that ingeniously relates the observations of celestial motions to deafness. He talks about the scientific contributions of deaf scientists. (My favorite is Anders Ekeberg, the discoverer of the element tantalum—a story that took me all the way to Sweden to visit the same university where he did his landmark work.) But most interesting is the very opening of the introduction of the book, specifically the story he tells about meeting Stephen Hawking, an encounter that provided the "impetus" for Dr. Lang writing his book, and how it related to his understanding about how others perceive deafness. Through the various interactions that I have had with Dr. Lang, I have no doubt that he also used the story of his encounter to deliver powerful messages about abilities and perceptions to his students through his own teaching.

I dedicate this chapter to all of the "giants" of teaching excellence in NTID's illustrious history.

Acknowledgments

I would like to direct special appreciation to individuals who assisted with certain aspects of this chapter. Thank you, Jim DeCaro, David Templeton, Larry K. Quinsland, and Mary Lou Basile for providing thoughtful and valuable information in support of this chapter.

Dr. Todd Pagano is a professor of chemistry, as well as the Associate Dean for Teaching and Scholarship Excellence at RIT/NTID.

Notes

1. Stephen Hawking. *On the Shoulders of Giants: The Great Works of Physics and Astronomy.* (Philadelphia, PA: Running Press, 2002).
2. D. Robert Frisina, personal communication, 2015.
3. Todd Pagano. "Teaching Perspective: Ex Ovo Omnia." *Journal of Science Education for Students with Disabilities* 16, no. 1 (2013): 40–42.
4. Harry G. Lang. *Silence of the Spheres: The Deaf Experience in the History of Science.* (Massachusetts: Bergin & Garvey, 1994).

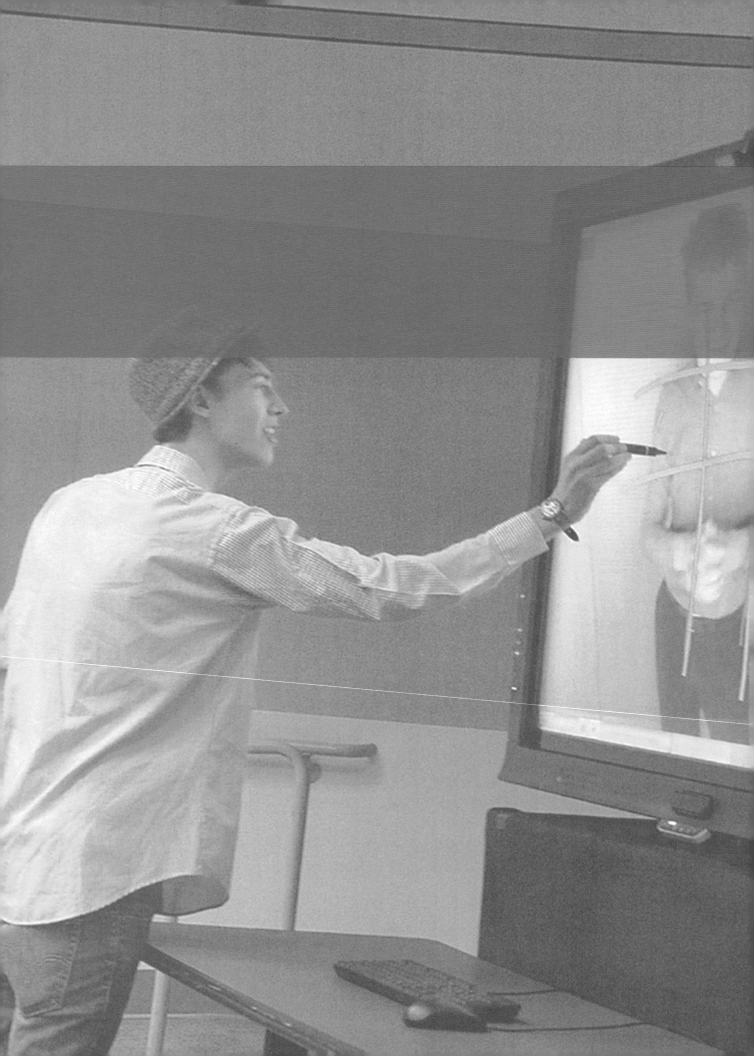

Section 3
The Purpose

From Roots to STEM
The Growth of STEM Education at NTID

Dr. Todd Pagano and David Templeton

Prologue

Science, technology, engineering, and mathematics (STEM) educational programs have been a consistent backbone of NTID's degree offerings over the course of its history, as would be expected of any technical institute of higher education. The T (for technology) in both NTID and RIT is derived from NTID's original purpose—to train deaf and hard-of-hearing students in technical fields. It also resonates with RIT's history, with roots dating back to the Rochester Mechanics Institute.

The authors of this chapter are trained as scientists and science educators. We do, however, also pride ourselves on being inter-disciplinarians, and we value the roles that arts, business, and other disciplines play in the logistics and quality of everyday life. In addition to its STEM offerings, NTID also has quality programs in these other fields. We are often approached, though, about whether the acronym "STEM" is too exclusive, as surely the arts, business, and other disciplines are also unquestionably important.

We agree with the importance of inter-disciplinarity and of the diversity of thought that comes from *all* fields. In fact, one of the most influential essays that we have read is "The Two Cultures" by C.P. Snow. Snow was both a physicist and a writer, and in his essay (published in 1959) he discussed the divide of "intellectual life of the whole of western society" into the sciences and the humanities.[1] He felt that this great divide and lack of communication between the two sides could hinder the problem solving of some of the world's most critical issues. The interesting timing of Snow's comments with respect to the planning stage of NTID might cause one to pause and wonder if the architects of NTID were cognizant of his (still fairly fresh at the time) message when they ingeniously designed the institute.

Today, STEM is born from the national priority of educational attainment to meet the demand for highly skilled technical workers in order to remain globally competitive, to create innovative products that improve the quality of life for humans, and to strengthen national security. Notwithstanding Snow's caution or the importance of *all* fields, for the purposes of this chapter, we are going to use this interpretation of the four standard strands of STEM. To our knowledge, there is no one all-encompassing and agreed-upon list of STEM academic majors.

Sometimes the lines between STEM and non-STEM majors can also be blurred. For example, the programs within NTID's Department of Visual Communication Studies have technical components related to graphics and visualization (including an exciting new focus in 3D graphics). One might argue that these great programs speak very directly to Snow's points. Another visionary whose philosophies were also the basis for the selection of the boundaries of STEM programs featured in this chapter is the first chairperson of NTID's first National Advisory Group (NAG), Dr. Ralph Tyler, who recognized the importance of the shift from "manual" jobs to "technically-oriented occupations" and the rise in market demand for graduates of engineering and technical programs.[2]

Introduction

STEM is the acronym used for science, technology, engineering, and mathematics, and it has become commonplace in today's job market and educational vernacular. Although the exact person to coin the term and the date of its coinage are still subject to interpretation, most trace the use of the acronym to the National Science Foundation (NSF) in the late 1990s or early 2000s.

However, the NSF was founded nearly a half-century before then, so it is evident that the United States was beginning to invest in science long before the acronym surfaced. In fact, President Lyndon Baines Johnson, who later famously signed the bill for the establishment of NTID, also had a paramount role in the formation of the National Aeronautics and Space Administration (NASA) in the late 1950s; an interesting coincidence is that the main NTID campus building and the NASA spaceflight hub have the same namesake.

Recognizing that a workforce educated in STEM fields has a significant influence on the competitiveness of the United States in a global economy, NSF funds early education through STEM-based career-preparation programs, including the S-STEM scholarship program and various K–12 programs.[3,4] Nearly 17 million jobs in the United States, based on the core STEM occupations, representing close to 13% of total national employment, were available in 2013.[5] STEM occupations are predicted to have a high growth potential in the future; average wages earned in these occupations are nearly twice the national average.

There have been workforce shortages of skilled STEM graduates in the United States required to fill some crucial jobs. In fact, special visas exist to address this shortage and to expand the talent pool, including the H–1B visa and Optional Practical Training visa.[6] The U.S. Department of Education continues to prioritize resources in support of teaching and learning in the STEM disciplines through a wide variety of grants and programs designed to prepare students for advanced degrees and to offer the ability to compete for technology-based careers in a global economy.[7]

The prioritization of STEM is also, in part, related to innovation that results in the creation of new designs and the development of products and bodies of knowledge that ultimately lead to enhanced quality of life for people around the world. A population that is well-educated and trained in STEM curricula is well-situated to contribute to innovation as career professionals and to enjoy both the economic benefits and enhanced quality of life that can accompany STEM careers. By placing an emphasis on education, training, and the integration of disciplines within the STEM curriculum over the past two decades, the NSF and Department of Education have acknowledged how critical a role innovative advancement plays in the strength and vitality of our economy and leadership in the global marketplace, creating a need to remain globally competitive.

More useful ideas lead to more products, the increased need for products leads to more jobs, and a combination of innovation and jobs is the gateway to an improved quality of life. Research and development is viewed by many as the vehicle that drives innovation, and research of this type is built on applying knowledge and skill in the fields of science, technology, engineering, and mathematics.

Since its inception, NTID has embraced education and training for entry into the workforce in the STEM fields, even before they were emphasized as having so much importance in the growth of the global economy (and certainly before the term "STEM" was coined). A core mission of NTID has always been to train students to be employable, to be competitive in the job market, and to meet the needs of industry. It is important to note that the recent focus on STEM involves more than just teaching additional courses, offering more degree programs, and encouraging more students to enroll in STEM-related programs. A focus of NTID is also on how STEM disciplines are taught and integrated.

Early in its first year of teaching students in the charter class, educators at NTID realized that more efficient and successful educational strategies needed to be developed and evaluated. Participation by deaf and hard-of-hearing students in existing classes offered at the various colleges of RIT with interpreting and tutoring support was not always producing the anticipated success. Over the past 50 years of involvement in the STEM disciplines, NTID faculty have created and employed numerous innovative teaching strategies, always with the goal of increased knowledge acquisition, and enhanced competence and confidence in the future workplace.

A myriad of strategies in support of learning have been successfully implemented among many of NTID's STEM disciplines over the years: computer assisted instruction (CAI), individualized instruction, hands-on learning, project-based learning, writing across the curriculum, capstone courses, concept mapping, spiral curriculum, distance learning, flipped classrooms, writing in the disciplines, scaffolding, cooperative work experiences (co-ops), and undergraduate research, to name many (but not all). Hundreds, if not thousands, of presentations, articles, and research publications have resulted from the application and evaluation of these teaching/learning strategies. Today, discipline-based education research (DBER) is a field of scholarship in which some NTID faculty members are involved. Prominent in STEM fields, it addresses the investigation of strategies to improve learning within the discipline. And faculty in many of the departments across NTID are involved in the scholarship of teaching and learning (SOTL) in order to research ways to better educate our students.

NTID has hosted many STEM programs over the years. Programs have closed for different reasons, which led to opportunities to develop new and exciting programs. Below, we highlight the different STEM programs that NTID has offered over its history, culminating with its current offerings. The STEM curriculum has indeed been dynamic at NTID. Job opportunities and new technologies dictate cycles of program development and discontinuance, but the focus on creating and maintaining STEM programs has been a flagship of NTID's efforts throughout its 50-year history.

STEM at NTID
Science, technology, engineering and mathematics have always been major foci of NTID's mission and development, beginning 30 years prior to the coining of the term, STEM. Resonating with RIT's long-time commitment to cooperative education, co-ops have been a visible and important part of the educational requirements of NTID's STEM programs over the years. Hands-on, co-operative education, combined with continually advancing curricula that are rich in applied focus, have formed the basis of highly enrolled and successful STEM programs at NTID. It is interesting to note, at least in the science-related programs, that

NTID's enrolled and graduating student cohorts have historically had female majorities in many of the institution's programs. Although currently, the ever-important thrust to encourage more female students to enter STEM fields is a significant focus on the national level, NTID has been doing a remarkable job of this in some disciplines since its beginning.

A historical perspective of NTID's involvement and evolvement in these four strands can best be described through an examination of progressive thematic eras of time that have occurred through NTID's 50-year history. In many ways, STEM-based curricula at NTID have followed similar patterns to that of natural evolution, beginning with the fight for survival, followed by development and growth, aging (and sometimes extinction), and finally, rebirth as stronger, more efficient organisms. Curricula must adapt to remain viable in support of a rapidly changing job market in today's high-tech industry.

In this chapter, NTID's STEM offerings have been divided into several eras along a timeline, and they have been categorized according to the following themes that capture some commonalities of the programs and the state of the institute at that time: *Carpe Diem*, Curriculum or Bust, STEM Takes Flight, and STEM 2.0. The text of the themes below lend detail to the accompanying Table 1. And for the benefit of referencing the table, program abbreviations are given alongside their full program names.

Carpe Diem, 1968–1969
The *Carpe Diem* era was an immediate response to an assessment by the NTID faculty and administration of the need to enhance the success rate of the charter class beginning in 1968. Borrowing from the natural evolution metaphor, the fight for survival began at the beginning of the second academic quarter; more than 50% of the entering cohort of students were struggling academically, due to their challenging transition to college-level course content as they were mainstreamed into RIT classes.[8] The moment was seized, so to speak, mostly within the first year by the rush to develop programs and interventions, such as the initial NTID Math Learning Center (MLC), the Vestibule Program, Physics Learning Center, and computer-assisted instruction

(CAI), all of which had the common goal of fostering increased student success. A Vestibule Program was established by the beginning of winter quarter 1968 to address the gaps in knowledge that kept students from being successful in their courses, with most of these gaps being related to mathematics and science concepts, as well as written English.[9] CAI in mathematics and the MLC were available to students for individualized instruction to help them prepare for calculus coursework at the beginning of the second year.

Math Learning Center

Dr. Vince Daniele, NTID faculty member from 1981 to 2013, offers this account of the MLC. When NTID first opened, the original vision was that deaf and hard-of-hearing students would enter mathematics courses taught in RIT's College of Science, and that NTID faculty members would provide tutoring and support for those courses. However, it was determined that, despite the fact that virtually all NTID students had taken mathematics in high school, a high percentage of students could benefit from a review of topics typically found in courses such as algebra or trigonometry. Consequently, separate course sections for NTID students were established. Additionally, some sections of courses, like calculus, were offered for deaf, hard-of-hearing, and hearing students, and were taught by NTID faculty. However, in part because most NTID students had studied subjects such as algebra in high school, and because individualized education was en vogue back in those days, by the early 1970s, it was decided that providing mathematics instruction could readily be approached using an individualized instructional format. One perceived benefit of such an approach was that it would allow students to progress through courses as quickly as they needed or wanted to do so.

The MLC was established to permit students to take their courses by studying instructional modules in an individual setting. In fact, because of the individualized nature of the study, and because the work constituted a review, of sorts, for many students, some students were able to move through more than one mathematics course in a given academic quarter. Although some small number of NTID students took mathematics courses in classroom environments from time to time, the individualized format of MLC instruction dominated until the late 1980s or early 1990s, when national societies of professional mathematics educators began to place more value and emphasis on problem-solving and communication in the mathematics classroom, as opposed to focusing on numerical computation or manipulation of algebraic symbols. That nationwide shift in instructional emphasis initiated a move toward the use of more traditional classroom instruction for NTID mathematics, since communication and problem-solving could often be more readily fostered through group settings. Little by little, more and more courses were taught in classroom formats, until the MLC was finally dismantled in the mid 1990s.

Physics Learning Center

Dr. Harry Lang, NTID faculty member from 1970 to 2011, offers this account of the Physics Learning Center. Similar to the MLC, the NTID Physics Learning Center also applied the concept of individualized instruction. It was established in 1970 and continued into the early 1980s. Approximately two dozen courses were tailored from single-concept, self-paced learning modules to meet the specific knowledge and skill requirements of various STEM-related majors. For example, Physics for Ophthalmic Optical Finishing Technology (affectionately known as Optical Finishing Technology, or OFT) focused (no pun intended) on lenses and how they were used to correct vision. Physics for Architectural Technology included modules on heat, light, insulation, and other topics relevant to that field of work.

Similarly, self-paced, modularized courses were offered for Electromechanical Technology and Civil Technology. Four courses were offered through the Physics Learning Center to prepare NTID students for baccalaureate-level physics in the College of Science (COS) at RIT. These courses offered more flexible hours than did the self-contained COS College Physics courses since the NTID courses were built around self-instructional physics modules. As a result, these NTID physics courses were also offered to non-traditional hearing students who had difficulty scheduling College Physics through the COS and served, in a small way, as a reverse mainstream program at NTID.

The Evolving Math and Physics Instructional Methodology
Although the practicality of the MLC and Physics Learning Center faded in favor of group instruction in self-contained classrooms, the need for technical math and physics courses has continued into the present day. Although no degree programs at NTID are offered in mathematics or physics, the need for instruction, either individualized or through credit-bearing courses, has persisted throughout NTID's 50-year history and is an integral component of all STEM-related programs and general-education degree requirements.

It is difficult to fathom the flurry of brainstorming, decision-making, and development that led to both the establishment of such a myriad of programming focused on increasing student access to majors in the other colleges of RIT, and the preparation required for the onset of STEM programming to be offered as NTID's first curriculum.

Curriculum or Bust, 1969–1978
The early STEM-related programs in this era were three of the first four programs offered by NTID: Architectural Drafting (AD), Mechanical Drafting (MD), and Machine Tool Operations (MTO). One year later, these were followed by Electronics (E) and Optical Finishing Technology (OFT), which all offered the diploma degree option. In 1970, the Technical Science Department initiated the first STEM-related program to offer an Associate in Applied Science (AAS) degree, the Medical Laboratory Technology (MLT) program.

Four years after the MLT Program was established, four related certificate/diploma programs were established: Histology Technicians (HT), Hematology Technicians (HMT), Microbiology Technicians (MT), and Clinical Chemistry Technicians (CCT). In 1974, a burst of AAS degree programs were established: Data Processing (DP) from the technology strand of STEM; and Architectural Technology (ArchT), Civil Technology (CT) and Electromechanical Technology (EMT) from the engineering strand. (The EMT program replaced the retired diploma-level Electronics program.) At the onset of the 1974–75 academic year, there were 10 new STEM-related programs, offering 19 certificate/diploma/AAS degree options.

The longest running-programs (without changing their program titles) were Architectural Drafting (AD), from 1969 until 1998, and Optical Finishing Technology (OFT), from 1975 until 2004. These programs trained students for 29 years. Both of these programs were discontinued a few years on either side of the millennium. Since both Optical Finishing Technology (OFT) and Architectural Drafting (AD) no longer exist, Applied Computer Technology (ACT) is the next program in line for the longevity award, surpassing the 29-year mark set by OFT and AD, by the year 2022.

The shortest existence of a program title was Numerical Control (NC), between 1974 and 1978. The Numerical Control program combined with the Machine Tool Operation (MTO) program, established in 1969 as one of the first four programs offered by NTID, to become Manufacturing Processes (MP). With the addition of Manufacturing Processes Technology (MPT) in 1992, the degree offerings in this field were expanded to include the Associate in Occupational Studies (AOS) degree.

An excellent example of how the continual advancement of technology stimulates the advancement of a select field of engineering, the integration of computer technology in the machining field necessitated another program title change. By consolidating Manufacturing Processes (MP) and Manufacturing Processes Technology (MPT) into a new program, Computer-Integrated Machining Technology (CIMT) was created in 1997 and remains a viable program today.

Combining all four of these program offerings, beginning with Machine Tool Operation (MTO) and eventually transitioning to Computer-Integrated Manufacturing Technology (CIMT), establishes the longest-running series of STEM programs at NTID to date. Housed in the engineering strand of STEM, Computer-Integrated Machining Technology (CIMT) and its foundation programs have been accepting students over the past 48 years.

The second longest-running program in a specific field, the STEM strand of technology, incorporates computer technology. The Data Processing (DP) program, running from 1974 through 1992, changed its title to Applied Computer Technology (ACT) in 1992, as personal computers (PCs) continued to grow in popularity and function, replacing mainframe computers. The combined Data Processing (DP) and Applied Computer Technology (ACT) programs have been graduating students for 43 years, from 1974 to 2017, and will continue into the future.

Early in this era of curriculum development and expansion, the Vestibule Program, originally designed to better prepare students for the rigor of coursework in a degree program offered by one of the other colleges of RIT, was replaced by a pre-baccalaureate (pre-bacc) experience. A new pre-technical program (pre-tech) was also developed for students who aspired to degrees offered by NTID. Students who demonstrated talent and interest in certain technical programs, but did not have all the necessary knowledge to begin NTID's technical programs of study, were required to complete a pre-technical year. Pre-technical programs helped students build basic skills in English, general education, mathematics and science before beginning their technical courses. Programs that did not have pre-technical years would incorporate basic mathematics, science and technical skills into their regular curricula.[10]

The pre-technical program was eventually replaced by the science and mathematics general-education requirements for all graduates, and additional science and mathematics courses were designed to satisfy the needs of specific degree programs at NTID. In total, 18 new STEM-related programs were established during this era of Curriculum or Bust. Again, these programs are visualized in Table 1.

STEM Takes Flight, 1978–2000

As shown on Table 1, nine STEM-related programs flourished during this 20-year span of NTID's history, many of them in the engineering strand of STEM, as well as one very popular program in the emerging field of computer technology. In 1992, as reliance on mainframe computers and data input gave way to reliance on PC computers and networking, the original Data Processing (DP) program modified its curriculum to address this advancing area of technology and changed its name to Applied Computer Technology (ACT). It is worthy of recognition that the Data Processing (DP) program was enrolling an enormous number of students in the first year of its program (upwards of 150 in the early years of the STEM Takes Flight era). During

this era, the impact of the German measles (or Rubella) epidemic resulted in increased enrollment at NTID, reaching a high of 1,319 in 1984, the peak year of the "Rubella Bulge".[11] Programs were functioning at full capacity, and resources were stretched to accommodate the increasing numbers of students arriving each fall.

By 1983, four AAS degree programs in the engineering strand of STEM—namely, Architectural Technology (ArchT), Civil Technology (CT), Electromechanical Technology (EMT) and Industrial Drafting Technology (IDT)—received accreditation from the Accreditation Board for Engineering and Technology, Inc. (ABET). Accreditation recognizes the high standards of program quality provided to NTID students and an expected level of rigor. Credits earned in an accredited AAS degree program tend to be more transferable to continued study in a baccalaureate degree program in a related field and may support graduates in employment, promotions, and salary increases, according to the 1994–1995 *RIT Undergraduate Bulletin*.

According to the 1990–1991 RIT undergraduate bulletin, the Optical Finishing Technology Program (OFT) also received accreditation by the Commission on Opticianry Accreditation in 1990, as did the Laboratory Science Technology (LST) program, by the American Chemical Society.

In 1987, the Industrial Drafting Technology Program (IDT) offered NTID's first STEM AOS degree, followed by the Optical Finishing Technology Program (OFT) in 1988. Presently, AOS degrees are offered in Applied Computer Technology (ACT), Laboratory Science Technology (LST), Computer Assisted Drafting Technology (CADT) and Computer-Integrated Machining Technology (CIMT) among STEM-related NTID programs. Certification at the AOS degree level permits students to enter their careers directly and is not necessarily designed for transfer into higher-level degree programs.

This era of STEM Takes Flight runs out of gas, so to speak, in the latter part of the 1990s due in part to several circumstances: the declining population of students now that the Rubella Bulge cohort had passed through the system, Congressional budget cuts, and reviews by accrediting bodies. During the end of each Summer Vestibule Program (SVP) in the 1990s, academic programs held informational events in the Street area of the Lyndon Baines Johnson (LBJ) building, and as the years of declining enrollment continued, the pressure to attract students during these activities increased. Faculty who recall those years refer to the term, critical mass, to describe the number of students enrolled in a program in order to maintain financial and logistic viability.

The U.S. Congress proposed a 10% budget reduction for NTID as a result of their "Republican Budget Revolution" during the 1990s, and as a result, 117 of NTID's 640 faculty and staff positions were eliminated over a two-year period.[12] During this time, the Middle States Association Commission on Higher Education conducted a formal accrediting process that involved a self-study by NTID as part of the commission's self-regulation and peer-review requirements.[13] Several technical programs were identified for discontinuance as a result of this self-study and the Commission's recommendations. The final outcome of this series of interrelated events was the discontinuance of the Medical Laboratory Program (MLT) in 1995 and Architectural Drafting (AD), Architectural Technology (ArchT), and Civil Technology (CT) in 1997, as well as Electromechanical Technology (EMT), Industrial Drafting (ID) and Industrial Drafting Technology (IDT) in 1998.

Thus ends the STEM Takes Flight era. Although the loss of so many programs with a viable and productive history was saddening, newly crafted and vibrant programs arose during the next era, STEM 2.0.

STEM 2.0, 2000–present

Technology has made significant advances since the millennium, which is the threshold of the STEM 2.0 era of NTID's STEM history, an era that encompasses most of the past two decades (2000–present).

In response to these rapid changes, the Applied Computer Technology (ACT) program offered a series of courses within its two-year curriculum that focused on more specific topics related to computer technology, with each series of focused courses called a "concentration." The very first concentration was Industrial Computer Electronics offered in the 1999–2000 academic year, followed by Computer Support and Introductory Programming the following year. By 2005, these concentrations were replaced by PC Technical Support, Networking & Cyber Security, and Web Development & Database concentrations. In 2013, the Web Development & Database concentration was retired, but the other two concentrations remain as natural spin-offs in the ever-expanding computer field.

One significant change in the scope and delivery of science, mathematics, and physics instruction occurred at the entry point of this STEM 2.0 era. Previously, science courses (followed by physics courses after the closure of the Physics Learning Center in the mid-1980s) were designed specifically to support individual technical programs. Those science courses were taught either as a component of a pre-tech program or they were an integral part of the program's credit requirements, thereby showing up in the program's course mask for degree attainment. Additionally, nine math courses were developed in the early 1980s as a progressive series of courses, with content ranging from entry-level college mathematics skills to calculus concepts. Students were placed in an appropriate level of math based on their performance on a math placement exam, and their progress through these courses was supported through the MLC.

The goal of new curriculum development efforts of the late 1990s was, in part, to replace the pre-tech program and MLC with strong and viable science, mathematics, and physics curricula offered by NTID. Curriculum Development Teams were established within the new NTID Center for Arts and Sciences to focus on the design and development of either math or science curricula. These new curricula were viewed as essential for student access and success in the various technical programs of study at the other colleges of RIT, as well as being critical to NTID's leadership role in the education of deaf and hard-of-hearing students in general.

Effective preparation in one or more of the basic scientific fields (physics, biology, and chemistry) had always been recognized as important to the success of technical programs in the college of NTID, as well as in other colleges of RIT. Additionally, general science literacy, defined as the basic knowledge and skills to communicate in science and technology, had become a serious national concern for all educators. Both content and intent goals were considered during the design of these curricula. Intent goals were related to critical understandings, general skills, attitudes, and values that students acquire in the course of studying science, that are essential to the development of scientific literacy and achieving success in college. Together with these broader needs, the new science curriculum content was also based on a thorough analysis of the specific science prerequisites of technical programs at NTID and the needs of career programs that previously did not have science prerequisites.

As a result of the times and educational foci, four levels of science courses were developed: Introductory, Fundamental, Intermediate, and Bridging. The Introductory level was designed to meet the needs of students arriving with minimal scientific knowledge, with the goal of preparing them to be successful in an upper-level course that would satisfy NTID's minimum general education requirements for graduation. The Fundamental courses were offered as general education courses that satisfied the NTID graduation requirement for non-science majors and provided for the development of general scientific literacy. The Intermediate courses satisfied the specific scientific concepts and skills necessary for student success in their NTID technical programs of study, whereas Bridging level courses were designed to satisfy the general education requirement of other colleges of RIT as a result of collaborative efforts.

This newly revised science and mathematics curriculum closely followed the spirit of the NTID Strategic Plan initiated in 1991. Two of the five goals of the new science curriculum related directly to identified STEM qualities: "Understand the role of science in solving the problems of society," and "Pursue life-long science learning in today's changing and technology-dependent society."

After the onset of the STEM 2.0 era, eight new technical programs were established, including Computer-Integrated Machining Technology (CIMT), which was established in 1997 at the very end of the previous era. Two programs, Applied Optical Technology (AOT) and Automation Technologies (AT), established early in this era, were discontinued in less than a decade. The precision-optics component of AOT was transferred to CIMT as an elective for a short duration. The Automation Technologies Program underwent program screening during the conversion process that transformed RIT's quarter system to the present semes-

ter system in 2013, and as a result of this review, the metrics required for program continuance were determined to be insufficient.

Six of the seven current STEM-related technical programs arose during this most recent era, the seventh being Applied Computer Technology (ACT), which has woven a continuous thread of computer-based technology instruction over several decades. An important feature of many programs present in STEM 2.0 is the establishment of articulation agreements with the other colleges of RIT. These articulations allow students who complete many of the NTID technical associate (AAS or AS) programs to enroll in baccalaureate degree programs and receive credit for much of their NTID coursework. In essence, these degrees can serve a dual purpose, where a graduate is well-trained to perform on the job and also as transfer degrees (sometimes in the form of +2 or +3 program masks).

Current Programs

The process of discovery and innovation in STEM fields often involves building upon the discoveries and accomplishments of others. That has also been the case for the development of STEM programs at NTID; all of the programs mentioned in the history of STEM programs have helped to pave the way for the current STEM program offerings at NTID. And in the true spirit of evolution, these current programs will undoubtedly transform and give way to newer programs that meet the needs of the workforce well into the future. These current programs, as of the writing of this chapter, conclude the STEM 2.0 era.

In line with RIT's recognized excellence in applied learning and career preparation, NTID's programs of today work in concert with the needs of industry. As with most technical programs, NTID's current programs tend to rely heavily on industrial partnerships in order to allow for a collaborative flow of information between the two entities. Industry can also provide advisement related to curriculum modifications, equipment acquisitions, career counseling, the establishment of co-op positions, and permanent employment opportunities. Academia's collaboration with industry for the ultimate benefit of student learning is brought full circle, as industry can benefit from better-prepared graduates entering their workforce.

As with other programs at NTID, co-ops are a requirement for graduation in the STEM programs. Along with program faculty, NTID's Center on Employment (NCE) helps students to secure meaningful co-ops, from which students often return with improved confidence in both their technical and professional social skills.

The Laboratory Science Technology (LST) program, established in 2001, is the current science program at NTID. It was developed primarily from an industry perspective and prepares deaf and hard-of-hearing students for employment as laboratory technicians. The program's foundation includes course sequences in Chemistry (Fundamental, Analytical and Organic/Biochemistry), Biology (including Biotechnology) and Instrumental Analysis. A flagship of the program is state-of-the-art classroom and research instrumentation laboratories.

The LST program awards AOS and AAS degrees, while also allowing for qualified students to transition to related baccalaureate programs. Graduates are prepared for work in a broad range of fields, including chemical, biological, biotechnical, pharmaceutical, environmental, forensic, industrial, and food analysis. LST students are well-trained to function in laboratory employment settings. Their program has focused on application and many hands-on experiences related to instrumental, volumetric, gravimetric, and biological techniques, as well as demonstrated proficiencies in general scientific "bench skills." Additional instructional emphasis has been placed on laboratory organization and safety, laboratory mathematics, technical writing, functioning as a member of a team, and critical thinking. The program was approved by the American Chemical Society's Chemical Technology Program Approval Service (CTPAS). The LST program has proven to be very popular, has experienced a very successful 16-year run, has some of the highest job-placement and degree-persistence rates at NTID, and is poised for continued success into the future.

The Applied Computer Technology (ACT) program is the only existing technical program that has followed the technology strand of STEM since sometime in the middle of the "Carpe Diem" era of NTID's early days, and its longevity is likely due to its ability to adapt. The program has kept up with technology changes, for example, by moving from mainframe computers with "dumb terminals" to personal computers (PCs) at the appropriate time. The program has also offered concentrations that match technology trends, established strategic-transfer agreements, and teaches an innovative capstone course.

Graduates can work as computer and network technicians, as well as computer support and network security specialists. Students can obtain AAS, AOS or AS degrees within the program. Offered through the same department at NTID, Mobile Application Development (MA) is a brand-new program that offers an AAS degree. It is taking advantage of the exponential increase in the use of mobile computing devices and is looking forward to placing its first cohort of graduates into much-needed technical careers in the workforce.

Keeping with one of RIT's greatest strengths, engineering maintains a significant presence at NTID. Two current programs, Computer-Integrated Machining Technology (CIMT) and Computer Aided Drafting Technology (CADT), have been longstanding staples of engineering technology programs offered at NTID.

CIMT students are trained in the precision machining industries and can pursue jobs in computer numerical control set-up, operation, and programming, as well as general machining, die- or mold-making, and precision optics manufacturing. The program, which offers AOS degrees, has historically boasted one of the highest co-op placement rates at NTID.

CADT students are trained for careers as drafters/technicians predominantly in the construction and architectural engineering industries, with foundations (no pun intended) in mathematics, building systems, construction regulation, site utilities, and engineering materials. The program offers AOS and AAS degrees for its students, and places an emphasis on computer-based two- and three-dimensional drawing. NTID's engineering department also offers two transfer degrees in Applied Mechanical Technology (AMT) and Civil Technology (CVTC). Students who complete these AAS programs can transition to RIT's College of Applied Science and Technology in Mechanical Engineering Technology or Manufacturing Engineering Technology (from the AMT program) and Civil Engineering Technology (from the CVTC program).

Science Programs (the "S" in STEM)
Medical Laboratory Technology (MLT) 1970–1995
Histologic Technician (HST) 1974–1992
Hematology Technician (HMT) 1974–1982
Microbiology Technician (MBT) 1974–1982
Clinical Chemistry Technician (CCT) 1974–1982
Laboratory Science Technology (LST) 2001–present

Technology-based Programs (the "T" in STEM)
Data Processing (DP) 1974–1992
Applied Computer Technology (ACT) 1992–present
    Concentrations (past):
        Industrial Computer Electronics
        Computer Support
        Introductory Programming
        Web Development and Database
    Concentrations (present):
        PC Technical Support
        Networking and Cyber Security
Mobile Application Development (MA) 2016–present

Engineering Programs (the "E" in STEM)
Architectural Drafting (AD) 1969–1998
Mechanical Drafting (MD) 1969–1974
Machine Tool Operations (MTO) 1969–1978
Electronics (E) 1970–1980
Numerical Controls (NC) 1974–1978

Industrial Drafting/ Industrial Drafting Technology (IDT)
   1974–1999
Manufacturing Processes/Manufacturing Processes Technology
   (MPT) 1978–1997
Architectural Technology (ArchT) 1975–1998
Civil Technology (CT) 1974–1998
Electromechanical Technology (EMT) 1974–1999
Optical Finishing Technology (OFT) 1975–2004
Applied Optical Technology (AOT) 2004–2012
Computer-Integrated Machining Technology (CIMT)
   1997–present
    Concentrations (past):
        Machining
        Precision Optics Manufacturing
Computer Aided Drafting Technology (CADT) 2001–present
Automation Technologies (AT) 2003–2012
    Concentrations (past):
        Applied Robotics
        Semiconductor Technology
Applied Mechanical Technology (AMT) 2007–present
Civil Technology (CVTC) 2015–present

Mathematics Instruction (the "M" in STEM)
Math Learning Center (MLC) 1970–1996
   Math courses and individualized instruction 1968–present
Physics Learning Center (PLC) 1970–1983
   Physics courses and individualized instruction 1968–present

Table 1. STEM programs.

Cross-Registered STEM Students

In addition to all of the programs mentioned that NTID offers, NTID students have long enrolled in STEM programs offered in the other colleges of RIT (which has been a recurring theme of this chapter). Students have enrolled in the Kate Gleason College of Engineering (KGCOE), College of Applied Science and Technology (CAST), College of Science (COS), B. Thomas Golisano College of Computing and Information Sciences (GCCIS), and more recently, the College of Health Sciences and Technology (CHST), Golisano Institute for Sustainability (GIS), and the School of Individualized Study (SOIS). As stated, the boundaries of STEM programs are not always easy to draw. For example, RIT's College of Liberal Arts offers a Psychology degree that is steeped in scientific and technical theory, as well as a science-rich concentration in Archeology. The College of Imaging Arts and Sciences has programs that emphasize science and technology. NTID-supported students have obtained either undergraduate or graduate degrees from all of these colleges or constituents of RIT, many of which also have focused co-op programs. NTID provides these students with access services in the classroom, academic support programs, job-placement programs, and audiology services, among others.

The types of degrees and programs that have been offered by the other colleges of RIT is too long to list, but NTID-supported students have obtained many of these degrees over the years. Students in the STEM programs at CAST learn applied technical and engineering concepts related to cutting-edge technology. Current STEM programs at CAST include engineering technologies; environmental sustainability, health and safety; and packaging sciences. Computer-science and information-technology programs at RIT are currently housed in the GCCIS, which has nationally ranked programs. These students are trained in constantly changing computer and information technologies, including database development, game development, network/systems administration, programming, and software engineering, to name but a few fields of study.

KGCOE is also nationally recognized. It trains engineers to solve many of the world's problems. These students major in chemical, electrical, and mechanical engineering, to say nothing of the many other specialized forms of engineering offered. RIT's COS offers degrees in the mathematical sciences, imaging and color sciences, chemistry and material sciences, and life sciences. And within COS, the School of Physics and Astronomy has recently been making waves (excuse the pun) as a part of the international 2016 news story related to the discovery of gravitational waves.

CHST is RIT's newest college and is working to satisfy the need for trained workers in the healthcare fields. CHST undergraduate students major in biomedical sciences, sonography, nutrition, and exercise science. The new SOIS had its start in earlier renditions within CAST, but is now its own school. Along with faculty advisors, students are able to tailor degrees to fit their needs and expand beyond a single program of study. Students in the exciting new GIS are able to pursue graduate degrees in sustainable architecture, sustainable systems, and sustainability.

RIT has demonstrated a real commitment to the inclusion of deaf and hard-of-hearing students on campus. In addition to all of the support services provided to students in the classroom, faculty members who teach in the other colleges of RIT have access to resources that can support the learning experiences of deaf and hard-of-hearing students enrolled in their courses. The RIT American Sign Language & Deaf Studies Community Center (RADSCC) is a centrally located space that was established in 2010 to allow RIT-wide faculty, staff, and students to interact and learn about ASL and Deaf culture. Among many other

functions, the center provides resources for RIT faculty to help improve the classroom experience for NTID-supported students.

Likewise, DeafTEC, an NSF-funded Center of Excellence located at NTID, is a clearinghouse of information related to teaching deaf and hard-of-hearing students. DeafTEC has the added feature of promoting specifically STEM education and employment. Before DeafTEC, Project Access was a program supported by the Department of Education designed to improve the educational experiences of deaf and hard-of-hearing students in classrooms with their hearing peers. Cross-registered students have benefited from RIT's commitment to their success and have been earning degrees from the other colleges of RIT throughout NTID's history.

A Word on Student Involvement in Research at NTID

True for other disciplines at NTID as well, the STEM offerings have been involving students in exciting research projects. Through involvement in research, students have unique opportunities to learn discipline-specific information, contribute to the advancement of their fields, disseminate technical information, take ownership of their original work, and have fun working on projects that are often logistically prohibitive in the traditional classroom setting.[14, 15, 16]

For students at the associate degree level, these student-centered efforts to conduct original investigations that help to promote student learning while contributing to the scholarship of the discipline are often scarce.[17] Through small-group or individualized interactions, our faculty members are able to advance their scholarly research, provide substantial student learning opportunities while teaching beyond the time limitations of a typical course, and integrate teaching and research efforts.

Although some NTID-supported students conduct research while they are in graduate and baccalaureate courses, many of the student-centered research initiatives at NTID have the additional goal of involving early undergraduate (1st and 2nd year students) and associate-degree-level deaf and hard-of-hearing students. Those students can present a challenge to work with for various reasons, such as the short length of their academic program, the varying level of academic preparation, and

How to Educate an Interpreter
50 Years of Interpreter Education

Dr. Linda Siple and Dr. T. Alan Hurwitz

The primary mission of NTID is to provide deaf students with an outstanding state-of-the-art technical and professional education. Additionally, NTID has a secondary mission to prepare professionals to work in fields related to serving individuals who are deaf and hard-of-hearing. This chapter discusses NTID's evolving and ongoing commitment to the preparation of professional ASL-English interpreters to facilitate communication between deaf and hard-of-hearing individuals and their hearing counterparts.

The early interpreters on campus were teachers of deaf students, children or siblings of deaf individuals, and religious workers or social workers who worked with deaf people. There was no formal interpreter education program—they learned by doing. In the late 1960s when NTID was established, the demand for interpreters quickly overwhelmed this meager supply. NTID was faced with a crisis of resources and had to respond with a creative solution. Dr. D. Robert Frisina, NTID's first director, recalled, "What better source of interpreters than RIT hearing students well versed in the technologies in which the deaf students were engaged?"[1] No one is certain who came up with the original idea to train RIT hearing students to be sign language interpreters, but that idea was the first step in an amazing journey.

I never met a deaf person until the fall of 1972 at RIT; I arrived on campus and was assigned to the third floor of Kate Gleason Hall. I remember walking down the hall to my room and feeling shocked

that many of the students on my floor were deaf. Many months later I learned that I had been randomly assigned to an experimental house that was half deaf and half hearing; every other room had two deaf students in it. Someone at NTID wanted to study the effects of having deaf students on campus and how hearing students would react.

At that time, the dorms didn't have any adaptive equipment for deaf students. There were no doorbell lights, no fire-alert strobes, no video relay centers, no cell phones, no personal computers. Deaf students had to depend on their hearing peers. Most of the hearing students on my floor quickly learned basic sign during the first few days. Over time, several of us took a real interest and regularly interacted with deaf students and learned enough sign to make phone calls for them. Five hearing students from my floor, including myself, applied for and were selected for the summer interpreter program to become student interpreters. The program only accepted 15 RIT students, so having deaf and hearing students live together had a very positive impact.

— Linda Siple[2]

Interpreting education at NTID started in the summer of 1969. The original program was called the Summer Interpreter Training Program. However, it became more commonly known as the Basic Interpreter Training Program (BITP). The BITP instruction,

Dr. Linda Siple

common for interpreters to become so proficient in such a short time of study.[3]

The BITP was a great success because it was cultural immersion. Not only did the hearing students experience formal classroom instruction, but every NTID student also became actively involved in the student interpreters' education and induction into Deaf culture.

The interpreting program ran simultaneously with NTID's Summer Vestibule Program (SVP). The interpreting students worked as Resident Advisors (RAs) and Program Directors (PDs) for the SVP students, as well as attending interpreter training classes, Monday through Friday, 9:00 to 5:00.

When I was in the summer interpreter program in 1972, and I was a Program Director, I would plan a variety of social events like movies, midnight broom hockey and special speakers and, because there were limited interpreting services at night, I would interpret. Also, frequently there would be a line of students at my door for interpreted phone calls late into the night. We were signing or interpreting 24/7. I even remember dreaming in sign language.

— Linda Siple[4]

In 1968, James Stangarone joined NTID as the Coordinator for Interpreting Services, and was responsible for the BITP. He pointed out that training in the field of interpreting was limited. Only one of the full-time interpreters on staff at the time had received any kind of formal training.[5] The student interpreters were young, but with training, they were able to provide a needed service. They worked as many as 15 hours a week interpreting in classrooms and then spent extra hours interpreting at RIT sporting events, student meetings, and dorm activities, and making phone calls for deaf students. It was physically hard work with long hours, but RIT students saw it as a very unique and satisfying job. A student interpreter who was majoring in biology received the rare opportunity to experience a photography lab, a business law class, and a social work seminar, all in the same week. The job was also financially

coupled with the NTID environment of several hundred deaf and hard-of-hearing students, was successful in producing a steady stream of home-grown interpreters who became remarkably competent in a short period of time, as described in this scene from the early days of the program:

Deaf professionals visiting the RIT campus immediately noticed the impact of the student interpreters. At one of the National Advisory Group meetings, Frank Sullivan and Robert Sanderson, two distinguished leaders in the Deaf community, watched an RIT hearing student interpret. During a break, they asked her if her parents were deaf. She told them they were not. Sullivan then asked her where she had learned to sign and she responded, "Here".

"'What do you mean – here?" he inquired.

She explained that she was an RIT student and had been trained to interpret at NTID. Sullivan and Sanderson sat there in utter disbelief. It was not rewarding. In 1970, the minimum wage was $1.60 per hour, but a student interpreter was paid $5.50 per hour. It was the highest-paid student position on campus!

Typically, the BITP received 60 to 70 applications for 15 to 20 slots. As Nowell and Stuckless reported in 1974, the RIT hearing students who were selected to attend the interpreting program were interviewed by both NTID faculty and deaf students.[6] They were looking for students who best satisfied the following criteria:

- Ability to sign before entering the program
- High motivation
- Ability to work well with others
- Quick mind/physically fit
- Representative of a variety of majors

The curriculum involved several different courses:

- Basic principles of interpreting
- Expression and the non-verbal aspects of interpreting
- Sign language vocabulary
- Comprehending sign language and reverse interpreting (known today as ASL-to-English interpretation)
- Basic knowledge about audiology, psycho-social aspects of deafness, educational practices for the deaf, speech development, and many other areas related to deafness
- Practice sessions

In their summary of the BITP, Nowell and Stuckless stressed that a short-term training program was insufficient to produce a skilled interpreter. "True skill in interpreting only comes with much experience. The greatest benefit for an interpreter, and for the deaf people for whom he is interpreting, is the availability of ongoing training."[7]

Marjorie Clere, a child of deaf parents and RID-certified (Registry of Interpreters for the Deaf) interpreter, was one of the lead instructors in the BITP from 1971 to 1975. Clere felt strongly that interpreters should be focusing on meaning. "A few persons entering the course were skeptical about learning [American Sign Language (ASL)]. They felt we should be teaching signed English. But now I think most of them feel that [ASL] is the best method when the major concern is meaning and communication."[8]

There were six RIT students in the first class of the BITP in 1969. Over the span of 19 years, the BITP awarded over 600 certificates of completion to students from across the United States and Canada. In 1972 and 1973, the program was expanded to include not only RIT students but also members of the Rochester community and students from the University of Massachusetts, Oberlin College, and Syracuse University. In 1976, Anna Witter-Merithew made several important additions: she changed the program name to the Basic Interpreter Training Program (BITP); provided tutoring to interpreting students; formalized the curriculum; added mock lectures for interpreting practice; weekly evaluations; and a performing-arts aspect. The BITP show was always a highlight for students and audiences alike. In 1978, the BITP graduated its largest class with 60 participants. In 1979 and 1980, in addition to the summer program, the BITP was offered during Winter quarter. The final class completed the BITP in the summer of 1988.

An important feeder program for the BITP was the "Free University," a program offered to students at night and held in the first floor of the RIT dorms. Originally, there were courses in learning how to play the guitar, photography, and sign language, among others, but over time, sign language became the most popular topic. By the mid-1970s, sign language was the only course offered. Michael Rizzolo became the director of "Free U," as it was commonly called, in 1976 after he attended the BITP as a student. Free U offered small-group instruction in basic sign and used the book *A Basic Course in Manual Communication,* published by the National Association of the Deaf (NAD).[9] At the time, this was the only opportunity for RIT students to take a course in sign language, and it was very popular with the Rochester community. Each quarter, Free U offered 15 to 20 classes of 6 to 8 students to accommodate all of the participants. The classes were taught by NTID students and student interpreters.

For the time period, the BITP was a great success in that hundreds of hearing individuals were exposed to ASL and Deaf culture and to the emerging career of sign language interpreting. A large percentage of students who attended the BITP went on to become full-time staff interpreters at NTID, and many of them are still working as interpreters on staff today. Additionally, many community graduates went on to interpret professionally or pursue other careers working with deaf and hard-of-hearing individuals (e.g., teachers of deaf students, counselors/social workers, medical personnel, audiologists, and speech/language pathologists). In the 1976 NTID *Annual Report*, the following was stated regarding a survey of the 1976 class: "It is significant to note that at least 68% of the trained interpreters are still employed in the field of deafness in some capacity."[10] In addition, the program employed many deaf and hard-of-hearing students to work as instructors and tutors, and for some of them, that experience led to a career as an ASL instructor.

Anna Witter-Merithew.

The idea of the student interpreter model was successful because the concept of interpretation in general was new to many deaf and hard-of-hearing students. They had no expectations regarding appropriate levels of interpreting skill or professionalism. This, coupled with the fact that the student interpreters were around the same age as the NTID students, created a strong alliance. As time passed, interpreting needs continued to grow as more and more deaf and hard-of-hearing students chose to attend NTID and then other colleges of RIT. Many deaf and hard-of-hearing students who used interpreters in high school came to NTID expecting more from the interpreters. Interpreters needed to develop more breadth and depth of knowledge, stronger language skills in ASL and English, and a deeper understanding of professionalism and ethical behavior. Thus, a short-term program became insufficient to prepare interpreters with the needed qualifications.

The demand for qualified interpreters was made more urgent by the passage of two federal laws: The Rehabilitation Act, Section 504, of 1973 and the Individuals with Disabilities Education Act (IDEA) of 1975. At this time, more than 8,000 children—born deaf as a result of a rubella epidemic between 1963 and 1964—created an overwhelming demand for interpreters as these children moved through K–12 and then into college during the 1980s.

In 1974, Dr. T. Alan Hurwitz assumed responsi-

bility for coordinating interpreting services and training interpreters, tutors, and note takers housed in the Office of Support Services. He made a decision that would change interpreter training at NTID. He hired Anna Witter-Merithew (Instructor, 1975–1980) to lead interpreting services, which included the BITP. In 1977, in response to the need for expanded training opportunities for interpreters, a decision was made to create an interpreter training department, separate from the Department of Interpreting Services. The Department of Support Services Education was established, chaired by Witter-Merithew and including Jeanne Wells (Assistant Professor, 1977–2009), Alice Beardsley (1968–1988) and several adjunct instructors who provided pre-service and in-service training to interpreters (McGill, 1980). In 1979, Jenna Cassell (Instructor, 1979–1981) and Linda Siple (Professor, 1979–2015) were hired.

A history of interpreter education at NTID would be incomplete without further discussion of Alice Beardsley. Beardsley was affectionately referred to as NTID's First Interpreter. Born hearing, Beardsley became profoundly deaf due to contracting measles and scarlet fever one month after her fifth birthday. She was enrolled at the Rochester School for the Deaf (RSD), where she learned the Rochester Method, which largely

Alice Beardsley leads interpreting students in their "morning exercises." This photo was taken on July 11, 1979, the day the space station Skylab fell to earth, so the participants are wearing paper plates with bull's-eyes drawn on them as hats.

consisted of fingerspelling words, rather than using signs. Later, she developed her ASL skills though her involvement in the Deaf community. Many years later, in adulthood, her hearing was surgically restored in one ear, which allowed her to interpret for many deaf and hard-of-hearing people in the Rochester community. In 1965, Beardsley served as the interpreter for the site-visit team that selected RIT as the host institution for NTID.

Once established, NTID hired Beardsley, where she served as a staff interpreter for more than 10 years.[11] A series of severe ear infections once again left Beardsley profoundly deaf; unable to interpret in the classroom, she moved to the Department of Support Services Education and started training interpreters. Those fortunate to have Beardsley as an instructor will remember her impish grin and lightning-fast fingerspelling developed when she learned the Rochester Method at RSD. Most memorable were "morning exercises" during the BITP, which Beardsley taught every day in the NTID quad at 8:00 a.m., accompanied by Barry Manilow songs. She loved a good prank and could take it as well as she gave it. One morning in the summer of 1977, Beardsley arrived to find a pile of papers and no students. The papers contained a variety of excuses explaining the students' absences (e.g., "Dear Alice

Beardsley, Please excuse Pat from exercise class. She has a hang nail. Signed, Pat's mother.")[12]

During this time, NTID made several important contributions to the field of interpreting and interpreting education. For example, in the late 1970s, a group of oral deaf individuals who were members of the Oral Deaf Adults Section (ODAS) of the Alexander Graham Bell Association for the Deaf (AGBAD) approached NTID with the expressed need to have trained oral interpreters. An oral interpreter, using silent lip movements, natural gestures and expression, reproduces what the speaker is saying to deaf or hard-of-hearing individuals who do not use sign language. The need for oral interpreters was particularly acute when the oral deaf individual was in a large group and needed to follow the conversation, such as in the classroom or a meeting.

Hurwitz, with Witter-Merithew, Stangarone, and faculty members Dr. Diane Castle and Marjorie Jacobs, proposed certification requirements for oral interpreters to representatives from the AGBAD, the National Association of the Deaf (NAD), and the Registry of Interpreters for the Deaf (RID) at a conference hosted by NTID. Shortly after the certification test was developed and approved, NTID hosted the first short-course to prepare and certify oral transliterators. Twenty sign language interpreters learned the specialized skill of oral transliteration and were certified by the RID. The curriculum was later packaged and disseminated to many interpreter training programs across the country.[13]

Another important contribution to the field of interpreter education was the establishment of a professional organization for interpreter educators. In 1979, Witter-Merithew and Hurwitz were instrumental in convincing NTID to co-sponsor a formal gathering of interpreter trainers from across the country at St. Paul Technical Vocational Institute (now called Saint Paul College). This meeting resulted in the establishment of the Conference of Interpreter Trainers (CIT). Siple served on the organizational board of CIT and maintained a published directory of all of the interpreter education programs in the United States and Canada from 1980 to 1988. The second meeting of the CIT was held at NTID in 1981, with Siple serving as conference chair.

In 1980, Witter-Merithew and Hurwitz wrote a new degree proposal that would establish an Associate

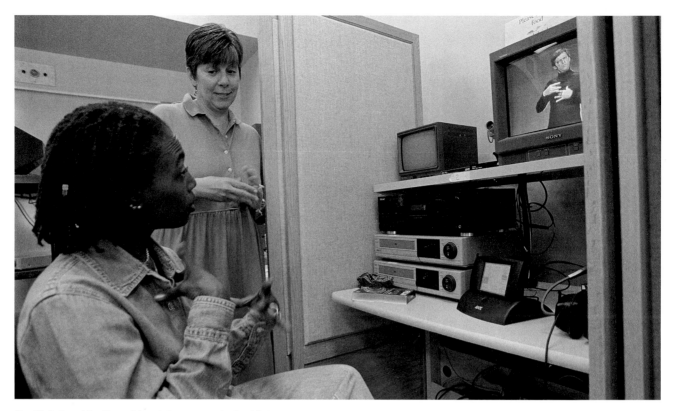

Dr. Christine Monikowski watches as a student interpreter practices in the sign language lab.

of Applied Science (AAS) degree in Educational Interpreting. The curriculum proposal was based on a growing need to train and educate interpreters to work in educational settings. This need came about as a result of Public Law 94–142, which was passed in 1975 to expand educational opportunities for students with disabilities, including deaf and hard-of-hearing students, in public schools. Also, at that time, there was a trend in offering AAS degree programs for interpreters in other colleges and universities across the United States.

NTID made a critical decision to focus on the preparation of interpreters in educational settings, particularly in K–12 and postsecondary education environments. Hurwitz and Witter-Merithew presented the curriculum proposal to various curriculum committees at NTID and RIT for their critique and endorsement. The proposal was subsequently presented to the RIT Faculty Senate (which eventually became Academic Senate); RIT academic administration, including the provost, vice presidents, and deans of other RIT colleges; and the

RIT Board of Trustees for their review and endorsement. Upon the Board of Trustees' approval, the proposal was submitted to the New York State Education Department (NYSED) for final approval and certification in 1981.

The AAS degree first appeared in the NTID 1982–1984 course catalog. The prerequisite for the program was "basic simultaneous communication competency." This meant the applicant needed to exhibit the ability to sign and speak at the same time, which would demonstrate signed English, not ASL. Looking back, one can only guess at the reasoning behind that decision, but it may be related to the scarcity of formal courses in ASL at the time. There were no courses formally identified as having ASL instruction as part of the content, although instructors from that time recall spending a great deal of time teaching ASL. In addition to coursework in interpreting and psycho-social aspects of deafness, students took "Principles of Tutoring and Notetaking" and "Mainstreaming". There was also a full course devoted to the ethics of interpreting, which was rare in any interpreting program at the time.

To prepare students sufficiently for entry to the program, all accepted students were required to attend a six-week intensive ASL experience the summer before entrance. The addition of the Pre-AAS Program outside of the AAS degree was necessitated by NYSED's requirement that associate degree programs be limited to no more than 60 semester credit-hours or 90 quarter credit-hours. The AAS degree program required 90 credits, making it impossible to incorporate the ASL experience into the curriculum.

NTID's attempt at offering the first degree for interpreters reflects a desire to professionalize interpreting, but also demonstrates a lack of understanding regarding the need to master language competency (i.e., ASL) before acquiring interpreting competency. At that time, the best interpreters were born into the field as children or siblings of deaf or hard-of-hearing individuals. There was little information or knowledge on how to educate students who didn't have a background in sign language, nor was there a clear job description in existence that could inform a formal curriculum.

The interpreting faculty members were pioneers, trying new and innovative approaches, and developing instructional and testing materials where none previously existed. As the faculty expanded their knowledge, the composition of the program also evolved. For example, the AAS degree eventually omitted course work in support services (e.g., tutoring and notetaking) and added credit-bearing coursework in ASL. However, not all of the changes were culturally appropriate by today's standards. In the 1982 – 1984 NTID course catalog, the title of the program was "AAS in Interpreting for the Hearing Impaired." Other terms that were used in earlier years evolved over time. For example, "reverse interpreting" came to mean "ASL-to-English interpretation", and "PSE (pidgin signed English)" came to mean "Signed English".

From 1981 to 1986, Joseph Avery was chair of the Department of Support Services Education. Under his leadership, the department completed the establishment of the AAS degree program. In 1985, Hurwitz and Avery co-chaired the National Task Force on Educational Interpreting, with representatives from various parts of the country. The purpose of the Task Force was to study

Joseph Avery

and investigate the growing need to formalize programs for the preparation of educational interpreters and to define the parameters that would enable educational interpreters to meet the requirements for employment in school systems.

The Task Force produced a report that was shared with the US Department of Education and state education departments. Among a number of recommendations in the report was the enhancement of academic rigor and certification requirements, including a baccalaureate degree for educational interpreters. These recommendations were supported by the RID.[14] In 1994, following the report of the National Task Force, a New York Advisory Committee on Educational Interpreting led by Avery was formed. Over a period of three years the Advisory Committee formulated the New York State Guidelines for Educational Interpreters, which was edited by Avery and Harry Karpinski (former employee of the Board of Cooperative Educational Services). Based on the national guidelines, many schools in several states followed in developing their own guidelines.

RIT/NTID continued to experience a high demand for interpreting services. Throughout the 1980s, each year of the NTID Annual Report (1980 to 1989) showed a steady increase in interpreting hours. In 1987, the Annual Report stated that NTID provided over 57,000 hours of interpreting services. Unfortunately, the high demand for interpreting came with consequences. An increasing number of working interpreters were experiencing physical injuries related to interpreting. "Repetitive motion injury (RMI) refers to a variety of inflammations of the hands, arms, neck, and shoulders caused by repeated hand and arm motions such as those required for educational interpreting."[15] It was not uncommon for classroom interpreters to be interpreting 30 or more hours per week, needing to keep up with highly technical lectures that might exceed 200 words per minute. NTID established a task force to investigate how to address the crisis. As a result, interpreting hours were reduced, breaks were built into schedules, and classes longer than an hour were interpreted by a team of two interpreters.[16]

The RMI crisis, and the ensuing modifications to working conditions, created a shift in how interpreters were educated. Students now needed to learn how to work with another interpreter to "team" an assignment. The concept of teaming was new to interpreters and required a different approach to the work—being in the "hot seat" every 15–20 minutes, yet paying attention, assisting, and supporting when in the "cold seat". Interpreting students needed to learn how to advocate for improved working conditions, recognize the onset of a repetitive motion injury, understand the ins and outs of seeking medical attention, and how to maintain physical stamina.[17]

As the profession of sign language interpreter was taking shape, so was the profession of the interpreter educator. Interpreter educators were acquiring advanced degrees in areas such as linguistics, intercultural communication, and translation theory. Across the country, departments of interpreter training were changing their names to "interpreter education", and moving from departments of communication disorders to departments of modern languages. In addition, short-term certificate programs were being replaced by associate and/or baccalaureate level programs.

From 1986 to 1996, Gary Mowl was chairperson of NTID's Department of Support Services Education (DSSE). He managed the AAS degree program and was instrumental in establishing the Summer Institute, which for several years provided course work for working interpreters. Lynn Finton (Professor, 1982–present) was the coordinator for the Summer Institute and taught several courses. In 1991, the department was renamed Center for Sign Language and Interpreter Education when DSSE merged with the Department of Sign Communication. The blending of faculty from both ASL instruction and interpreting education had a very positive and constructive influence on the development of curriculum and the quality of graduates. With the increase in personnel and programs, Mowl appointed William Newell (former Chair of Sign Communication) as Curriculum Coordinator for ASL and Siple as Curriculum Coordinator for Interpreting Education.

By the late 1980s, interpreter educators at NTID knew that students were not graduating with sufficient preparation. All of the changes to the AAS degree had maxed out the allowable number of credits permitted by the New York State Education Department. The logical next step was to undertake a proposal for a four-year baccalaureate degree—a more-than-10-year process, which would prove to be Herculean in scope. In 1993, the NTID Strategic Planning Committee granted permission to move forward with the development of a BS degree program in interpreting. In addition, they recommended the expansion of the AAS degree program from 60 to 100 students. This recommendation created an immense challenge for Mowl. He needed to hire many new staff members, find additional space, and expand and upgrade the interpreting audio/video lab facility, which is central to the preparation of sign language interpreters.

The establishment of a Bachelor of Science (BS) in interpreting was not an easy task for many reasons. At the time, NTID was designed to grant degrees only at the diploma, certificate, and associate levels. The thinking was that once deaf students completed their associate degree at NTID, they would transfer to RIT to complete a baccalaureate degree. The RIT administration decided that NTID should not duplicate BS degrees offered in other departments. However, they could propose a BS degree in an area not offered at RIT, and hearing students would be permitted to enroll. It was then agreed that NTID would be the best college to offer a BS degree for interpreters, which meant the curriculum had to meet NYSED's rigorous standards.

At the time, all proposed degree programs had to undergo a feasibility study to examine if the proposed degree was warranted, and whether there was a job market for graduates with a BS in interpreting. The design and content of the feasibility study was controlled by the NTID Curriculum Committee (NCC). Under the leadership of Mowl, Siple authored the feasibility study, which showed that there was a high demand for qualified interpreters and that the job outlook was very positive. Deaf people were attending college in record numbers, then entering highly technical and professional fields. Many were advancing into supervisory/management roles in the workplace and required interpreters with advanced skills. In addition, the RID passed a resolution that, starting in 2012, all candidates for certification must have a baccalaureate degree. Despite this support, the feasibility study was not accepted, thus denying approval to move ahead to a curriculum proposal. There was also great skepticism that there would be enough content to fill a four-year degree program in interpreting. Nevertheless, the faculty was not dissuaded, and they persisted with several iterations of the feasibility study.

In 1990, the Americans with Disabilities Act (ADA) was passed into law. This law was designed to improve accessibility for all disabled groups. For deaf and hard-of-hearing individuals, it significantly improved accessibility in employment, public service agencies, public facilities, and telecommunications. The latter grew to have the greatest impact on demand for interpreters. The ADA made way for the establishment of video relay service centers across the country, allowing deaf and hard-of-hearing individuals to have visual access to telephones. As a result of the enormous popularity of video relay services, there was a significant increase in the number of video relay centers. These centers employed large numbers of interpreters that would otherwise be working in the areas of employment, education, and/or health care—thus adding to the high demand for skilled interpreters and creating, yet again, another shortage of qualified interpreters.

After several years and numerous failed attempts to seek the approval of the NCC, the feasibility study was approved, and the design of a curriculum proposal could proceed, but not as a four-year degree. The proposal had to be a 2+2 program, and the additional two years had to focus on managerial skills. The NTID administration wanted a completely unique degree, thus pairing interpreting with management skills. However, the interpreting faculty knew that two years was grossly insufficient to prepare a competent entry-level interpreter. The interpreting faculty had to work against the misperception that the interpreting process was simply "message in and message out"—a verbatim process—and that all one needed to be competent was a sufficiently large sign vocabulary. After more than 10 years of persistence, the faculty finally convinced the NTID administration and the NCC that it was more appropriate to have a 2+2 degree that focused on ASL and interpreting skills. A curriculum proposal was developed and submitted to the year-long approval process.

From 1996 to 1999, Marilyn Mitchell (Associate Professor, 1977–2008) became Acting Chair for the newly named Department of ASL and Interpreting Education (ASLIE). Prior to serving as Chair, Mitchell taught in the interpreting program. In 2001, Mitchell was appointed Director for the New York State Board of Regents, SED Special Grant for the Preparation of Educational Interpreters in the State of New York, which was housed at NTID, where she served for eight years before retiring. The grant program provided in-service education to hundreds of working interpreters throughout the state.

From January to December of 1999, Siple took on the role of Acting Chairperson as the department searched for a permanent chair. Dr. Rico Peterson became the Chairperson of ASLIE from 2000 to 2005, and the 2+2 BS degree received official approval from NYSED in 2000. Under Peterson's leadership, the first

Student interpreter Gabrielle Nocciolino practices in the updated sign language lab.

service learning program in interpreter education was created. The service learning program involved volunteer work in the Deaf community, and interpreting students then reflected on their experiences as they learned about Deaf culture. Drs. Peterson and Christine Monikowski (Professor, 1993–present) created and incorporated a service learning course sequence into the BS degree curriculum, and presented the service learning program to a meeting of the CIT conference, along with a panel of students from the ASLIE program. This model program was subsequently adopted by interpreter education programs at several institutions, including the University of Arizona and the University of Northern Florida.

The 2+2 BS degree program ran from 2000 to 2008. After a few years, it was found to be difficult to recruit students, given the design. Potential applicants were concerned about the 2+2 model because graduates of the AAS program were not guaranteed a seat in the upper division BS degree. In 2005, ASLIE, under the leadership of Donna Gustina (Associate Professor, 2005–2009) and Siple, set about to formally propose modifications and establish a four-year, BS degree in ASL-English Interpretation and to modify the existing AAS degree. The interpreting faculty was fully committed to developing an outstanding curriculum, and in 2008, the four-year BS degree in ASL-English Interpretation was approved by NYSED. Since its inception, the BS degree has graduated more than 300 students and maintains a 95% employment rate.

A major challenge for ASLIE in running the four-year BS degree program was the provision of supplemental services required in a degree program, such as management and maintenance of the interpreting labs, enrollment management, academic counseling, and internship placement. The departments at NTID that house degree programs for deaf and hard-of-hearing students have affiliated departments that provide these services. However, the faculty in ASLIE had to not only provide instruction, but also provide all of the auxiliary services. Fortunately, ASLIE was given additional support positions, and Richard Smith (Curriculum Support Coordinator, 2000–present), Veronika Talbot (Academic/Personal Counselor, 2009–present), and Jackie Schertz (Practicum Coordinator, 2008–present) were hired. In addition, NTID's Department of Enrollment Management, headed by Scott Hooker, took over enrollment management. Hooker and the recruiters work closely with Finton, who was appointed Program Director in 2014. The interpreting program remains competitive, with an average of 200 applications for 50 accepted students. In addition, the program maintains a high retention rate, due to a careful screening process, which selects the right students with the right set of skills.

As part of the four-year BS degree program, students complete six courses in ASL/Deaf culture, three courses in interpreting foundation skills, eight courses in interpretation, an interpreting ethics course, a two-semester internship, and a research capstone course, along with extensive liberal arts and science coursework. Students also complete two professional electives, which are courses that focus on specialized interpreting skills above and beyond the required coursework. The following is a sample of courses currently offered and the instructor/developer:

- Introduction to Legal Interpreting - Jennifer Gravitz, Esq. (NTID Liberal Studies)
- Introduction to Health Care Interpreting & Mental Health Interpreting - Kathy Miraglia (ASLIE Lecturer)
- Introduction to Cued Speech & CS Transliterating - Jill Burress, (NTID Speech Pathologist)

- K–12, Elementary Interpreting & Secondary Interpreting - K. Williams (ASLIE Senior Lecturer)
- Interpreting Frozen and Literary Texts - Dr. Jason Listman (ASLIE Associate Professor)
- Deaf-Blind Interpreting - Jennifer Briggs (ASLIE Lecturer)
- Community Interpreting - Sarah Schiffeler (ASLIE Adjunct Lecturer)

This aspect of the BS degree also allows for the development of "special topics" courses, which may eventually become permanent course offerings. For example, Daniel Maffia (ASLIE Lecturer) designed and taught a special topics course that focuses on video relay interpreting.

BS interpreting students, like all RIT students, may also participate in study-abroad programs. However, there is a uniquely-designed program that affords students the opportunity to experience interpreting and Deaf culture in the Netherlands. In 2009, Drs. Marc Marschark and Alan Hurwitz, as President and Dean of NTID, developed an agreement with the Hogeschool Utrecht to establish an interpreting student and faculty exchange program. The program allows ASLIE to send eight interpreting students to the Hogeschool for five weeks in May and June and then, during fall semester, the Hogeschool sends four interpreting students to NTID for ten weeks.

While at the Hogeschool, the NTID interpreting students learn NGT (Dutch Sign Language), Dutch as a spoken language, Deaf culture in the Netherlands, interpreting for the Deaf-Blind, breathing and posture awareness, and interpreting in medical and welfare settings, and they receive weekly supervision. While at NTID, the Dutch interpreting students live in the NTID dorms and take courses in ASL, American Deaf culture, interpretation, and performing arts, and they receive weekly supervision.

The program was originally coordinated by Siple. Sandra Bradley (Senior Lecturer, 2007– present) took over in 2015. These programs have benefited both schools in that the interpreting students experience personal growth and broaden perspectives on the world. As part of this agreement, several faculty members from

Dr. Gerald Bateman, professor and director of the MSSE program.

need for excellent teachers of deaf students in junior and secondary school. The report concluded that "we have a unique set of resources and expertise on which to structure a rigorous and stimulating program."[2] The proposed program supported NTID's dedication to "offer[ing] educational programs that prepare individuals for careers related to working with deaf people." In the spirit of the Strategic Plan (1992) and the success of JESP, K–12 teacher preparation had found its place in NTID's secondary mission.[3]

The feasibility committee contacted a number of leaders in the field, including an administrator from the New York State Education Department (NYSED), and their comments emphasized a shortage of teachers of deaf and hard-of-hearing students and a long-standing need for content teachers at the secondary level. The committee was given the green light to develop a curriculum proposal.

In 1994, the curriculum proposal for the Master of Science program in Secondary Education of Students who are Deaf or Hard of Hearing (MSSE) was submitted to the NTID Curriculum Committee, RIT Graduate Council, RIT Policy Council, Provost, President, and RIT Board of Trustees Education Committee and was approved by all. Dr. Gerald C. Bateman was appointed

Interim Director of the new graduate program. In the meantime, the program was awarded a five-year grant from the U.S. Department of Education to provide tuition support to incoming students. Because the program had not been registered by NYSED, students could not be matriculated into a degree-bearing program.

For the first year (1994–1995), the U.S. Department of Education approved the MSSE program to sponsor a one-year special program to support selected students to earn additional credits toward their 36 semester credits in a content area (English, biology, chemistry, earth science, physics, mathematics, and social studies). Thirteen students participated in this program. Of those, six matriculated into the program the following year.

U.S. Department of Education Grants

Starting in its first year, the MSSE program has been awarded four grants for a total of $4,150,485 from the U.S. Department of Education. The four grant projects are:

- An Enrollment Incentive Plan to Increase the Number and Quality of Certified Secondary Teachers of Students Who Are Deaf or Hard of Hearing (1994–1999)
- Meeting the State and National Need to Increase the Number and Quality of Dually Certified Secondary Teachers of Students Who Are Deaf or Hard of Hearing (1999–2002)
- Meeting the State and National Need to Increase the Number and Quality of Dually Certified Secondary Teachers of Students Who are Deaf or Hard of Hearing Through Partnerships with Rochester, New York-Area Schools (2002–2008)
- An Accountability Initiative with Special Emphasis on Recruitment of STEM and Minority Teachers of Deaf and Hard-of-Hearing Students (2011–2016)

Dual Certification

In 1995, the curriculum proposal for MSSE was approved, and the program was registered by NYSED. Importantly, NTID would henceforth be able to award the master's degree and endorse students to be dually certified to teach deaf and hard-hearing students, grades K–12, and one or more of the following secondary-level content

Heather Maltzan Mooney, a 2002 graduate of the program, works with a student at the Rochester School for the Deaf.

areas (grades 7–12): English language arts, social studies, mathematics, biology, chemistry, earth science and physics (American Sign Language was added in 2001). The concept of dual certification established NTID as a model for teacher preparation in deaf education. Research with deaf students, their teachers, and school administrators has shown that content expertise is the most important characteristic of effective teachers.

MSSE opened in September 1995 with seven full-time students and two part-time students (all seven full-time students graduated in May 1997). Twenty-four NTID faculty members were appointed to teach courses in the program, including faculty members from the NTID research department. In 1996, Dr. Bateman was appointed as the director of the MSSE program. JESP was de-registered by NYSED and, in 1997, MSSE was granted program approval by the Council on Education of the Deaf (CED), an organization sponsored by major national organizations dedicated to quality education for all deaf and hard-of-hearing students.

Program Accreditation
Along with approval by CED, all teacher preparation programs had to demonstrate how they could address the new requirements set by NYSED. The MSSE

program was re-registered by NYSED in 2001. The program was also required to earn national accreditation by the Teacher Education Accreditation Council (TEAC). The five-year accreditation was granted in 2007 after a rigorous self-study and audit. After that, TEAC and the National Council for Accreditation of Teacher Education (NCATE) merged into one national agency called the Council for the Accreditation of Educator Preparation (CAEP), which affected the next round of accreditation.

To renew accreditation in 2012, MSSE went through a program audit and earned seven-year accreditation (2013–2020). In the meantime, the Council on Education of the Deaf granted the re-approval (2014–2019). To receive these recognitions, MSSE needed to affirm that its students were being prepared as "qualified, competent, and caring" (TEAC) teachers, and also "assure quality and support continuous improvement to strengthen P–12 student learning" (CAEP).

The MSSE program has emphasized a broad range of environments, mainstream, day and residential programs, issues related to inclusion and working with deaf and hard-of-hearing students with other disabilities. Evidence-based instruction is especially emphasized through research studies on effective teaching by the MSSE faculty and our graduate students who worked as research assistants. Faculty and graduate assistants have participated and presented at a variety of local, national and international conferences such as:

- Council of American Instructors of the Deaf (CAID)
- National Association of the Deaf (NAD)
- National Deaf Education Conference (NDEC)
- Association of College Educators of the Deaf and Hard of Hearing (ACEDHH)
- National Science Teachers Association (NSTA)
- National Council of Teachers of Mathematics (NCTM)
- Postsecondary Education Programs Network (PEPNET)
- International Conference of Education of the Deaf (ICED)

Instructional Innovations

To promote the use of innovative technology in the MSSE program, Dr. Bateman worked with Drs. Christopher Kurz and Harry Lang in developing the first library of veteran teacher videos (VETFLIX), a Microteaching program, remote student teaching observations and the Structured Online Academic Reading (SOAR) approach. Technical Sign Language lexicons were also developed online for science, mathematics and social studies terms.

New York State requires teacher candidates in graduate teacher education programs to observe experienced teachers for 100 hours. This "field experience" is partially satisfied during student teaching and visits to local schools such as Rochester School for the Deaf and Board of Cooperative Educational Services (BOCES). VETFLIX has emphasized an innovative approach to providing resources to the program faculty for demonstrating "best practices" in teaching. The VETFLIX online library includes a variety of teaching episodes from real classrooms in K–12 science, mathematics, social studies and English. Other best practices, such as the use of teacher aides with deaf students having secondary disabilities, are also included in the library. In addition, teleconferencing allowed for occasional discussions between MSSE students and groups of experienced teachers in schools serving deaf students.

Along with a variety of workshops and courses, MSSE introduced the innovative concept of "Microteaching," where graduate students present simulated lessons to a small group of deaf student actors trained to provide constructive feedback and suggestions. Working closely with the NTID Performing Arts Program, the deaf student actors were trained in improvisation to serve as elementary or secondary students during the microteaching lessons. Microteaching benefited MSSE students by allowing them to experiment with teaching strategies, technology devices, and language delivery. Pre- and post-measures of self-efficacy indicated that the teacher candidates were developing significantly more confidence in their ability to teach through the microteaching experiences.

Educational experts project that much of future postsecondary education will be online. MSSE has experimented with a variety of online courses, including its "History of Deaf Educational Thought and Practice," "Psychology and Human Development" and "Special Education in the Social Context." It has successfully offered its "Educational and Cultural Diversity" course online since 2006. As mentioned earlier, MSSE has experimented with different forms of remote teaching observation, in which teacher candidates who are practice teaching around the country are observed by the program faculty through video technologies. After the candidates finish a class, they meet privately online to discuss the MSSE faculty member's observations and suggestions. The program mixes live observation and the use of remote video technologies. Observing teaching strategies in both residential and mainstream programs, and receiving comments and suggestions from the cooperating teachers and the college supervisors have been instrumental in keeping the program current in evidence-based practices in preparing our students to become teachers.

Related to the projections for increased online K–12 education as well, MSSE faculty members have also experimented with teacher candidates to develop online lessons that address the reading difficulties many young deaf students demonstrate, since online education places increased demands on reading skills. Dr. Harry Lang was instrumental in the development of Structured Online Academic Reading (SOAR) training sessions for MSSE graduate students. SOAR allows the deaf reader to click vocabulary terms and receive text or ASL signed definitions, images and links to other websites. Special notes are sometimes added to enhance the reading of content, and adjunct questions with answers are inserted to improve factual recall. The experiments completed by several teacher candidates have shown much promise.

Faculty and Student Research

The MSSE faculty and students have also participated in a variety of research efforts over the years. Drs. Harry Lang, Christopher Kurz, Gerald Bateman, Susan Lane-Outlaw, Jessica Trussell, and Professor Nora Shannon conducted research studies on such topics as:

- Characteristics of effective teachers
- Learning styles
- Self-efficacy through microteaching

- Motivational factors in learning ASL
- Academic ASL
- Imagery in learning mathematics
- Technology reading and writing development
- Center schools
- Literacy
- Writing to Learn

Before the semester system was implemented, the MSSE program required students to complete capstone projects in the area of curriculum development, research and review of literature. The MSSE students pursued successful projects with support from the faculty in such topics as:

- "A Descriptive Analysis of Standardized Entrance Exams and Deaf Cross-Registered Students at the National Technical Institute of the Deaf" (Dr. Jessica La Sala Cuculick)
- "The Portrayal of Deaf People in Television and Film, and the Potential Effect on the Successful Transition of Deaf Adolescents into Adult Life" (Dr. Steven Singer)
- "Language-Delayed High School Students: English Syntax Acquisition and English Language Organizers" (Katie Locus)
- "Development and Evaluation of Electronic Portfolios for Future Teacher Candidates in the MSSE Program" (Cristina Trefcer Di Paolo)
- "A Study of Perceptions of Mathematics Signs: Implications for Teaching" (Paul Glaser)
- "Edgar Allan Poe's 'The Fall of the House': Bilingual Approaches" (Michelle Johnston)
- "eBeam in the Science Classroom: Action Research" (Emily Schriener)

International Impact

The MSSE program has had international impact on the education of deaf and hard-of-hearing students. For example, a group of MSSE students and MSSE/NTID faculty members participated in a project called "Project Inclusion" (2000–2002). It was an international course on educational inclusion of deaf students with four partner countries: Sweden, the Netherlands, Greece and the United States. There were lively discussions and

Chi Man "Chloe" Ho, a 2016 graduate of the program.

presentations on how educational inclusion is practiced within each of the four partner countries. All of the participants valued the sharing of ideas, strategies and issues, and debated the pros and cons of inclusive education and the impact it has in their respective societies.

The program has accepted a number of international students from China, and Fulbright scholars from Greece, Thailand, Vietnam, Portugal, Philippines, Hong Kong, Uganda, Nigeria, Ethiopia, India and Japan. For almost all of the international students, their goal is to bring what they have learned from this program to their home countries to set up new educational programs, improve their existing programs and expand opportunities for deaf and hard-of-hearing people.

In addition, research publications by MSSE faculty have been disseminated to many countries.

Not only has the MSSE program worked with a number of international students on campus, some of the MSSE faculty members have worked with other countries to promote teacher education and education of deaf and hard-of-hearing students in other countries through the Postsecondary Education Network-International and the Pre-College Education Network. For example, Nora Shannon and Thomastine Sarchet have served as consultants and instructors in the Philippines; Professor Sarchet and Dr. Christopher Kurz served the same roles in Cambodia, Vietnam and Hong Kong. The program has worked with professionals from Vietnam, Ethiopia, Uganda, Rwanda, India and Myanmar to share the wealth of experience all parties have gained in teacher preparation and schools for the deaf.

Post-Graduate Success

By the time NTID celebrates its 50th anniversary, MSSE (and its precursor program, JESP) will have prepared more than 500 students to become teachers. They have represented NTID well. They have taught in residential schools for the deaf, day schools for the deaf, mainstream programs, and public school programs in at least 39 states. Among these alumni, 24 have become faculty members at NTID. This shows how the MSSE program assists NTID in growing our own teachers.

In the recent MSSE employer feedback survey (2016), school administrators commented that MSSE graduates "demonstrate knowledge in their content areas, a passion for teaching and compassion for their students." They also mentioned "for newer teachers, they possessed the confidence and engagement to learn and grow into seasoned professionals" (2016). They also offered helpful areas of improvement that support our efforts in making continuous improvement related to teaching deaf students with secondary disabilities, classroom management and IEP writing. The program faculty and students value the partnerships we have with the many schools we work with. Their advice and wisdom have contributed to the quality of our program.

MSSE alumni have shown great satisfaction with their education at RIT. A few quotes are provided below:

The faculty were world-class and very supportive, and my classmates and I all bonded through our shared experiences. I remember the 4–8 p.m. classes on cold winter days, the portfolio requirements, and vying for our student teaching placements.

— Katie Cue[4]

Enrolling in the program was one of my best decisions because I was able to broaden my options after graduating with a Bachelor of Fine Arts in Film. There were many memories I got to share with my fellow classmates during the two years in the program. One of the best memories is when I got the wonderful opportunity to teach at New Mexico School for the Deaf. Everything we had been learning in the program truly helped me prepare for that student teaching experience. It also led me to Philadelphia, where I have worked at the Pennsylvania School for the Deaf since 2013. The city has been a great place to me, and I cannot see any reason for leaving there any time soon. I want to say thanks very much to Gerald Bateman, Christopher Kurz, Susan Lane-Outlaw, and Harry Lang for their endless support for the Class of 2012. Also, a huge thank to Jeanette Tydings, who is the heart of the MSSE program.

— Daniel Brucker[5]

Attending the MSSE program was the hardest and most rewarding experience of my life at the time. I met so many wonderful people, and we created our own family. We supported each other through tough times and through wonderful times, and I wouldn't trade my experience for anything.

— Cristina Trefcer Di Paolo[6]

From the very beginning of my teaching career, I felt extremely prepared with the best knowledge and strategies of how, not only to teach content to my students, but create a community of students who love to learn.

— Michael Lawson[7]

Before I came to MSSE, I was lost. I had graduated from RIT with a degree that I was not overall thrilled with. However, I did benefit from a big Deaf community from RIT that I never had while growing up as an oral Deaf person. So I applied to MSSE, where I realized it was a win-win situation because I was able to learn more about the Deaf culture that I fell in love with and to gain an ability to teach future generations of Deaf students to fall in love with what I learned. I did not have the best qualifications to get into your program, but you saw that I deserved a chance, and I am forever grateful you did because you changed my life. You successfully molded me into a teacher by showing me an example of how to be one. Now, because of you, I have been given numerous compliments and praise on how I positively affect my students' lives as a teacher of the deaf and as a baseball coach. Here's to you, creator of teachers, a man with a heart of gold, and my "grandpa" whom I went to for guidance. I am forever grateful to be your pupil.

— Jonathan Furman[8]

The MSSE program was transformative for me in many ways. I will forever be grateful to the faculty, colleagues, and students that have shaped me so profoundly. As a teacher once said to me, "Here's to changing the world!" In the 21st century, MSSE is poised to lead the transformation of deaf education.

— Michael Skyer[9]

A Special Recognition

In closing, the authors would also like to thank Jeanette Tydings for her outstanding service and support to the program faculty and students during her years with the program.

---

*Dr. Gerald Bateman, Professor, is the Director of the Master of Science in Secondary Education (MSSE) program. **Dr. Christopher Kurz**, Associate Professor, is a faculty member in the MSSE program. **Dr. Harry G. Lang**, Professor Emeritus, is a former coordinator of the Office of Faculty Development and a former faculty member of the MSSE program.*

Notes

1. Education of the Handicapped Children Act of 1975. Public Law 94–142. United States Congress. (1975). https://www.gpo.gov/fdsys/pkg/STATUTE-89/pdf/STATUTE-89-Pg773.pdf
2. National Technical Institute for the Deaf, *Feasibility Study for Graduate Teacher Preparation Program at the Junior and High School Levels*. Committee Report. Rochester, NY: NTID. (1993).

3. NTID. *Strategic Plan: An Agenda for Action Report*. Rochester, NY: NTID. (1992, June).
4. Katie Cue, personal communication, 2017.
5. Daniel Brucker, personal communication, 2017.
6. Christina Trefcer Di Paolo, personal communication, 2017.
7. Michael Lawson, personal communication, 2017.
8. Jonathan Furman, personal communication, 2017.
9. Michael Skyer, personal communication, 2017.

Big Ideas Everywhere
Innovation as Education

Dr. W. Scot Atkins

During NTID's formative years in the late 1960s, the first NTID director, Dr. D. Robert Frisina, said, "Try new things that have never been tried before." This set the tone for innovation at NTID, and innovation has been a hallmark of RIT/NTID's education ever since. Dubbed "The Grand Experiment," NTID led the way in terms of new pedagogies and strategies for teaching deaf and hard-of-hearing students. One example of this approach is the requirement of cooperative education experiences for students, which provides them paid work experience before they graduate.

Efforts in student innovation have been significant aspects of the RIT/NTID experience from the beginning. Student teams are often called to provide consultations to external clients on various projects. For one, the town of Henrietta, where RIT makes its home, called upon the expertise of our students to create the town's logo.[1]

Since 2000, student innovation has become a more formalized part of an RIT education, and NTID students have benefited greatly from RIT's mandates in this area. As an indicator of the current results of RIT's efforts regarding student innovation, in 2015, RIT ranked among the "Most Innovative Schools" by US News and World Report. RIT placed seventh in the "Best Regional Universities" category, among hundreds of schools that offer a full range of undergraduate majors and masters degree programs. Says former RIT President Dr. William Destler, "RIT is on the cusp of greatness and a university today where our students can flourish in an environment rich with innovation, creativity and entrepreneurial spirit."

It has been a very exciting time in NTID's history. Newly established programs have been created to harness the "innovation spirit" among NTID's student body. Faculty and staff have been diligently engaged in efforts to foster this spirit. This chapter will outline some of the programs and projects in which innovation has been showcased among our deaf and hard-of-hearing students. The Center on Access Technology (CAT), created in 2006, capitalizes on student innovation to develop and provide new technologies for an external clientele. RIT's Simone Center for Student Innovation and Entrepreneurship, established in 2007, helps student teams to develop products and build companies. The Imagine RIT: Innovation and Creativity Festival, established in 2008, is a major annual event in the RIT community; it attracts approximately 35,000 members of the Rochester community each year. ZVRS's "The Next Big Idea" contest for deaf and hard-of-hearing students, loosely based on the *Shark Tank* television show, was established in 2011. NTID's Rosica Hall, a newly-created center for research and innovation, opened its doors in 2013. Each of these programs and examples of student innovation activities will be outlined in this chapter.

The Center on Access Technology

The Center on Access Technology (CAT) was created by Dr. James DeCaro in March 2006 to meet a growing need for more effective access solutions for deaf and

Ping Liu demonstrates an ASL-based storytelling app to Thomastine Sarchet.

instructional technologies, health care technologies and services, and more. A multi-year collaboration with a business partner to conduct research and assessment on innovative uses of technology continued through 2015.

Designing and Building a Smart Cane Prototype for People who are Deaf-Blind

CAT continues to develop a "smart cane" device to aid Deaf-Blind individuals in navigating their surroundings. The advanced cane provides real-time force feedback guidance. The unique feature of CAT Director Gary Behm's patented IBM invention (US 8,077,020 B2 - Method and Apparatus for Tactile Haptic Device to Guide User in Real-time Obstacle Avoidance) involves exploiting the features of a tactile haptic device to enable real-time obstacle avoidance by Deaf-Blind users. Hearing blind users may benefit from it, as well.

See-through Life-size Interactive Monitor (SLIM)

The SLIM applies a technical solution that allows an instructor to communicate and write/display information on the monitor board at the same time without losing eye contact with deaf and hard-of-hearing students in the classroom.

Making Laboratory and Medical Instruments User Friendly for Deaf and Hard-of-Hearing Students.

Students are engaged in developing a prototype sound-recognition system that would discriminate sounds from different laboratory and/or medical instruments, and then send alert messages via email or text messaging.

Notification Device and System

CAT has been developing a lightweight portable device for a smartphone that will allow deaf or hard-of-hearing students to use it for notifications (phone, email, text) and wake-up calls through Bluetooth technology.

Various notification devices.

The lab has a subcontract for the FCC Access to Communication for Everyone Program to develop the front end of a new VRS product in the United States. The project is expected to have a minimum duration of five years.

hard-of-hearing people. One part of the center's model is the contracting with business clients to create new products that will enhance access in a variety of areas. The other part of the model is the utilization of funding from external grants, mostly federal grants, to develop access technology for deaf and hard-of-hearing people. Both parts of the CAT model help provide greater opportunities for real-world learning. RIT/NTID students have played an enormous role in the development of these technologies since CAT's inception, and many of the students who have been involved in CAT projects have gone on to work in high-level positions outside of NTID.

The NTID Center on Access Technology Innovation Laboratory ("CAT Lab"), a first-of-its-kind initiative, provides a place for students to get involved in the innovation process. The CAT Lab, located on the first floor of NTID's Lyndon B. Johnson Hall, brings together faculty and associate degree-level deaf and hard-of-hearing students to collaborate on multidisciplinary projects related to developing and adapting access and

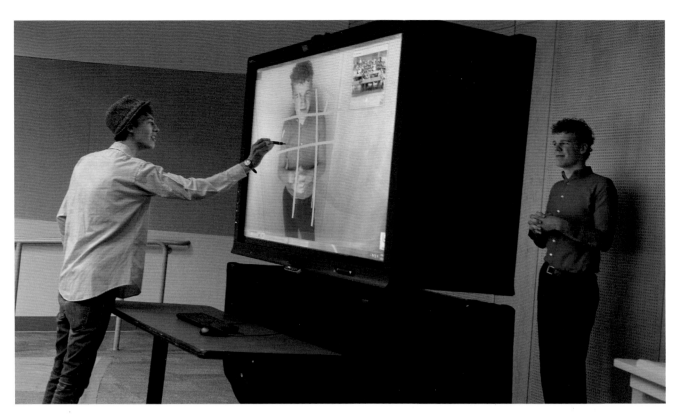
An instructor demonstrates SLIM in the classroom.

The Center on Access Technology, thanks to a healthy demand for new technologies to improve the lives of many, is continually tapping into NTID student expertise to create the next generation of products and services.

The Simone Center for Student Innovation and Entrepreneurship

During the early 2000s, two separate entities on campus, the Center on Entrepreneurship and the Center on Student Innovation, provided programs that focused on entrepreneurship and innovation, respectively. Eventually, both centers merged in 2007 to become what is now known as The Albert J. Simone Center for Student Innovation and Entrepreneurship. In recognition of his many contributions to academics and strong support of local businesses, the center was named for RIT President Emeritus Simone. The Simone Center includes both the RIT Student Incubator and the Venture Creations Center. The goal for this new center was to boost student innovation and entrepreneurship efforts on campus.

Leaders of the then newly created Simone Center formed an institute-wide innovation council, with representatives from all of the colleges of RIT, including NTID. Dr. E. William Clymer, a faculty member, was the first NTID representative to sit on this council. Since its inception, the Simone Center has seen 10 different teams of NTID students, primarily through the E. Philip Saunders Summer Start-up Program. Currently, NTID student teams have made up 10% of all Simone Center entrepreneurial teams. In the past six years, the amount of entrepreneurial activity through the Simone Center has doubled. Dr. Richard DeMartino, current director of the Simone Center, states, "Our deaf teams have usually had more clarity of thought about the needs of their customers, who tend to be deaf themselves. This has helped them to innovate new products that benefit the deaf and hard-of-hearing market. Many of these products are also appealing to a broader customer base."

The Saunders Summer Start-up Program is a summer-long program in which student teams take various classes and receive intensive coaching to convert their business ideas into viable products. Student teams are given a small amount of seed funding to help develop their products and businesses. The first all-deaf team to take advantage of this Summer Start-Up program was Team Galari, led by Professional & Technical Communications student Youmee Lee. In 2011, after having taken an entrepreneurship course at the Saunders College of Business, Lee decided to enter the summer program to learn more about how to create a product and run a business. Lee recalls, "I wanted to look for a product that deaf people needed and technology was starting to take off. I wanted to capitalize on this, and it has always been my personality to try new things."

Lee assembled a team of people from a variety of disciplines to help to create a new type of alarm clock for deaf and hard-of-hearing people. When asked about what the team did during the program, Lee responded, "I put together a team to work on a product that was attractive and functional for deaf and hard-of-hearing people. We looked for several investors and made several pitches."[2]

Because NTID student teams tend to be larger than the traditional Summer Start-Up teams, some of these teams have received additional funding from NTID to cover the cost of the additional members. As part of the program, student teams make several pitches to outside investors; some of these pitches have also resulted in additional funding for these student teams. The goal for the summer program is for the teams to learn transferable skills in establishing a new business venture, to "graduate," and then enter the next phase of their venture creation.

The next phase is located at Simone Center's Venture Creation Center, a business incubator located in an industrial park close to the RIT campus. At this center, the teams receive a different level of mentoring and support, and they are required to bankroll their start-up activities through a variety of funding sources. The goal is to have these teams become full-fledged companies and eventually move to their own spaces.

NTID students learn real-world skills through the various programs offered by the Simone Center. Currently, Lee is employed as a full-time graphic designer with several major clients. Lee reflects,

Now that I am a freelance graphic designer, the experience [I gained] during the Saunders Summer Start-up Program has helped me with the business aspect of what I am doing now. I learned important things like self-discipline, pricing, marketing and business ethics.... The summer program provided mentors and interpreters to help with the launch of the business.

Dr. William Destler and the Imagine RIT Festival

In 2007, the newly-installed RIT President, Dr. William "Bill" Destler, outlined his new vision for RIT, stating that the university "indeed has an unfair advantage," noting that RIT had a vast variety of both technical and creative disciplines that took advantage of "the collision of the right brain and left brain."

After his arrival on campus, Destler also commented, "Where else do you have electrical engineering and computer science students rubbing elbows with photographers and artists? We are not going to try to be the next Stanford or Berkeley. We're going to basically continue to be the unusual place we are, and try to do it better. That makes it a lot of fun."

This set into motion the new vision for RIT as an "Innovation University." This vision helped to further drive programs that focused on student innovation on campus.[3]

One such major event, Imagine RIT: Innovation and Creativity Festival, has since its founding in 2008 attracted tens of thousands of members from the Rochester area each year to witness many student and faculty projects, many of which focus on innovation and entrepreneurship.

Each year at this festival, RIT/NTID has showcased many student projects that reflect the innovative nature of the student experience. As an example, the NTID Information and Computing Studies Department (ICS) offered an elective to build 3-D printers in the spring semester of 2015. Ten students built printers from a kit, which started as a box of assorted nuts and bolts. As they put together these advanced printers, the students gleaned a wealth of knowledge and information about science, technology, engineering, the arts, and math. In addition, they learned the merits of working on a team to complete a project. During the Imagine

At Imagine RIT, students Amie Sankoh and Robb Dooling discuss a device-locating technology they developed as members of Team Champ, which won second place in the 2013 Next Big Idea competition.

RIT festival, these students demonstrated their printers and explained the nuances of building these machines.

The Smart Cane Systems Integration technology, developed through the Center on Access Technology, was demonstrated at this festival, as well. Visitors were able to hold the cane and get a sense of how it works for Deaf-Blind consumers.

Each year, NTID teams who are finalists in the Next Big Idea competition display their ideas at the Imagine RIT festival. All of the exhibits and activities showcase the innovative thinking and creative energy that are unique to RIT. This, in turn, has shaped RIT's reputation as a hub for innovation and entrepreneurship.

The Next Big Idea

The "Next Big Idea" contest was created through a joint partnership between NTID Outreach and ZVRS, a video relay service provider, with the main idea of promoting more interdisciplinary student teams at NTID. As Mark Sommer, Senior Director of the NTID Outreach Consortium, remarked, "ZVRS wanted to create a synergy and encourage members from different backgrounds to work together." Team projects have now become a mainstay in many modern companies, creating the need to teach students how to cooperate towards a common goal.

The goal of the contest is for multidisciplinary student teams to innovate a business idea that could have a lasting impact on the community. For example, in the competition, in order to qualify, each team has to be made up of full-time students in different majors. The competition itself is made up of several qualifying rounds, culminating in a final round that is open to the general public in the springtime. During the initial rounds, judges are selected from among NTID's faculty members. Lab sessions are available to the final five teams to prepare for the final round. During the final round, judges from ZVRS select the three winning teams. The judges select the winners based on the originality of the idea, its relevance to the deaf and hard-of-hearing

The V-Sports team, the first winners of the Next Big Idea, receive a $5,000 check from ZVRS CEO Sean Ballanger, Christopher Wagner, also of ZVRS, and Dr. Gerard Buckley, President of NTID. The team members are (l-r) Michael Della Penna, Tyler Swob, and Jeremiah Thompson.

community, feasibility, thoroughness of research, evidence of collaboration among team members, and the use of facts about the product and the market.

The inaugural Next Big Idea in the 2011–2012 academic year attracted a total of 57 RIT/NTID students to the competition. The final five teams represented a total of 16 students. The first faculty judges were W. Scot Atkins, Gary Behm, Wendy Dannels, Annemarie Ross, and Alicia Lane-Outlaw (as the only outside member). The winning team, earning $5,000, was V-Sports, made up of team members Jeremiah Thompson, Tyler Swob, Michael Della Penna, and Shane Qualls. V-Sports pitched their winning idea of creating a device to facilitate communication via vibration notification for deaf and hard-of-hearing athletes. As Jeremiah Thompson said in their pitch, "Communication has always been a major difficulty in sports. It can be very frustrating. We really want to solve that problem."

Second place and $3,000 went to the team of Get Dancin', which consisted of team members Nicole Hood,

Nic Shaw, and Samantha Braidi. This team pitched the idea of opening a dance studio for deaf and hard-of-hearing people. According to Hood:

I had been dancing since I was three years old, and it was always with all hearing people. I was the only deaf person in the classes, and I felt I needed to change all of that. When I came to NTID, I realized that I finally had dance teachers who signed. That's when I decided that I wanted to set up a dance studio for Deaf people. I met lots of faculty and staff who said they had deaf kids whom they wanted to bring to dance class, but they said they would feel more connected to a deaf dance instructor. I saw that there was a need and did some research to find out what was available out there. I found nothing, so it was time for a change. [4]

Third place and $2,000 went to team Watersocket. Casey Jaeger, Matthew Hente, and Richie Prilenski created a prototype for a waterproof cover for the receiver portion of cochlear implant processors using a superhydrophobic spray.

"All five teams did an outstanding job," remembers Christopher Wagner, an RIT/NTID alumnus and senior vice president of ZVRS. In his address to the participating teams, Wagner said, "I was so impressed; the dreams and aspirations you have makes me even more proud to be an alumnus. And, at RIT, it is all about the opportunity to grow."

NTID President Dr. Gerard Buckley remarked after the contest, "This competition shows the talent, creativity and entrepreneurial spirit our students have. This is the hallmark of a RIT/NTID education, and these are the innovators of the future."

The Next Big Idea has now become an annual tradition at RIT/NTID, drawing crowds in venues such as the CSD Student Development Center or the Panara Theatre. Each year, 10–15 teams compete for the coveted cash prizes. Over the years, many creative projects have won prizes.

InvisibleCAPTIONS, First Place, 2013

The team for InvisibleCAPTIONS, represented by students Samantha Braidi, Cory Behm, Daniel Moreno, and Melissa Kielbus, won first prize in 2013. The team pitched the idea of creating special glasses with lenses that have a custom filter to capture ultraviolet light. A movie projector would send out the UV light, but only the people with these glasses would see the captions. The glasses would be a cheaper and much lighter alternative to the options currently offered in movie theaters today.

MotionSavvy, Third Place, 2013

2013 third-place winners Wade Kellard, Ryan Hait-Campbell and Jordan Stemper would go on to form a company, MotionSavvy, which is still developing software that enables deaf and hard-of-hearing people to be able to convert their sign language to speech. Capitalizing on a new technology called Leap, this team went on to attend the Saunders Summer Start-up Program. Subsequently, MotionSavvy has received several rounds of investment funding to further develop their product, including a large grant from Wells Fargo. Ryan Hait-Campbell, who provided leadership for the

efforts to start up the business, said, "I realized that there is a big divide between two worlds [hearing and deaf]. Interpreters help solve the problem to a certain point, so I wanted to solve [it] head-on." Explaining his motivation for the business, Ryan continues, "We didn't start a business to start a business. We saw a problem that needed to be solved."[5]

Cenify, First Honors, 2014

Cenify was created by students Sophie Phillips, Patrick Seypura and Alex Satterly, and this team took first honors. Their concept would allow alarms to be programmed days in advance from a smartphone, even for different times of the day, through Bluetooth technology. During the final pitch, Seypura picked up a bulky vibrating alarm clock entangled in wires, and said, "This is a huge hassle; we have got to change this." Cenify also went on to continue the development of their products. Satterly led efforts to continue building Cenify as a company, stating, "Some people are in it for the money, but I am not. I really want to see people benefit [from the product] and live life in a simpler way by using automation and the connected society."[6]

HZ Innovations, First Place, 2015

HZ Innovations's winning team included students Greyson Watkins, Zack Baltzer, Nick Lamb, Chrystal Schelenker, Keith Delk, and Jason Lee. The team devised a cutting-edge wireless sound recognition system for deaf and hard-of-hearing homeowners. Sound-capturing devices plugged into ordinary electrical outlets are wirelessly tied into a single central processing unit. As an example, when the doorbell rings, smoke alarm beeps, or a water faucet drips, the unit notifies the homeowner via smart phone, smart watch or a tablet. Practically all sounds in the house that are important to the homeowner can be recorded and "memorized" by the system.

"I moved into a house, and I started noticing all of the important things I was missing," said Watkins, a fourth-year computer security student from Durham, North Carolina. "I missed the sounds of my friends knocking on my front door. My washer and dryer are in the basement and I wouldn't be able to hear the buzzing of the dryer, My food would burn because I would leave the oven on. There are a lot of people out there,

Philip Rubin discusses plans for Rosica Hall with architects from HBT Architects of Rochester.

including senior citizens, who have similar issues. I just came up with the idea, and it took off."

The HZ Innovations team were subsequently accepted into the Saunders Summer Start-up Program and eventually graduated into RIT's Venture Creation Center. The team has received seed funding for manufacture of the product, dubbed "Wavio," and is positioning to sell thousands of units to customers around the world.

Team Ugyo, First Place, 2016
Students Ethan Young and Nicole Dugan won first place for developing an innovative way for low-vision deaf people to be able to follow a conversation in a group discussion. The technology, using a combination of indicator lights and tactile output, will help point the user in the direction of the person speaking.

BAGMAG, First Prize, 2017
Hans Kohls and Wade Kellard won first prize for their solution to making skateboards more easily portable on the back of a backpack. The solution consisted of two strong magnets—one in the backpack and one on the bottom of the skateboard—allowing one to affix the skateboard to the backpack using only one hand.

Given that the "Next Big Idea" competition has become a major feeder into the innovation pipeline for deaf and hard-of-hearing students at RIT/NTID, there is continued commitment that this will become one of the major mainstays of the student innovation ecosystem on campus.

Sebastian and Lenore Rosica Hall: "A Dream Has Become a Reality"
As part of RIT/NTID's Strategic Decisions 2020, plans were developed for a new building that is dedicated to innovation and research for students, faculty and staff. Sebastian and Lenore Rosica Hall was made possible by a $1.75 million donation from the William G. McGowan Charitable Fund. The $8 million, two-story,

23,000-square-foot building, attached to the Shumway Dining Commons, officially opened on October 11, 2013. "Rosica Hall is a facility where center-based research can take place," Buckley remarked. "It will be the hub for important work that will benefit generations of deaf and hard-of-hearing people, and I am proud that this dream has become a reality." The building currently houses several research centers and several student-based innovation projects. For example, space is dedicated to the Center on Access Technology's development of new VRS technology.

The design of the building was done with the intention of making it deaf-friendly, incorporating maximum use of natural light, open line-of-sight paths, safety features such as strobe lights, and the minimization of vibration from the building's air conditioning and heating units. Philip Rubin, an RIT/NTID alumnus and architect in Palm Springs, California, consulted with Rebecca Barone of HBT Architects of Rochester on designing the building to be deaf-friendly. "We wanted to have deaf eyes on the building project from the beginning," said RIT/NTID Dean Emeritus James DeCaro, who oversaw the design and development of the building.

An important highlight of the process of building Rosica Hall was the involvement of RIT/NTID students. When plans for the building were announced, Engineering Studies Assistant Professor James Fugate suggested that a 3-D model of the building be constructed by students. As a result, a group of NTID Computer-Aided Drafting Technology students turned blueprints for Rosica Hall into a 3-D model, offering a more tangible version of the building, while at the same time developing their engineering skills.

Student Brandon McCarty, of Lake Geneva, Wisconsin, who intended to become an architect, created an animated tour of the proposed building and helped make the windows on the model, which had to be constructed and angled at just the right position so they would look natural. He said he learned a lot from this project and that the experience would help him in his future career. Another student, Justin Katich, of New Castle, Pennsylvania, grew up making models, "but this is the largest so far."

The greatest challenge came two weeks before their deadline, when the design for the building was changed. The roof, walls, and windows of the model all had to be rebuilt. Andrew Crawford, of Science Hill, Kentucky, who planned to become a civil engineer, built the model's Shumway Dining Commons and the connecting structure that joins the Dining Commons to Rosica Hall. During the unveiling of their model, he explained that the actual Rosica Hall would be built using a sustainable construction process, including using energy-efficient heating and lighting, and recycled local materials whenever possible.

Innovation Funding at NTID: Reinforcing an Innovation Culture at NTID

In 2010, RIT/NTID faculty, staff and students were encouraged to submit grant proposals that responded to Strategic Decisions 2020 (SD 2020) and related to innovative instruction/student services, innovative scholarship/research or professional growth. A total of 92 proposals were received; 27 were funded, 9 in each of those areas. Projects included the development of a prototype for a see-through monitor that would allow teachers to write on the monitor while maintaining eye contact with students; establishing a personal finance club that would enable students to create and monitor the club's portfolio with any interest/dividends going to student scholarships; developing a multi-disciplinary course that focuses on developing students' entrepreneurial experience; developing a prototype of an imaging system for image relocation on a head-mounted display for deaf and hard-of-hearing students with Usher's Syndrome (low vision); and targeting the "glass ceiling" for deaf and hard-of-hearing students by looking at the long-term growth of NTID graduates in the workplace.

RIT I-Corps Site

As part of RIT's increasing commitment to student innovation, RIT has received Innovation Corps (I-Corps) funding for student teams and mentoring from the National Science Foundation (NSF). RIT has been designated an I-Corps University Site, and the Simone Center has received NSF funding since 2014. This designation allows for the creation of the Student I-Corps Co-operative Education Program and provides stipends to students advancing a commercialization project. The

Electric bicycles are demonstrated during the Brick City Festival of 2012.

NSF I-Corps Grant provides teams with the necessary resources and I-Corps funding of up to $3,000, with the goal of conducting market research and testing startup viability. In order to qualify for the I-Corps program at RIT, teams must have a product or service that is related to, and benefits, the fields of science, technology, engineering, and mathematics (STEM). These projects must also be team-based.

If chosen, teams are paired with a mentor who will oversee and assist the team as they complete their business model canvas and develop a better understanding of their product and industry as a whole. After successful completion of the program, teams are given the opportunity to apply for other I-Corps grants of up to $50,000 to further develop their businesses. In addition, these teams receive comprehensive mentoring from industry mentors.

Other Examples of Student Innovation on Campus
There have been other significant efforts that have

showcased our student efforts on campus. In 2012, the RIT/NTID Bike Club was created to bring deaf and hearing students together to build light plug-in electric vehicles. These vehicles were designed to incorporate battery, motor, and controller innovations to reduce carbon emissions. The team utilized innovation funds to create this bike. The electric bike fleet went live just in time for the Brick City Festival in 2012 and was showcased at the 2013 Imagine RIT Festival.

The Future of Student Innovation on Campus: Carrying the Flame
If current activities are indicative, the future is certainly bright for our students in terms of innovation on campus. As part of RIT's new strategic plan for 2015–2025, RIT will be "a center of innovation, creativity, and entrepreneurship that serves as an important economic engine for Rochester, the region, and the nation."[7]

As part of these efforts, the goal for RIT is to support the launch of 20 start-ups each year, leverage university resources and expertise in entrepreneurship to create entrepreneurship criteria, applied research, business development, and technology transfer. In addition, RIT must develop an investment model to fuel entrepreneurial activities.[8] RIT/NTID is well positioned to support these efforts and to foster interdisciplinary collaboration on campus through formal and informal programs on campus. Student innovation has made it possible for many of our RIT/NTID alumni to utilize their skills in their careers, develop new technologies, create their own companies, and help to educate new generations of students.

Dr. W. Scot Atkins is a faculty member in NTID's Business Studies program.

Notes

1. James DeCaro, personal communications, 2016.

2 . Youmee Lee, personal communication, 2017.

3. "President Bill Destler Champions RIT's 'Unfair Advantage,' " *RIT University Magazine*, (Winter 2007). http://www.rit.edu/news/umag/winter2007/10_features_focus_innov.html

4. "Where are they now?" 2016. http://www.ntid.rit.edu/outreach/nextbigidea/wherearetheynow

5. "Where are they now?" 2016. http://www.ntid.rit.edu/outreach/nextbigidea/wherearetheynow

6. "Where are they now?" 2016. http://www.ntid.rit.edu/outreach/nextbigidea/wherearetheynow

7. "Greatness Through Difference: 2015–2025 Strategic Plan," (Rochester, N.Y.: RIT, 2015). https://www.rit.edu/president/strategicplan2025/pdfs/strategic_plan.pdf

8. "Greatness Through Difference," 2015.

From Classrooms to the Workforce
Job Placement and Success

Mary Ellen Tait

Laying the Groundwork

The Congressional legislation signed in 1965 by President Lyndon Baines Johnson that provided for the establishment and operation of a National Technical Institute for the Deaf (NTID), Public Law, 89–36, stated that NTID was "For the purpose of providing a residential facility for postsecondary technical training and education for persons who are deaf in order to prepare them for successful employment..." Rochester Institute of Technology (RIT), in Rochester, NY, competed with a number of other universities to be the host institution for NTID.

There were several reasons why RIT, established in 1829, was a good fit. RIT had a long history of success in technical education. It had one of the oldest and largest collegiate cooperative education (co-op) programs in the country. It was felt that deaf students would benefit particularly from having required work opportunities related to their studies before graduation. And, RIT had space for NTID.

Deaf students could be prepared for working with hearing people while on campus, as they interacted in academic, living, and social situations. Rochester had thriving businesses that had hired RIT students and could also employ NTID students. Due to the presence of the Rochester School for the Deaf (RSD), established in 1876, it also had an established deaf community, deaf services, and support of deaf education.

Research had shown that, historically, deaf people experienced more unemployment, more underemploy-

ment, and lower wages than their hearing counterparts. When the first class of 70 deaf and hard-of-hearing students enrolled at NTID in 1968, a full curriculum in selected fields was planned to match entry-level technical jobs that it was thought the students could qualify for. With such specialized training, it was hoped that such bleak employment prospects would reverse.

NTID sponsored a two-day job placement workshop in Rochester in early 1970. NTID staff met with representatives of state employment services, job placement services for the "disadvantaged," vocational rehabilitation (VR) workers, unions, businesses, and industry. Also in attendance were members of NTID's National Advisory Group (NAG), a committee comprising leaders from business, industry, education, and government. They discussed plans, objectives, and programs related to the placement process of young deaf and hard-of-hearing adults.

The moderator of the workshop was Dr. Jack Clarcq, Director of the Division of Student Development at NTID, who was responsible for the job placement of students. As NTID developed in the year that followed, the organizational structure shifted, and Dr. Clarcq was named Assistant Dean for Technical Education, reporting directly to Dr. William Castle, the Dean of NTID. Despite the disbanding of the Division of Student Development, Clarcq continued to lead NTID's role in placement.

First Co-ops

In fall 1970, as part of their educational program, 17 NTID students were the first deaf persons to participate in RIT's cooperative educational plan. Students spent one or more terms working off-campus, applying what they had learned in the classroom. Said Clarcq at the time:

> RIT has a long history of success in cooperative education, and we are fortunate to be able to capitalize on this history...For years the deaf have been categorized as people who must be shut off by themselves because of their supposed inability to communicate. These students are proving they can communicate and perform many jobs throughout industry that in the past have not been available...It's the responsibility of NTID and RIT to prepare deaf students to meet these opportunities.[1]

The first co-op students worked for a variety of employers, many in Rochester. They developed their technical and interpersonal skills through these opportunities. Both employers and students interviewed said they felt the experience was beneficial. Some employers hired additional co-op students after initial positive outcomes. Some students worked for employers near their home, and some worked in co-op opportunities on campus at NTID and RIT. NTID used the co-op program to evaluate deaf students' progress, and as students completed their co-ops and coursework, NTID prepared them for placement after they earned their degrees.

Placement after Graduation

To better prepare students for employment, NTID aimed to have flexible academic programs and to keep up with broader market trends. When faculty members were hired, they were selected in part because of their ability to make contacts in the field, along with their disciplinary knowledge and experience. Said NTID Director Dr. Robert Frisina in 1971:

> Our specific mission and professional commitment is to prepare each deaf student for a responsible role in the hearing world of work...But our placement will only be as good as our preparation. Everyone in NTID will participate in our nationwide job placement effort. Anything short of a comprehensive program will not succeed.[2]

In response to Frisina's charge, NTID took on the responsibility of placing its graduates. RIT had a placement program already established for hearing students, and it would support NTID in the placement of deaf and hard-of-hearing students earning baccalaureate degrees from the other colleges of RIT.

Kay Hartfelder, Assistant Director of the RIT Placement Program at that time, shared an experience she had with a representative from a major firm interviewing RIT graduates on campus. She asked his opinion on hiring people with disabilities, and he told her about how his company was wonderful about that sort of thing. She then told him he had a highly qualified deaf student on his interview schedule that day, and "...he turned white as a ghost. It was another indication of the effort NTID must make if it is going to educate employers to the contributions technically skilled deaf students can make to industry."[3]

NTID started hiring staff with experience in industry to undertake placement efforts. A former Ford Motor Corporation Supervisor of Education and Training, Victor Maguran, Jr., started at NTID in October 1970 as a Career Development Specialist. By mid-1971, he was named Coordinator of Career Development, responsible for developing NTID's job placement program. He demanded a business-like approach with detailed records and constant feedback.

Richard Giandana, a Personnel Researcher at Xerox Corporation, joined NTID as a Career Development Specialist in 1972. So did Richard Elliott, who had been employed at General Motors (GM) in industrial/labor relations for nine years, and then moved to Rochester and coordinated a youth job development program. The placement team stayed in touch with students and employers during the initial stages of employment to assist as needed. They used telephone and mail to communicate, and welcomed employers to campus to meet faculty, staff, and students. Parents, NAG members, VR counselors, and state employment agency staff also became involved in helping students connect with employers and develop their careers.

Victor Maguran at his desk.

NTID's *FOCUS Magazine*, Film, and Television Publicity

NTID's *FOCUS Magazine* published several issues devoted to employment in the 1970s. In 1972, Dr. Frisina is quoted as saying, "Although we have an aggressive job placement program,...someone must open the door." In the same article, Maguran says, "Unlike many placement efforts where employers come to the college to seek graduates, NTID must carry its program to employers across the country."[4]

Featured on the front cover of that magazine was a still from a 22-minute film NTID had recently produced, *The Silent Drum*. Narrated by writer and announcer Rod Serling, it was made for hearing audiences, especially employers. While the film featured NTID, it was designed to help make employers open to hiring deaf people nationwide.

That same year, NTID offered another film that could be shown to service organizations, human resources groups, and others who could be influential in the employment of more deaf people. A shorter film to promote understanding of the nature and implications of hearing loss, as well as the modes of communication used by and with deaf people, was also made available. All three films, as well as a publication on career development of deaf students for teachers or counselors who worked with them, could be borrowed from NTID at no charge.

To support employment development activities, NTID also produced a short film, shown in regional seminars, featuring graduates working in drafting and computer programming. Called *Getting the Job Done*, it explained the benefits of hiring deaf employees and encouraged potential employers to find out more about what NTID graduates had to offer. Also, the Office Products Division of IBM Corporation sponsored a one-minute Public Service Announcement (PSA) filmed at NTID, to be produced and shown on television throughout the country.

Working with Students and Graduates

Maguran also felt it was important to teach students about the details involved in placement. NTID started designing a course in interviewing techniques, developing a résumé, and understanding the realities of work. Counselors also worked with placement staff in helping students get ready for employment, learn about the job market, and prepare to look for jobs.

Maguran said in early 1974, "We can help open the door to employment, but in the end the deaf graduate must help sell himself to industry and then produce, once employed."[5] To help with this, NTID Developmental Education developed mini-courses in job-seeking strategies and interviewing, interpersonal relationships, and money management.

That year, Anthony Finks joined the placement staff. He had worked in banking, as well as in setting up programs for unemployed people in New York City, and he had been a production control planner at the Xerox Corporation in Rochester. One of his responsibilities was to work with a group of students who wanted to organize a committee to keep students informed regarding placement and opportunities, and to provide feedback on services. Said Finks at the time:

> We want students to understand our function...We are here to help students find the best employment possible. And we want to know how they feel about working, what they don't understand, what they're apprehensive about, so we can be sure we are meeting their needs.[6]

In addition, the Placement Office implemented an annual feedback system to help NTID find out about graduates' success on the job, salary levels and upward mobility, communication skills, socialization, and job satisfaction. Both employers and graduates were surveyed, one year after the initial hire. About 75% of the supervisors responding said they had never supervised deaf employees before. Graduates felt they were trained, but they thought even more emphasis was needed on co-op, lab work, and simulated on-the-job training.

Graduates also gave feedback in person when they returned to NTID to talk with current students. Many were the first deaf persons to be hired by their companies, and they were aware that their success could pave the way for their younger peers. They shared their experiences, provided tips, answered questions, and learned from each other.

Employment Development and Regional Employment Seminars

As the college grew, so did the staff of the Placement Office. Placement activities began to function separately from employment development and occupational research. Along with the student body, the need to foster good relationships with potential employers increased, and employment development took on an even more important role in paving the way for job development and placement.

The staff of the Placement Office began to develop a new way to contact and educate potential employers about the advantages of hiring deaf workers in large cities: a series of regional employment seminars. They usually were a half-day in length. The first was held in 1975 in Philadelphia. Area leaders from business, industry, VR, government agencies, and the local deaf community attended. This event was sponsored by a major employer in the area and the Philadelphia Chamber of Commerce, who provided contacts in the community. The seminar was titled, "Taking a Look at the Employment of the Deaf". The NTID employment development staff gave a historical view of deaf employment, which was followed by an explanation of the preparation given to NTID students and the work of the Placement Office. Their presentation ended with a discussion of the benefits of hiring trained deaf employees, and suggestions about how employers could help to remove job barriers they might face, with communication and safety tips provided.

Later seminars around the United States grew more interactive, with activities designed to simulate deafness. NTID alumni, along with their employers, would present. Occasionally, *The Silent Drum* would be screened. The purpose was to meet employers on their home turf and introduce them to the idea of hiring deaf employees. Said Maguran, "Providing information and allowing opportunities for open discussion regarding employment of the deaf is often the first step in creating a positive attitude toward hiring a deaf worker."[7]

Afterwards, employers who were interested in learning more about NTID were encouraged to contact a staff member to discuss organizational needs and to schedule meetings with representatives of the employer, preferably at NTID in order to showcase the college. "It's only after a carefully thought-out process where we work with the employer to determine if the organization and the deaf worker can meet each other's needs, do we begin to talk of specific placements," said Maguran.[8]

Employer Relationships

NTID developed relationships with major corporations that had hired its students and graduates, and had supported NTID in other ways. During a regional employment seminar in San Francisco, Maguran presented Dr. Steven Jamison from IBM a certificate of appreciation. Jamison, a personnel consultant, was recognized for his support in expanding career opportunities for deaf people around the country. He had been instrumental in setting up the IBM Work-Experience Program for deaf college students in 1974.

Co-op hiring at NTID began with computer-related experiences, but then expanded to include other fields that fit with student skills and IBM needs. Annually, Jamison would interview interested students at various colleges, and then match the students with summer positions at various IBM locations in the United States. IBM also sent an employee through its Faculty Loan Program to teach management and data processing to NTID students for one year.

Other mutually beneficial ongoing relationships had been established by that time with companies, such as US Steel, AT&T, Mobil, Kodak, Xerox, 3M, and GM.

Tony Finks, right, senior career opportunities advisor, and Katherine Lomoglio, placement coordinator at Eastman Kodak, take a moment between interviews to discuss job applicants.

These large national corporations had multiple facilities in various cities, and some corporate offices that were visited shared information about NTID students and graduates with their branches in other locations.

NTID Professional Interns

Early on, NTID started a unique Graduate Internships program, giving students and graduates of master's-level degree programs and prospective employers an opportunity to have supervised experience with deaf students. Some of the interns were eventually hired full-time at NTID. One such intern was Deborah Lawless, a former rehabilitation counselor in Massachusetts. In 1974, she finished a special internship to learn placement techniques for use with deaf people. Afterwards, she was hired by NTID, and she joined the Employment Office.

In 1977, Robert Menchel, a deaf scientist who had worked as a research physicist for Avco Corporation and Xerox, was selected as a national role model for the disabled by the American Association for the Advancement

of Science. He took a leave from Xerox, and traveled for a year all over the country, speaking to students, teachers, parents, and counselors. He then joined the NTID Employment Office and decided to stay at NTID, where he worked most of his career.

Employment Opportunities

In late 1978, the NTID Employment Office (still led by Maguran) was organized into two areas: Employment Opportunities and the National Center on Employment of the Deaf (NCED). Debbie (Lawless) Veatch, Dick Elliott, and Tony Finks stayed in placement with Employment Opportunities. Additional staff members were hired from various businesses and educational institutions, some of whom remained with the office for many years.

In the past, placement staff and career counselors at NTID worked individually with students and co-taught classes about seeking employment, including videotaped practice interviews. When students watched themselves, they saw how they handled the interaction, which gave instructors the opportunity to provide specific feedback.

Veatch, for example, used role-playing in the classroom to demonstrate both successful and unsuccessful interviews. Through NTID's Instructional Television Department, Veatch had videotapes made of similar demonstrations with deaf people as interviewees. She started receiving outside requests for the videotape, so she and instructional developer Dr. Michael Steve created an activities guide to go with the videotape.

Veatch also compiled a placement manual with curricula for the informal and formal classes. She wrote a workbook for students, *How to Get the Job You Really Want.* These materials served as the basis for a formal, credit-bearing course taught by Employment Opportunities and NCED staff. The course, Job Search Process, became a requirement for all NTID associate-level students.

How to Get the Job You Really Want was adapted by Veatch for general use outside of NTID and was published in 1982 by the National Association of the Deaf. It was made available for purchase by the public and proved to be very popular, with more than 1,000 copies sold in two years.

Employment Information Center

Another way students were encouraged to take a more active role in their job search was through the development of the Employment Information Center (EIC), housed in the Employment Opportunities office suite. It was created in 1977 to be a library of employment-related information, such as directories and employer literature, as well as to provide space and equipment for students. There were job opening announcements, as well as information on services available for deaf people.

Eventually NTID hired a placement aide to obtain and update the resources, and to assist students in researching employers for their co-ops and permanent jobs. Students would then send letters of introduction and résumés by mail to the contacts they found from their research. The EIC was also available to local recent graduates and alumni. It was open during regular office hours, and was staffed by deaf student workers during some evenings and weekend hours. Some of those student assistants would later become NTID faculty members.

In addition, the EIC was also used by Employment Opportunities staff in assisting individual students and NCED staff in employment development and occupational research. The EIC became a central location for information formerly kept in individual staff offices. In 1982, the EIC was named the Victor J. Maguran Memorial Employment Information Center in a formal dedication ceremony after Maguran's passing in 1981.

National Center on Employment of the Deaf

Kathleen Martin, who had been with the employment office since 1976, working on research and placement, was named Manager of the NCED in 1979. NCED continued the employment office's occupational research and employment development, supporting Employment Opportunities placement activities. New undertakings included developing a national clearinghouse of research information regarding employment of deaf persons, and training programs for VR counselors and other professionals working with deaf individuals.

The aim was for NCED to become a national resource and authority on the employment of deaf people in the United States, and to expand employer training programs. NCED became involved in NTID Project Outreach, through which NTID would collaborate with other postsecondary institutions and rehabilitation agencies.

As the NTID employment office expanded, some key partners continued to provide support. In addition to IBM, AT&T collaborated with NTID in different ways. Hiring NTID graduates and co-op students since 1972, AT&T provided accommodations for deaf employees such as teletypewriters for the deaf (TDD) for use in typed telecommunications and interpreters for group meetings.

AT&T also undertook a job analysis project with NCED, studying nine NTID graduates employed there, and examined the limited upward mobility the majority had. One factor, among others, could be the inexperience of many supervisors in working with deaf employees. AT&T made several recommendations to NCED that included training for would-be supervisors and identification of positions that would allow for suitable accommodations. This collaboration with NTID and NCED, first led by Jay Rochlin, district manager of their equal employment opportunity/affirmative action policy, continued with Frank Blount, president of AT&T Network Operations Group.

Employer Training Programs, Recruiting, and Information Sharing

To work on creating and expanding training programs, Mary Rees and Eleanor Stauffer were hired in 1980. Experienced with counseling and teaching, Rees and Stauffer met while volunteering at the Women's Career Center in Rochester. Together, they developed a four-session course that was given at local colleges and to industries. The time and travel required for their work kept them from their families more than they liked, so they came up with the idea of job-sharing. Although it was a somewhat new concept at the time, NTID decided to give it a try, and hired them. Over time, they became known as "Mary and Ellie," and that reflected their partnership since they functioned "jointly as one" in their job.

They developed a number of training sessions for supervisors of deaf employees, human resources managers and company policy makers, job placement staff working with deaf people and for those who trained deaf and hard-of-hearing employees. Their training incorporated some activities that had been developed at NTID. For example, in "The White Noise Experience," participants listened to "white noise," which prevented them from hearing other things. The sound, similar to the noise a waterfall makes, drowned out everything else, similar to the experience of a deaf person, surrounded by others with whom it could be challenging to communicate.

Training workshops were held in various U.S. cities and at NTID. Some employers who came to NTID stayed to interview students. Employer representatives visiting NTID in the early 1980s came from firms such as Ford Motor Company, Texas Instruments, and McDonnell Douglas. Sometimes employer development staff would also go on site to present to various employers, as well as handing out employer information packets developed by NCED to inform employers about NTID, its students and graduates, and communication methods.

NTID started compiling an annotated bibliography in 1980 on employment of deaf persons after conducting a literature review, believed to be the first such search that was published. A media search on the topic was also done, and those results were compiled. These resources were intended to serve employers and service providers seeking information about employing deaf people, and also deaf job seekers. The bibliography was updated for over a decade.

Additionally, NCED staff member Georgene Fritz co-wrote a book with Nancy Smith in 1985, designed as a practical manual for supervisors, human resources managers and trainers on employing deaf and hard-of-hearing workers. Many NTID faculty and staff contributed to the work, as well as an industrial task force made up of employer representatives from IBM, AT&T, 3M, GM, US Steel, and Hewlett-Packard.

Rubella Bulge and Employment Office Expansion

A rubella epidemic from 1963 to 1965, as mentioned elsewhere in this book, resulted in thousands of children born deaf. Those children, known as the "rubella bulge" or "rubella bubble," came of age in the early 1980s. NTID student enrollment reached record levels, so the employment office was faced with an unprecedented number of students seeking co-op and permanent

Mary Ellen Tait works with a student.

employment, and hired more staff.

The EIC was moved to the first floor of the Shumway Dining Commons building, where it had space to expand. It was coordinated by new hire Mary Ellen Tait, who had worked previously in the Career Center at the University of Rochester. The formerly separate Employment Opportunities and NCED also merged, and kept the name National Center on Employment of the Deaf. All staff members became involved in working with employers as well as students.

A number of graduate and professional interns came to work in NCED temporarily during the '80s, including some who came from other countries. Some NTID faculty also left their departments for one year to work in NCED as well, bringing with them their academic knowledge and expertise. Elizabeth Ewell, who had joined NTID's Instructional Television Department in the mid-1970s after working at Kodak, joined NCED in the early 1980s and became manager of the department within a few years.

Deepening Relationships with Employers

In 1986, NCED began to honor employers who repeatedly hired NTID students with a "Recognition of Service Award." Some had long-standing relationships with the NCED, while others were newcomers. Citicorp, GE, New York State Department of Transportation, the University of Rochester, and the U.S. Department of the Navy were among the honorees.

During this time, the demand for employer training increased. Rees and Stauffer developed a training program for both managers and co-workers of deaf employees, called "Working Together: Deaf and Hearing People." The main topics were understanding deafness, communication on the job and integration and accommodation of deaf employees. This program proved to be quite popular, and has remained so. As of this writing, more than 1,000 "Working Together" employer workshops have been conducted since 1984, at NTID and all over the United States. In 1984, a former CIA recruiter named Linda Iacelli was hired into NCED, and went on to lead the department's employer outreach and training efforts for many years.

In 1987, with input from various NTID faculty and staff, Rees and Stauffer wrote training manuals for trainers and participants. These, together with audio and video tapes, and overhead transparency masters, were put together into a package. NCED offered a new "Train-the-trainer" program around the country to teach corporate and academic trainers, as well as human services staff, who were interested in learning to present "Working Together" themselves in their own companies and cities. The "Train-the-trainer" presenters demonstrated and outlined use of the package.

As part of NTID's Educational Development Outreach Project, NCED continued to target specific cities every year for training, while also providing it for individual employers upon request. The "Working Together" training package and participant manuals were distributed to those trained as part of the trainer workshop fee, which made it possible for "Working Together" to be offered to many more audiences than NCED staff could reach on their own.

Institutional Employment Research

Also in the mid-1980s, NTID became the first educational institution to collaborate with the Internal Revenue Service (IRS) in collecting aggregate information about the earnings of its graduates. This analysis found only a 7% gap in earnings between deaf and hearing baccalaureate degree earners. Previous national research had reported the earnings gap between deaf and hearing employees at 28%. The study also found that baccalaureate graduates returned to the federal government what it had invested in the cost of their education through taxes paid in 10 years, and sub-baccalaureate graduates did so in 13 years.

Qualitative research was conducted on the employment experiences of deaf graduates. Those interviewed generally felt comfortable with their ability to perform the work and communicate one-on-one. However, it was more difficult for them in group situations, and they did not always have access to the exchange of informal information in the workplace. Many of those interviewed were anxious about communication, and felt that could be a potential barrier to upward mobility. NCED staff used this research to help graduating students in their preparation for the world of work.

New Decade, New Law, New Technology

In July 1990, the Americans with Disabilities Act, known as the ADA, was passed. Title I went into effect in 1992 and required employers with 15 or more employees to provide "reasonable" accommodations to applicants or employees with disabilities. NCED staff received many employer inquiries about the new law and was able to provide basic information as well as use the opportunity to raise awareness about NTID as a source for possible hires.

Title IV of the ADA called for the establishment of telephone-relay services (TRS) nationwide by 1993, using TDDs, more commonly known as text-telephones (TTY). Each person on the end of a telephone call needed to have this device to type messages back and forth to each other, displayed on a screen or printed out. TRS were service centers that connected a caller with a TTY to a hearing caller who did not have one through relay operators, who conveyed the conversation between callers. This enabled deaf or hard-of-hearing individuals to call anyone at any time, and gave deaf and hard-of-hearing employees the opportunity to make and receive calls from hearing people at work.

TRS was one new way by which deaf and hard-of-hearing individuals could communicate, and other technologies came into play as well. E-mail, collaborative document editing and instant-messaging began to emerge. Some systems allowed several users to "chat" at the same time. For employees who went out of the office frequently, an alpha numeric pager that vibrated when a message was sent could be carried, precursors to today's smartphones.

Co-op Continues

Co-op hiring of NTID students continued, including some new employers. In 1992, Liz Ewell, NCED manager, noted that in addition to appreciating students' skills, these new employers may have been motivated to hire by the need to comply with the ADA. "Employers want to do a better job of hiring disabled people. NTID students can help employers accomplish that goal as well as provide the skills they need."[9]

One of the ways NTID supported co-op employers was by having faculty and staff visit selected co-op students and their supervisors, a practice that continues to this day. During visits, faculty discuss how things are going, provide information and answer questions. The "in-person" interaction can help strengthen the connection with the employer. This support, and student success, helps influence the hiring of additional NTID co-op students, and some of those become permanent employees.

A Bigger Picture Emerges

Congress allowed NTID to begin admitting international students in 1990, and some of those students stayed in the United States for their co-ops while others returned to their native countries. Some were hired in the United States permanently, and some went back home to seek work after graduation, so NCED expanded its employer development into other countries. NCED also hired individuals from different countries, such as Shahin Monshipour from Iran, Ndey Kumba Hinds from The Gambia, and deaf RIT alumna Regina Kiperman-Kiselgof, who came from the Ukraine and attended a deaf school in Moscow before moving to America.

For U.S. citizens in particular, the federal government has had a long history of employing people with disabilities. One federal worker in particular, Paul Meyer, did much to advance co-op and permanent employment of NTID students. He was employed for 24 years at the David Taylor Naval Ship Research and Development Center in Carderock and Annapolis, Maryland, where he worked on developing equal employment opportunity networks and the hiring of people with disabilities.

His program recruited students with disabilities at about 25 colleges, including at NTID, beginning in the mid-1970s. After interviews were finished, Meyer compiled evaluations of the applicants, and made copies to share with employers throughout the Departments of Defense and Agriculture. He also organized an annual conference for federal employees on the employment of people with disabilities. Meyer was honored by NCED in 1987, and received a special citation from NAG in 1989 for his service and commitment to the college. When interviewed in 1993, Meyer said, "I can't speak highly enough about the abilities of the NTID students. They come to the workplace with tons of enthusiasm, energy and the skills necessary to perform well on the job."[10]

In 1992, Meyer became deputy executive director of the President's Committee on Employment of People with Disabilities. His recruiting program continued, becoming the Workforce Recruitment Program (WRP), and still is in operation as of this writing. Annually, federal employees conduct telephone interviews with disabled students all over the country, and make applicant information available in a database to interested employers.

The U.S. Department of Labor's Office of Disability Employment Policy and the U.S. Department of Defense's Office of Diversity Management and Equal Opportunity manage the WRP, which is successful with the participation of many other federal agencies and the private sector as well. Since the program's expansion in 1995, more than 6,000 students and recent graduates with disabilities have been hired for temporary and permanent employment through the WRP.

The Nineties Arrive with Plenty of Change

In the early 1990s, the National Center on Employment of the Deaf became, and remains, the NTID Center on Employment (NCE). NCE maintained and enhanced employment development efforts, through correspondence, calls and visits to employers as well as networking and exhibiting at national meetings of professional organizations and employer conferences. It continued to offer employer training programs all over the United States through the Employer Outreach Project. Training was added in the spring for employers who expected to hire NTID students and graduates in the summer, and in response to requests from individual employers.

The World Wide Web began to emerge during this time as well. Information sharing increased and job-vacancy announcements started to be passed along online. In 1997, the decision was made to close the EIC. Some books and printed materials were still made available centrally in the Lyndon Baines Johnson building (LBJ). NCE developed a website with information for job seekers and employers, which included links to online employment resources, and job postings submitted by employers were added over time. Tait, who had been hired to coordinate the EIC in 1982, returned to LBJ and took on a caseload of students as an employment advisor in NCE (where she remains as of this writing).

Allen Vaala

NTID at Thirty

In 1998, NTID celebrated its 30th anniversary. NTID's *FOCUS* interviewed the now-retired Dr. Frisina, who said:

> The biggest change I've seen relates to the acceptance of deaf graduates into private sector business and industrial employment. NTID has made a dramatic contribution to the economic status of deaf people, both in terms of the number and types of positions. Our alumni have earned their way in technical and professional fields. Moreover, through the influence of NTID, deaf people are better understood and more accepted generally throughout all of society.[11]

The Kodak Connection

At the turn of the century, NTID hired a former employer who had been trained by the NCE. Allen Vaala had been director of university relations and college recruiting for Kodak, and learned about NTID through an NCE workshop onsite. He also oversaw the hiring of some NTID students in co-op positions at Kodak. In December 2000, the company held its first-ever "Kodak Day" at NTID, meeting with students and collecting resumes, interviewing and giving technical demonstrations. Vaala helped generate excitement about working with NTID students within the company, and decided he wanted to enhance opportunities for all companies to work with them. He became NCE director in 2001.

During Vaala's tenure, the NCE website expanded, with enhanced student and employer sections. NCE eventually added a section for "visitors," including parents, who were encouraged to share their potential employer contacts with their children and NCE staff, including those in the organizations employing them. These leads from family and friends benefited not only their sons and daughters, but other students and graduates, in finding employment and helping spread the word about hiring and working with deaf and hard-of-hearing people.

NTID Job Fair

As a service to students and to employers, NTID held its first ever NTID Job Fair in 2001, on the first floor of LBJ, in collaboration with the New York State Department of Labor. This was a chance for students to meet employers from all over the country, find out about potential job opportunities and share their resumes. Some employers also conducted interviews on campus after the job fair.

Employers participating that initial year included Rochester-based companies such as Kodak and Paychex, as well as a local utility company, a manufacturer, and a hospital. Representatives from federal agencies, such as the Defense Contract Audit Agency, the Defense Contract Management Agency, and the U.S. Geological Survey also attended. National employers included IBM, URS Corporation, and the Educational Credit Management Corporation.

An employer presentation preceded the event to provide information on employing deaf and hard-of-hearing students and communication techniques. Said NCE director Allen Vaala at the time, "the job fair showcases the strengths and breadth of disciplines and majors and the strengths of our technically educated students. And it gives NTID faculty, staff and students a glimpse of the needs of businesses and of the job opportunities out there.[12]"

The NTID Job Fair has been held in subsequent years during October, which is designated as National Disability Employment Awareness Month. The number of employers represented has risen from 17 to more than 50 in 2016. Many of them do not know American Sign Language, and an interpreter is provided at each employer table. This is done in person, and more recently, through a video link to an interpreter in a remote location (Video Remote Interpreting, or VRI). At the same time, there has been a steady increase in NTID alumni sent to represent their employers at the event.

Warren Poe, a deaf RIT computing graduate from 1982, was asked by his employer, ITT, to attend the 2007 Job Fair. He and his employer saw it as a chance to increase the diversity of employees in that division. At the time, Poe had three sons attending RIT, including Jonathan, a business student who said at the time, "Having alumni recruiters is good because they show students that companies hire from RIT, and their being here

creates a great relationship between students and alumni. This relationship becomes part of the student's network, and that's a very important result of the job fair."[13]

After the 2014 NTID Job Fair, Loriann Macko, NTID Director of Alumni and Constituent Relations (and a deaf RIT alumna) said, "I repeatedly witnessed alumni representatives commenting that 'The students are great,' and 'I'm so excited about the interviews we have lined up for tomorrow.' Our alumni see the quality and work ethic of our students on display, and they can look back with pride on their experiences as students here. In turn, our students see terrific role models in the alumni who return to campus to represent their companies. It's a win-win all the way around."[14]

Paying it Forward

Some alumni have become employment advisors in NCE; for example, deaf RIT business graduate John Macko obtained a position as a financial reviewer at the Prudential Asset Management Company after an on-campus interview at NTID, then joined NCE in 1994. After several years of sharing his experiences with students, he became the director of NCE in 2007, a position he holds to this day.

Just as alumni share what it is like to work for their employers with students and recent graduates, students who have been on co-op tell other students about their successful experiences. Students become unofficial ambassadors for their employers, and help fellow students prepare for their co-op interviews. The Department of Defense has begun a program where it employs a deaf student at RIT to educate other RIT students and alumni about employment opportunities during the academic year, especially those with disabilities.

Outstanding Employer Partner Awards

NTID's relationships with employers over the years have helped bring about employment opportunities for deaf and hard-of-hearing students and graduates. Employers benefit by having students and graduates with state-of-the-art skills that bring talent and diversity to their workforce. Many, after having success with initial hiring, continue to hire. To recognize these valued partnerships, NCE began in 2010 to present an "Outstanding Employer Partner Award" annually to corporations and smaller businesses, government agencies, educational institutions and non-profit organizations. The awards are given during the NTID Job Fair employer luncheon. Early recipients included the Defense Finance and Accounting Service, BNY Mellon, and the City of Los Angeles.

Economic Benefits of Completing a Degree from RIT/NTID

In 2013, the results of a study conducted by NTID in partnership with Cornell University, the Internal Revenue Service, and the Social Security Administration showed that, at age 50, deaf and hard-of-hearing RIT/NTID graduates with bachelor's degrees earn 178 percent more than such graduates who obtain degrees from other colleges and universities. Those with NTID associate degrees earn 95 percent more than such graduates earning degrees elsewhere. By age 40, deaf and hard-of-hearing persons who graduate from other postsecondary institutions collect Supplemental Security Income (SSI) at more than twice the rate of those who graduated from RIT/NTID. The study also found that an RIT/NTID education results in higher rates of employment and longer careers.[15]

In addition to the societal contributions of RIT/NTID graduates, said NTID president and alumnus Dr. Gerry Buckley,

> ...[This] study has demonstrated that completing an RIT/NTID education has significant economic benefits for deaf and hard-of-hearing graduates, allowing them to contribute to society through taxes on wages earned...[We] are proud that we continue to accomplish what Congress had originally envisioned: providing the best technological postsecondary education for deaf and hard-of-hearing students and helping them secure careers upon graduation.[16]

Mary Ellen Tait is Assistant Director in the NTID Center on Employment.

Notes

1. "NTID students are pioneers in co-op educational program" and "Three Assistant Deans Appointed." *FOCUS Magazine* (December 1970–January 1971): 2–3, 4.

2. "Placement called 'Mission Possible.'" *FOCUS Magazine* (February–March 1971): 6, 12.

3. "Maguran gears up placement." *FOCUS Magazine* (May–June 1971): 5, 13.

4. "Your part in the show." *FOCUS Magazine* (April–May 1972): 6.

5. "Graduates' skills needed by industry." *FOCUS Magazine* (January–February 1974): 6.

6. "Business, industry receptive to hiring graduates." *FOCUS Magazine* (November–December 1974): 19.

7. Joan Cooley, "Getting the job done in the 'Big Apple.'" *FOCUS Magazine* (Winter 1978): 12.

8. Cooley, "Getting the job done."

9. Deborah Waltzer, "Co–opportunity." *FOCUS Magazine* (Fall 1992): 24–27.

10. Pamela Seabon, "Paul Meyer: A friend, in deed." *FOCUS Magazine* (Winter/Spring 1993): 22.

11. Kathryn Schmitz, "Reflections of the Elite Eight." *FOCUS Magazine* (Fall 1998): 4.

12. Kathy Johncox, "Hitting the ground running." *FOCUS Magazine* (Spring/Summer 2002): 10–11.

13. Kathy Johncox, "Alumni return as recruiters." *FOCUS Magazine* (Spring/Summer 2008): 6–7.

14. Kathy Johncox, "Job fair brings alumni recruiters back to campus." *FOCUS Magazine* (Fall/Winter 2015): 3.

15. Greg Livadas, "An RIT/NTID Education: A Worthwhile Investment." *FOCUS Magazine* (Spring/Summer 2013): 3.

16. Greg Livadas, "An RIT/NTID Education: A Worthwhile Investment."

Conclusion
NTID 2043: A Living, Evolving and Thriving Institute

Dr. Peter C. Hauser and Dr. Jess Cuculick

Introduction and Overview

In 2017, Dr. William Destler, RIT's ninth president, described NTID as "one of the brightest jewels in RIT's crown for decades." As NTID prepared to celebrate its 50th anniversary, Destler reflected on the college's many accomplishments over half of a century:

> The education provided by NTID to thousands of deaf and hard-of-hearing individuals has, of course, opened up a world of opportunities for them, and NTID's record of placing these students in meaningful positions upon graduation is second to none. But just as important, the presence of NTID faculty, staff, and students on RIT's campus has brought to our campus a special kind of diversity unavailable anywhere else, and RIT has been a richer and more humane institution as a result. Congratulations, NTID! For 50 years, you have represented the best that RIT has to offer.[1]

We agree with Dr. Destler that NTID has become a part of RIT's identity and culture, experienced by students when they come to campus to receive a higher education. NTID's existence at RIT has expanded and evolved over time, and there are some useful benchmarks for measuring that evolution. For example, in 1988, when NTID celebrated its 20th anniversary, the faculty and staff at that time paused to recognize the college's remarkable achievements. They dreamed that NTID's relationship with RIT would solidify, creating a document known as *Vision Quest*.[2] This document is the source of any predictions in this chapter that are noted to have been made in 1988.

One such prediction was made when the NTID Faculty Council (NFC) at the time was asked what NTID would be like when it celebrated its 50th anniversary. The members predicted that the president of RIT would sign the commencement address every year. This prediction was realized earlier than they anticipated. In 1993, RIT's eighth president, Dr. Albert Simone, signed a portion of his inaugural address. He was the first RIT president to take ASL classes and eventually began to sign his commencement address every year. When Dr. Destler became the RIT president, he did the same.

The NFC was not the only group in 1988 that made accurate predictions of what NTID would be like in 2018. The staff of NTID's former Division of Public Affairs (now NTID's Communications, Marketing, and Multimedia Services office) stated 30 years ago, "Just as we snicker at the ditto machine [a hand-cranked contraption that produced single, purple copies], you probably can't imagine how we survived using primitive TDDs [Telecommunication Devices for the Deaf] and paper news releases."[3]

They also predicted that in 2018, their department would produce "videotaped viewbooks and other recruiting materials...Prospective students get a taste of NTID at RIT by interacting with teachers and other students in the classroom, experiencing the challenges of a successful lacrosse season, and participating in student government—all through video."[4]

The Division of Public Affairs' predictions were not far off the mark. At that time, they probably did not imagine the sophistication of networked communication and information exchanges that are typical in children's and adults' lives today. They probably could not imagine social media, nor children and grandparents posting personal videos on Facebook or other digital platforms.

As technology has improved, access to education has also improved for NTID students at RIT. In 1988, Stephanie J. Flagg, an interpreter from the Department of Interpreting Services (now Department of Access Services) suggested that "All movies shown on campus (especially in the classroom) [will be] captioned. Now, in 1988, there is a two-year waiting list from the captioning department." As NTID celebrates its 50th anniversary in 2018, the RIT Office of the Provost has made it clear for almost a decade that it expects that "all media used in face-to-face, blended, and online courses will be transcribed and captioned…[and] uncaptioned audio-visual materials may not be provided as course content."[5] RIT/NTID has gone above and beyond the 1988 predictions in ensuring captioning for its classrooms. RIT's Teaching and Learning Services now captions media for faculty and students with a short turnaround period.

In compiling this chapter, we asked NTID faculty, staff, students, and alumni to share their predictions on what NTID would be like in the year 2043. We identified six themes: 1) NTID students and alumni, 2) NTID faculty and staff, 3) access services, 4) NTID facilities and technology, 5) NTID global reputation and impact, and 6) employment. We present quotes that highlight the six themes.

NTID Students and Alumni

In 1968, NTID had its first class of 70 deaf and hard-of-hearing students. This number grew to 1,130 when NTID celebrated its 25th anniversary. In 2009, NTID had its highest enrollment of 1,450 students. As the college celebrates its 50th anniversary, there are approximately 1,300 students enrolled. The number of NTID students "cross-registered" in baccalaureate programs in other RIT colleges has grown from 15% in 1982, to 30% in 1992, to 42% in 2017. Dr. Gerard J. Buckley (SVP

'74, BS '78; sixth president of NTID Student Congress), current President of NTID and Vice President and Dean of RIT, predicted that in 2043, the NTID workforce will reflect the diversity of the NTID student population.

Dr. Christine Licata, past NTID Associate Vice President of Academic Affairs and current Senior Associate Provost for RIT, hopes that by 2043, "the number of deaf and hard-of-hearing students who receive a bachelor's or master's degree from RIT hits a record of at least 75%." Licata also hopes that NTID "continues to represent a living and learning microcosm of what it means to be situated in a fast-paced, global environment and that this will drive curriculum and educational programming."[6]

Dr. Charlotte Thoms, NTID Director of Diversity Recruitment and Retention, said:

Our students [will] hail from diverse backgrounds (urban/suburban, national/international)…[All] the students have one goal and that's to create a better world for everyone regardless of their different abilities. I don't see the battles over language, race, and maybe not even culture because I envision a transculturalized society where what is today considered the minority culture will become in the future the majority culture. The transculturalized society is accepting of the unique qualities that make human interaction interesting and enriching. NTID will be known worldwide for developing leaders with this same philosophy.[7]

Dr. T. Alan Hurwitz, who started working at NTID in 1970 as an Educational Specialist for RIT's College of Engineering, became the first deaf dean of NTID in 1998. He served many roles on campus and ended his illustrious career in Rochester in 2010 as the president of NTID and Vice President and Dean of RIT. He predicted in 1988 that NTID would have at least 10,000 alumni by its 50th anniversary and that:

The Alumni Association of NTID will be a strong, vibrant and viable organization to work with its alma mater…[and]…many alumni will have gone on for their advance[d] degrees at RIT and in other colleges and universities elsewhere…and support services will have become a way of life with these alumni everywhere.[8]

As of the Spring of 2017, NTID has around 9,000 alumni. Loriann Macko ('94), Director of Alumni and Constituent Relations, stated:

With the growth of our alumni population has come strength in our alumni involvement and connections. Alumni regularly network and assist each other in cross-collaboration that bridges innumerable fields and various cultural and geographic regions. Our more experienced alumni mentor young alums as they graduate, and they provide support and guidance, as well as connections to employment opportunities...As NTID celebrates 75 years, our alumni will be close to 16,000 strong and continue to grow annually, with approximately 300 new alumni added to the fold each year. NTID has enjoyed steady success, and our alumni population continues to flourish. RIT/NTID alumni can now capitalize on a truly global network and routinely connect with fellow alums for global outreach and community service, as well as recreational travel. This applies not only to our deaf alumni, but also our hearing alumni from interpreting and teaching programs, both of which enroll and graduate top candidates in their fields.[9]

Joseph Riggio (SVP '88, AAS '92, BS '01), the current president of the NTID Alumni Association and the Sales Manager at ZVRS, reflected on the past 25 years and wrote that "Deaf and hard-of-hearing students and graduates broke the glass ceiling in their workplaces, and we will continue to see glass ceilings being broken for the next 25 years to the point that there will be no ceilings left to break."[10]

Dr. Robert Q. Pollard, the Associate Dean of Research, predicts that the "75-year NTID reunion will bring a record number of alumni back to their alma mater, including hundreds who hold doctoral degrees, are CEOs of successful companies, and alumni who have held high-visibility positions in the national and state governments."[11] Buckley also believes that by 2043, at least 10 NTID alumni will be CEOs of Fortune 500 companies.[12]

NTID Faculty and Staff

Patrick Graybill, who joined the National Theater of the Deaf in 1969 and served as a performer and as a director, has taught courses at the Department of Performing Arts at NTID. He is also the current Deacon for the Emmanuel Church of the Deaf at St. Monica Church. Graybill stated that:

In 2043, I will rest well in my gravesite in the Resurrection Cemetery. My spirit will soar in awe of certain changes on the RIT campus: an increasing number of deaf and hard-of-hearing administrators, professors, and researchers of varied races...and also that a deaf female alumna will serve as the new NTID president.[13]

The 1988 NTID Faculty Council predicted that by 2018, at least 50 percent of the faculty would be deaf or hard-of-hearing. As of December 2017, 41% of NTID faculty were deaf or hard-of-hearing. Pollard believes that at least by 2043, the proportion of deaf to hearing faculty at NTID will surpass the 50-50 ratio and that all faculty will hold a terminal degree in their field of study.[14]

Dr. Scott Smith, medical doctor and research faculty member agrees, and Dr. Buckley is even more optimistic. "[I believe that by 2043, NTID will have at] least 75% deaf faculty and administrators and staff, well-represented by all members of all different diverse backgrounds and on par with RIT with academic and training opportunities for all D/HH students," says Smith.[15]

Buckley adds, "NTID's faculty in 2043 will be made up of 85% Deaf and hard of hearing individuals. More than 90% of these individuals [will] have terminal degrees with outstanding records of scholarship and productivity."[16]

Dr. Denise Kavin, an NTID alumna, Assistant Dean and Executive Director of NTID Outreach, Placements, and Special Projects agrees, predicting that in 2043, "the majority of the NTID administrators will be deaf themselves."[17]

Dr. Kim Brown Kurz, (SVP '88, BS '93, MS '95), Chair of NTID's Department of American Sign Language and Interpreting Education, believes that "25 years from now, NTID will have some of the most innovative degree programs for deaf and hard-of-hearing students in the area of STEAM (Science, Technology, Engineering, Arts, and Mathematics), including health care."[18]

The emphasis on developing more training opportunities for NTID students in STEAM and especially healthcare has been a priority in the 2010s. Dr. Daniel Ornt, vice president and dean of RIT's College of Health Sciences and Technology (CHST) stated that his college "is proud to play a role in NTID's commitment to this effort through offering access to programs in healthcare professions and biomedical research."[19] Kurz noted that:

> Currently, we are struggling to find qualified Deaf people who are working in the STEAM fields to come and teach at NTID. That will change as NTID will produce and graduate more and more successful deaf and hard-of-hearing people in the field of STEAM. I predict that NTID will have more master's and new doctoral degree programs to prepare our people working with the Deaf community, especially in the STEAM areas. NTID will continue to lead and prosper as the "MIT" of the Deaf Education.[20]

Kavin also believes that there will be more graduate programs at NTID, as well as more bachelor's degree programs. Pollard predicts there will be five master's degree programs and two doctoral degree programs. Additionally, Buckley predicts that by 2043, NTID will have graduated at least 75 PhD students with more than 25 of them returning to NTID as faculty members. He also believes that "NTID's emphasis on health and science careers [will have] resulted in the career success of more than 400 deaf scientists and health care professionals who are practicing in the USA and abroad."[21]

Jamie Munro (STOP '90, BS '94), Associate Director of NTID Admissions and Data, foresees that:

> NTID [will become] a true global education hub, still serving at the intersection of progressive deaf education and technology. Virtual learning will take place around the world with the NTID faculty leading the way. The new mandate for NTID will be delivering training and information to students beyond the RIT campus, tapping into the vast potential of deaf talent across continents.[22]

Regina Kiperman-Kiselgof (SVP '95, BS '00, MS '01), Assistant Director of the NTID Center on Employment, thinks that by 2043 at least half of all courses offered by NTID will be online.[23] However, Christopher Knigga (SVP '89, AAS '93), Director of NTID Facilities Services and Sustainability, predicts that all of the classes will be online and faculty will not need to live in Rochester.[24]

Access Services

Kiperman-Kiselgof predicts that NTID will provide different types of access services to students in the same classroom through the provision of multiple video remote interpreting in spoken English, cued English, and ASL.[25] Dr. Michael Stinson, Professor and NTID Researcher, predicts that:

> ...classroom instruction will become more and more interactive, including the use of small group work and various combinations of online and in-class learning. Accommodations such as professional sign language interpreters, real-time captioning, and note takers in classrooms will be challenged because these services are geared primarily for traditional lecture courses.[26]

Buckley predicts that the "NTID Department of Access Services (DAS) and Department of American Sign Language and Interpreter Education (ASLIE) [will be] viewed as international models of excellence, which are frequently sought out for consultation services."[27] Dr. Robert R. Davila, NTID vice president and CEO from 1996 to 2006, also notes that "NTID is already one of the world's largest trainers of sign language interpreters and it will continue in the future. This is a field that critically needs world-wide access, especially in the developing world."[28]

Munro believes that "access technologies will bring people closer together than ever, making the term 'inclusion' a word of the past,"[29] while Buckley believes that NTID will remain on the cutting edge of access technology and that the use of Automatic Speech

Recognition (ASR) will be commonplace in 2043. He and several others suspect that ASR technology will be prevalent throughout campus, saying that "[NTID will serve as] a model for businesses and corporations throughout the US and the world."[30]

"Advances in speech recognition technology will provide individuals with directionally controllable, mobile, efficient, effective, reliable, anywhere/anytime speech-to-text services," says Dr. James DeCaro, (Professor Emeritus, Dean of NTID from 1985 to 1998, and Interim President of NTID 2009 to 2011).[31] Similarly, Dr. Rico Peterson, Assistant Dean and Director of NTID Access Services, says that ASR "will revolutionize classroom access, and will be more ubiquitous and more accurate."[32] Furthermore, Pollard believes that by 2043, ASR will have:

...long been perfected. All non-signing teachers at RIT, with deaf or hard-of-hearing students in their classes, use ASR equipment that instantly and accurately shows their comments on a display that follows them wherever they walk and differentiates teacher comments from fellow students' comments, which also are captured by ASR technology.[33]

The idea of ASR technology is not new, as back in 1988, Hurwitz predicted that by 2018 "real time graphic displays, including an automatic voice recognizer and synthesizer, will be part of the classroom environment wherever deaf students are."[34] NTID is not there yet, but it is very likely by its 75th anniversary.

NTID Facilities

In 1988, the NFC hoped that the Dining Commons would have low-calorie gourmet options by the time NTID celebrates its 50th anniversary. The authors of this chapter agree that the food at the Commons has improved over the years with a greater number of healthy food options. There are low-calorie (non-gourmet) options and gourmet options (not low-calorie). Kavin predicts that in 2043,

...we would have new mini-cafes in LBJ and SDC run by deaf students, offering organic, vegan and gluten-free food options...One third of the parking

lot would be reserved for electric cars. There would be several meditation and yoga rooms available, with mini-classes offered throughout the day.[35]

During NTID's 25th anniversary, the NFC predicted that by 2018 there would be strobe lights in all of the offices in LBJ. Today, the offices at NTID have doorbells that activate strobe lights when pressed. Additionally, throughout RIT there are red boxes on the walls with strobe lights for fire alarms. Strobe-light fire alarms can also be found in many buildings outside of RIT because of the Americans with Disabilities Act of 1990. RIT continues to build new buildings each year, and their accessibility to different groups of students is taken into consideration during the initial planning. This was especially true for the CSD Student Development Center that was added to LBJ in 2007 and the Rosica Hall addition in 2013. Of special note, Rosica Hall has been certified as a Leadership in Energy and Environmental Design (LEED) building, which is a prestigious honor.[36]

Dr. Alim Chandani (SVP '98, BS '02; 30th president of NTID Student Congress), founder and CEO of Global Reach Out Initiative, predicts that "as technology continues to evolve at a brisk pace, [there will be] many technological advances with NTID being at the center of it all."[37] Several current NTID administrators, faculty and staff, to our surprise, predicted in the year 2043, there would be widespread use of holograms. For example, Dr. Robert Q. Pollard, NTID Associate Dean of Research, predicts that "experiments in distance-rendered, holographic image interpreting, pioneered at NTID, are proving quite promising, not only at RIT/NTID, but in elementary and secondary educational settings collaborating in these studies."[38]

Loriann Macko (BS '94), Director of Alumni and Constituent Relations, also foresees that the NTID Alumni Relations Office will stay in touch with alumni: "largely through more modern avenues like video hologram messages, and routinely hosts large events which any alum can virtually join in."[39]

Some of the faculty and staff predicted that when NTID celebrates its 75th anniversary, there will be some new buildings. Interestingly, each person who mentioned new buildings specified that the buildings would be used for Science, Technology, Engineering, and Mathematics (STEM) majors and for research laboratories. For example, Knigga predicts that NTID "will be full of research labs, conference rooms and training rooms."[40] Pollard goes a little further, claiming that by 2043, "the physical plant at NTID has seen the major renovations of several buildings, including a significant expansion of discipline-based laboratory space to complement the center-based research that continues to fill Rosica Hall, but also has taken up residence in NTID's newest building."[41]

Thoms takes her speculation even further, foreseeing that:

> [NTID will have two new structures that will be both] environmentally sound, self-sufficient...[with] compartments with students and robots working collaboratively with worldwide industries to improve the issues that the world will face politically, environmentally, socially and technologically. Campus will have overhead highways with train-like transporters that make navigating across campus in seconds without braving the weather. A see-through substance, but more durable than plastic and clearer than glass, developed by a group of RIT/NTID Imagineers absorbs heat from the air in the winter and cool from warmth in the summer to allow the two buildings to have the same temperature year-round without exhausting the funds to RG&E.[42]

NTID Global Reputation and Impact

When asked about NTID's reputation in the future, Sasha L. Ponappa (SOAR '01, BS '05) replied, "I know that in 25 years NTID will continue to be a premier university (or institute) that empowers deaf and hard-of-hearing students to achieve their dreams of higher education."[43]

Thomastine Sarchet (BS '03, MS '09) Associate Research Professor and Director for NTID International Education Outreach makes a similar prediction. "My heart tells me that NTID will be a national and international resource center of excellence. We will be providing cutting-edge academic programs, preparing students for a global society, and serve as the preeminent

model of interdisciplinary research and practice in Deaf Education."[44]

Dr. Ryne Raffaelle, RIT Vice President of Research and Associate Provost, wrote:

> It has been very gratifying to see the tremendous growth in research at NTID...as we look to the future, I definitely see this trend continuing. I'm often asked in what areas do you see this growth? Will it be in regards to research on deaf education, or the development and use of access technology, or simply just more deaf and hard-of-hearing faculty and student researchers participating in domain specific research? My answer is: all of the above. Whether it is developing the training to help teachers, or preparing the deaf and hard of hearing for careers in specialized fields such as healthcare, or developing new tools to help the deaf and hard of hearing, these are all areas in which we excel. In 25 years, I see us as the absolute national and international leader in research in this domain.[45]

Dr. Mary Karol Matchett (SVP '85, BS '88), Assistant Vice President for Student and Academic Services, agrees:

> NTID will continue to be the pipeline for promoting success in our deaf/hard-of-hearing/hearing students' academic/career advancement and also, a resource center for professionals, parents and colleagues around the world due to the new additional academic programs, grants, online courses and strong partnerships with professionals, parents, alumni and stakeholders.[46]

Dr. Buckley, however, gets more specific in his prognostication, saying that by 2043,

> NTID has established regional centers on each continent, which provide critical outreach services to Deaf individuals and their families. The Gulf Region International Center now serves over 2,000 students annually. More than 3,000 students are served through the Chinese Center. Many of these students complete their initial degrees on their

home campuses prior to coming to RIT to complete advanced studies.[47]

Rick Postl (SVP '90, BS '95), NTID Senior Associate Director of Admissions, believes that "when NTID reaches its 75th year of existence, it is going to have a solid presence, a tremendous captivating effect on the quality of life and how deaf individuals are perceived around the world."[48] Jules Chiavaroli (MS '83), former Program Coordinator for NTID Arts and Imaging Studies and current Professor at RIT's Golisano Institute of Sustainability agrees with Postl, saying, "...I could also see [NTID] becoming a stronger central institution that takes on the world of Deaf education. Perhaps it becomes an agency of the United Nations. Are we ready for the International Technical Institute for the Deaf (ITID)?"[49]

Dr. Todd Pagano, 2012 United States Professor of the Year and NTID Associate Dean for Teaching and Scholarship Excellence, stated:

Through an ongoing student-centered educational approach focused on teaching knowledge that is directly applicable to success in professional careers, NTID will have effectively eliminated the employment and degree attainment gaps for deaf and hard-of-hearing students—further showcasing this talented pool of valued members of the workforce.[50]

Tracy Ivy (SVP '89, BS '96, MS '00, MS '09), NTID's first Black Deaf NSC president, has a similar vision for the future:

In 25 years, it is my hope that NTID becomes a mecca of multicultural communities where entering Deaf, Deaf-Blind and Hard-of-Hearing students with multifarious modes of communication have outstanding services and resources met by culturally affirmative staff and administrators. As they enter the working world, our students are empowered, well-rounded, and successful with their endeavors in their lives as they emerge into the real world.[51]

The 1988 NFC predicted that by 2018 all faculty/staff will sign proficiently. Similarly, in 1988, Hurwitz

also predicted that by now "[s]tudents will no longer complain about their teachers' communication skills."[52] Unfortunately, neither prediction came true. We hope NTID commits the next 25 years to ensuring that the college becomes a place where all communication barriers no longer exist, while embracing the culture and language of the Deaf, and of deaf people with emerging identities. Munro agrees:

...Our foundation of ASL and Deaf culture cannot change. NTID is all about the Deaf experience and the journey we take together. NTID should continue to provide what other colleges cannot do—the opportunity for students to embrace their Deaf identities. By celebrating ASL and Deaf culture at its core, NTID can continue its long history of providing deaf students a world class education, personal growth and the opportunity to reach for what is beyond our imaginations today.[53]

Lastly, Buckley predicts that as NTID celebrates its 75th anniversary, "NTID's Sunshine 4.0 is performing before thousands of students each year, bringing national and international recognition of ASL and the theater to our campus."[54]

Dr. Jess Cuculick is Associate Director for the Center on Cognition and Language. **Dr. Peter Hauser** is the Director for the Center on Cognition and Language, an on-campus research center.

Notes

1. William Destler, personal communication, 2017.
2. Christine Licata and Laurie Brewer, eds., *Vision Quest.* (Rochester, N.Y.: National Technical Institute for the Deaf, 1988).
3. Christine Licata and Laurie Brewer, eds., *Vision Quest.*
4. Christine Licata and Laurie Brewer, eds., *Vision Quest.*
5. Rochester Institute of Technology Division of Academic Affairs, "Guidelines for Captioning Audio-Visual Media." (2015) https://www.rit.edu/academicaffairs/sites/rit.edu. academicaffairs/files/images/Captioning%20Guidelines%20 rev.%202.15.pdf.
6. Christine Licata, personal communication, 2017
7. Charlotte Thoms, personal communication, 2017.

8. T. Alan Hurwitz, personal communication, 2017.

9. Loriann Macko, personal communication, 2017.

10. Joseph Riggio, personal communication, 2017.

11. Robert Q. Pollard, personal communication, 2016.

12. Gerard Buckley, personal communication, 2017.

13. Patrick Graybill, personal communication, 2017.

14. Robert Q. Pollard, personal communication, 2016.

15. Scott R. Smith, personal communication, 2016.

16. Gerard Buckley, personal communication, 2017.

17. Denise Kavin, personal communication, 2016.

18. Kim Kurz, personal communication, 2017.

19. Daniel Ornt, personal communication, 2017.

20. Kim Kurz, personal communication, 2017.

21. Gerard Buckley, personal communication, 2017.

22. Jamie Munro, personal communication, 2017.

23. Regina Kiperman-Kiselgof, personal communication, 2016.

24. Christopher Knigga, personal communication, 2016.

25. Regina Kiperman-Kiselgof, personal communication, 2017.

26. Michael Stinson, personal communication, 2016.

27. Gerard Buckley, personal communication, 2017.

28. Robert R. Davila, personal communication, 2017.

29. Jamie Munro, personal communication, 2017.

30. Gerard Buckley, personal communication, 2017.

31. James DeCaro, personal communication, 2017.

32. Rico Peterson, personal communication, 2017.

33. Robert Q. Pollard, personal communication, 2016.

34. T. Alan Hurwitz, personal communication, 2017.

35. Denise Kavin, personal communication, 2017.

36. Christopher Knigga, personal communication, 2017.

37. Alim Chandani, personal communication, 2017.

38. Robert Q. Pollard, personal communication, 2016.

39. Loriann Macko, personal communication, 2017.

40. Christopher Knigga, personal communication, 2017.

41. Robert Q. Pollard, personal communication, 2016.

42. Charlotte Thoms, personal communication, 2017.

43. Sasha L. Ponappa, personal communication, 2017.

44. Thomastine Sarchet, personal communication, 2017.

45. Ryne Raffaelle, personal communication, 2017.

46. Mary Karol Matchett, personal communication, 2016

47. Gerard Buckley, personal communication, 2017.

48. Rick Postl, personal communication, 2016.

49. Jules Chiavaroli, personal communication, 2016.

50. Todd Pagano, personal communication, 2016.

51. Tracy Ivy, personal communication, 2017.

52. T. Alan Hurwitz, personal communication, 2017.

53. Jamie Munro, personal communication, 2017.

54. Gerard Buckley, personal communication, 2017.

Index

Note: Page numbers in italics indicate illustrations. Those with a *t* indicate tables.

on, 115; scholarship related to, 104–5

Doctor, T. Jane, *110*

Dooling, Robb, *199*

Downes, Susan, 8

drama club. *See* Masquers Drama Club

Driscoll, Matthew, 6

Dudis, Paul, 18

Dugan, Nicole, 202

Dupor, Susan, 53, 54, 57, 59–60, *60*

Durr, Patti, 25t, 35, 47–50, *49*; documentary films of, 49; on Dyer Arts Center, 57; *HeART of Deaf Culture* by, 49; outstanding teaching award of, 153

Dyer, Helen, 55–57, 59, 117

Dyer Arts Center, 51–61, *52–61*, 95, 117

Dyer Gallery, 40

Eastman Kodak Company, 53, 98, 210, 216

Eaton, Isaiah, 22

Ebony Club, 66–67, 72, 112

Education of the Handicapped Children Act, 187

Educational Development Outreach Project, 214

Egelston-Dodd, Judy, 187

Eickman, Jordan, 25t

Eisenhart Award for Outstanding Teaching, 152–53

Ekeberg, Anders, 154

Electromechanical Technology (EMT), 164

Ellingson, Mark, 117

Elliot, Lisa B., 131t

Elliott, Peter, 30

Elliott, Richard, 208, 211

Ely, Newby, 25t

Emerton, Greg, 48

Emmorey, Karen, 25t

Emperor Jones (multimedia production), 36, 113

Employer Training Programs, 212–14

Employment Information Center (EIC), 212, 213

Enders, Marilyn, 140

English Learning Center (ELC), 44

Enify, 201

entrepreneurship, 195, 197–98

environmentalism, 2, 168, 225, 227

Épée, Abbé Charles-Michel de l', 22

Epstein, Eric, 57

Equal Access Now movement, 68

Equal Employment Opportunities program, 102t, 103

Esposito, Erin, 6, 71

Ethiopia, 108, 191, 192

Etkie, Gary J., 8

Evans, Ashleen, 74t

Evenstad, Colleen, 23

Everts, Joanne DeRoller, 30

Ewell, Liz, 215

Experimental Educational Theatre (EET), 31, 32–33

Expressions of Diversity Annual Conferences, 107

Facilities Management Services (FMS), 104

Faculty and Staff Sign Language Program (FSSL), 15–16, 18

Faculty Loan Program, 210

Faculty Teaching Development, 150–52

Fagan, Garth, 31

Fair Labor Standards Act (FLSA), 139

Faison, Eva, 66

Fallon, Barbara M., 8

Farrell, Scott, 24t

Feder, Mark, 8, *64*, 65, 73t

Feeney, John, *37*

Felo, Chris, 30

Fergerson, C. Tim, 51

Finks, Anthony, 209, *211*

Finton, Lynn, 153, 180, 184, 185

Fischer, Susan D., 26t, 27t, 105

Fjeld, Juliana, 22

Flagg, Stephanie J., 222

Flanagan, Sean "Skip," *77–83*, 77–84

Fleischer, Flavia S., 24t

Fleischer, Lawrence, 26t

Flowers, Amy, *35*

Flying Words Project, 44, 45

Forbes, Sean, 29

Forestier, Claudius, 22

Foster, Susan, 104, 131t

Foundation for Encouragement of Social Contribution (FESCO), 93

Fox, Barbara, 49

Fox, Joe, 39

Francis, Pamela, 141

Frawley, Pat, 33

Frelich, Phyllis, 35, 41

Holocaust, 49, *58*, 105
Hong Kong, 191, 192
Hood, Nicole, 200
Hooker, Scott, 183
Hurwitz, T. Alan, 3, 68, 95–97, *96*, 154; on Alumni Association, 222–23; on automatic speech recognition, 225; on interpreter education, 136, 173–85, *177*, *178*, *182*
Hurwitz, Vicki, 25t, *48*, 49
HZ Innovations, 201–2

Iacelli, Linda, 214
IBM Corporation, 209, 210, 217
Imagine RIT: Innovation and Creativity Festival, 198–99, *199*
India, 191, 192
Individuals with Disabilities Education Act (IDEA), 19, 135, 176
Industrial Drafting Technology (IDT), 164
Information and Computing Studies, 198
innovation as education, 195–205, *196–204*
Institute Curriculum Committee (ICC), 19
Instructional Television Department, 211
Intercity Upkeep, Inc., 109
inter-disciplinary education, 159
International Center for Hearing and Speech Research, 92
international regional centers, 226–27
internships, 211
interpreters, 3, 95, 135–39; education of, 173–85, *177*, *178*, *182*; in health care settings, 184–85; overuse syndrome among, 138
InvisibleCAPTIONS, 201
Isobe, Gerald, 8, *78*
Ivy, Tracy, 227

Jackson, Susan, 35, 71
Jacob, Philip J., 8
Jacobs, Marjorie, 177
Jacobson, Andrew, 8
Jacques, Tabitha, 54, 57
Jaeger, Casey, 200–201
Jamison, Steven, 210
Japan, 191
Jeter, Camille, 29

Jewish Deaf Week, 103
job placement, 207–18
Johnson, Claudia Alta "Lady Bird," 117
Johnson, Ellen Renee, 108–9, *109*
Johnson, Robert, 27t
Johnston, Michelle, 191
Johnston, Paul, 51, 53, 56, 57–58, *58*
Joint Educational Specialist Program (JESP), 92, 187
Jones, Alex, 105
Jones, C.J., 29
Jordaan, Braam, 24t

Kachites, Donna, 44
Kalinoski, Richard, 37
Kannapell, Barbara, 25t
Kanter, Ann, 102
Karpinski, Harry, 180
Kate Gleason College of Engineering (KGCOE), 168, 169
Katich, Justin, 203
Katz, Charles, 26t
Kauppinen, Liisa, 24t
Kavin, Denise, 223–25
Kegel, Judy, 21, 27t
Keiffer, Robert, 153
Kellard, Wade, 201, 202
Kelly, Ronald R., 125–33, 127t, 131t, 132t
Kelstone, Aaron, 29–41, 49
Kemp, James, 74t
Kennedy, Kent, 73t
Kenney, Patricia, 48
Khalsa, Baldev Kaur, 14
Kiel, Paul, 73t
Kielbus, Melissa, 201
King, Frances Carlberg, 53, 56, 59
Kinuthia, Waithera, 104
Kiperman-Kiselgof, Regina, 215
Knigga, Christopher, 2, 226
Kodak. *See* Eastman Kodak Company
Kohls, Hans, 202
Kononenko, George O., 8
Kulakowski, Adriana, 153
Kuntz, Ann Marie, 141
Kuntze, Marlon, 26t
Kurz, Christopher, 24t, 153, 187–93
Kurz, Kim Brown, 3, 13–23, 24t, 184, 185, 223–24

Oral Deaf Adults Section (ODAS), 177
Ornt, Daniel, 224
Orr, Jim, 29–41, *32, 37*
Osugi, Yutaka, 26t
Outstanding Employer Partner Awards, 217–18
overuse syndrome, among interpreters, 138

Padden, Carol, 25t
Pagano, Todd, 129–30, 153, 154, 227; on STEM edu-
    cation, 159–70, 168t; on teaching excellence,
    145–54
Panara, Robert F., xi, *48*, 153; commemorative stamp of,
    23, *47*; death of, 50n1; Ginsberg and, 44; influ-
    ence of, 47–48; Pagano and, 145; performing arts
    program and, 31; poetry of, 34, 43–45; recruit-
    ment of, 30
Panara Theatre, 29, 34, 43–45, 117
Parasnis, Ila, 101–15, *107*
Parker, Mary Beth, 153
Partnerships in Pluralism, 115
PeaceArt International, 114
Pecot, Jeff, 66
Penny, Tom, 73t
Performing Arts program, 29–41, *32–39*; certificate in,
    35; future of, 39–41; teacher training in, 38, 190
Peterson, Paul, 153
Peterson, Peter N., 47, 119
Peterson, Richard "Rico," 3, 135–43, 181–82, 225
Petronio, Karen, 26t
Phatsgiving, 66
Philippines, 191, 192
Phillip, Marie Jean, 26t
Phillips, Sophie, 201
physical education program, 33
Physics Learning Center, 161–63, 165
Pidgin Signed English (PSE), 16, 179
Pierce, David H., 8
Poe, Jonathan, 217
Poe, Warren, 217
poetry, ASL, 43–45
Pollard, Robert Q., 223, 225, 226
Pollock, Greg, 20, 63–73, *72*, 74t
Ponappa, Sasha L., 226
Poor, Geoff, 13, 16, 17
Portugal, 191

Postl, Rick, 3, 227
Postsecondary Education Network–International, 53,
    93, 192
Pouliot, Oliver, 24t
Pre-College Education Network, 114, 192
Price, Beverly J., 153
Price, Martin, 74t
Prilenski, Richie, 200–201
Prince, David, 74t
Professional Development Program, 103
Project Inclusion, 191
Project Outreach, 212
Pumphrey, Kriston Lee, 40

Qualls, Shane, 200
Quinsland, Larry K., 146, 150, 151
Quinto-Pozos, David, 25t
Quiroga, Jeremy, 53

Raco, Thomas, 56
Radford, Curt, 24t
Raffaelle, Ryne, 226
Ramey, Carmella, 8
Rapazzo, Mary, 53
Rashid, Khadijat, 24t
Ratchasuda College for the Handicapped (Thailand),
    92
Ray, Meredith, 82–83, *83*
Real-Time Captioning (RTC), 140–43
Rees, Mary, 212–14
Riggio, Joseph, 223
Registry of Interpreters for the Deaf (RID), 135, 136,
    177
Rehabilitation Act (1973), 19
Reid, John T. "JT," 47, 79, *110*, 110–11
Relentless Tiger Leadership, 83
Rennie, Debbie, 29, 44–45
Research on Employment and Adapting to Change
    (REACH) Center, 128
research programs, 125–33, 127t, *128–30*, 131t,
    132t; departmental responsibilities for, 127t;
    faculty role in, *130*; funding options of,
    130–31, 131t; influences on, 132; mission
    statement for, 125, 126; scholarly dissemina-
    tion of, 131–32, 132t

Technical Sign Language, for STEM courses, 190

telephone-relay services (TRS), 214–15

Templeton, David, 159–70, 168t

Thailand, 92, 191

Thayn, Paul, 31

Thomas, Michael, 33, 35, 36

Thompson, Jeremiah, *200*

Thoms, Charlotte, 101–15, *106*, 222, 226

Timm, Rosa Lee, 22, 29

Ting, Simon, 49

Tom, Rickey, 67

Tooley, James, 38

Toothman, Timothy, 33

Trumble, Ron, 53

Tsukuba Technical Institute for the Deaf (Japan), 92

Tullier, Tate, 53, 54

Tutor/Notetaker Training Program (T/NTP), 140

Tydings, Jeanette, 192

Tyler, Ralph, 159

TypeWell program, 141

Tyson, Ronnie Mae, 102

Uganda, 191, 192

US Deaf History website, 49

Vaala, Allen, *216*, 217

Valli, Clayton, 27t, 44, 45

Van Hook, Alexander, 72, 74t

Vargas, Jeannette, 67

Veatch, Debbie, 211

Veditz, George W., *22*, 23

Vedock, Jo Carol, 137

Venture Creation Center, 198, 202

Vestibule Program, 161–62

veteran teacher videos (VETFLIX), 190

Video Remote Interpreting (VRI), 217

Vietnam, 192

Villareal, Leo, 60, *61*

Virnig, Dack, *38*

Vision Quest, 221

Visual Communication Studies, 159, 169

Viva, De'VIA art exposition, 53–54

vocational rehabilitation (VR), 207

Vreeland, Mary, 34

V-Sports team, *200*

Wagner, Christopher, 8, *200*, 201

Wagner, Staci, 8

Waldinger, Lois, 74t

Walla, Albert, *77*, 77–78

Wallace, Anthony, 81–82, *82*

Walter, Gerard, 2, 16, 89–99, 129–30

Warfield, Thomas, 37, 113–14, *114*; *AstroDance* production by, 40; recruitment of, 36; *West Side Story* production by, 35

Washburn, Cadwallader Lincoln, 59

Washington, Tracy, *34*, 74t

Watersocket cochlear implant cover, 200–201

Watkins, Greyson, 201

Web Development courses, 165

Webster, Dennis, 35

Weikart, Steve, 65

Weir, Barb, 137

Wells, Jeanne, 176, 184

Westlake, Mel, 35

White, Barry, 27t

"White Noise Experience," 213

Wilcox, Sherman, 27t

Wildbank, Charles, 53

Wilkins, Dorothy, 17, 22, 26t

Williams, Elizabeth W., 53, 55, 57, 59

Williams, Hope, 103, 104, *109*, 109–10, 152

Williams, Kevin, 183

Williams, Leonard, *78*

Williams Gallery, *53*, 57

Wilson, Jimmie, 139

Wilson, Nat, 35

Wing, Ed, 30

Winston, Elizabeth, 26t

Witter-Merithew, Anna, 136, 175–78, *176*, 185

WOLK Deaf Jewish Culture Club, 67

Women of Color, Honor and Ambition (WOCHA), 115

Women's Career Center, 212

Women's Studies, 49, 105

Wonder, Guy, 25t, 51, 54

Wood, Barbara Jean 'B.J.', 8, 27t

Woosley, Harry, Jr., 73t

Wooten, Alicia, 67, 71

Workforce Recruitment Program (WRP), 215

World Games for the Deaf, 79

Yoshida, Minoru, 68
Young, Ethan, 202
Yussif, Abdul, 68

Zaurov, Mark, 24t
Zawerucha, Stefa, 33
Zion, Amber, 40
Zola, Evelyn, 27t
Zollo, Carl, 53, *119*
Zulkifl, Antilla, 36
ZVRS, 195, 199–201, *200*

Photo Credits

Unless otherwise noted, all other photos are courtesy of the Deaf Studies Archive.

p. 5	Mark Benjamin
p. 14	Mark Benjamin
p. 15	Jorge Samper
p. 22	Mark Benjamin
P. 33	Mark Benjamin
P. 37	Mark Benjamin
p. 38	A. Sue Weisler
p. 47	Courtesy of the United States Postal Service
p. 49	Mark Benjamin
p. 53	Mark Benjamin
p. 55	Mark Benjamin
pp. 58–60	Mark Benjamin
p. 61	A. Sue Weisler
p. 71	A. Sue Weisler
p. 72	A. Sue Weisler
p. 81	A. Sue Weisler
P. 82	Mark Benjamin
p. 90	Mark Benjamin
p. 93	A. Sue Weisler
p. 94	Mark Benjamin
pp. 96–97	Mark Benjamin
p. 104	Mark Benjamin
p. 107	A. Sue Weisler (right)
p. 107	Mark Benjamin (left)
p. 108	A. Sue Weisler
p. 109	Mark Benjamin
P. 110	Mark Benjamin (left)
p. 110	A. Sue Weisler (right)
p. 111	Jorge Samper
p. 114	A. Sue Weisler
p. 119	Jorge Samper (upper)
p. 120	A. Sue Weisler (lower left)
p. 121	Mark Benjamin
p. 122	A. Sue Weisler
p. 122	Mark Benjamin (upper left)
p. 123	Mark Benjamin (right)
p. 128	Mark Benjamin
pp. 156–157	Mark Benjamin
p. 178	Mark Benjamin
p. 182	Mark Benjamin
p. 188	A. Sue Weisler
pp. 189–194	Mark Benjamin
p. 196	Ann Mochinski (right)
p. 197	Mark Benjamin
pp. 199–204	Mark Benjamin
p. 216	Mark Benjamin

Colophon

Design
Marnie Soom

Typefaces
Minion Pro and Franklin Gothic

Paper
80# Huron Gloss

Printing and Binding
Thomson Shore